The Making of the Chinese Industrial Workplace

For decades one of the most important institutions in Chinese politics and society has been the "work unit" (*danwei*): the organization of China's urban state sector workforce into tightly enclosed communities offering lifetime employment and extensive welfare benefits. The work unit has also served the Chinese state as a means of direct and indirect control over China's historically contentious working class. While the work unit is often explained as part and parcel of Chinese communism or of Chinese culture, in this book Frazier shows how particular elements of the work unit structure emerged during different crises that swept through China's industrial sector. China's industrial workplace was made, in effect, through a process of conflict and coalitions among workers, managers, and state officials over several critical decades that bracketed the Communist regime's founding in 1949. The author traces important continuities and changes in state and society relations across the Nationalist and Communist regimes during the pivotal decades of the mid-twentieth century.

Mark W. Frazier is an Assistant Professor of Government and the Luce Assistant Professor in the Political Economy of East Asia at Lawrence University.

Cambridge Modern China Series

Edited by William Kirby, Harvard University

To Karen and Shelby

The Making of the Chinese Industrial Workplace

State, Revolution, and Labor Management

MARK W. FRAZIER

Lawrence University

CAMBRIDGE
UNIVERSITY PRESS

PUBLISHED BY THE PRESS SYNDICATE OF THE UNIVERSITY OF CAMBRIDGE
The Pitt Building, Trumpington Street, Cambridge, United Kingdom

CAMBRIDGE UNIVERSITY PRESS
The Edinburgh Building, Cambridge CB2 2RU, UK
40 West 20th Street, New York, NY 10011-4211, USA
477 Williamstown Road, Port Melbourne, VIC 3207, Australia
Ruiz de Alarcón 13, 28014 Madrid, Spain
Dock House, The Waterfront, Cape Town 8001, South Africa

http://www.cambridge.org

First published 2002

Printed in the United Kingdom at the University Press, Cambridge

Typeface Times New Roman 10/13 pt.   *System* QuarkXPress [BTS]

A catalog record for this book is available from the British Library.

Library of Congress Cataloging in Publication Data
Frazier, Mark W.
    The making of the Chinese industrial workplace : state, revolution, and labor
management / Mark W. Frazier.
        p.   cm. – (Cambridge modern China series)
    Includes bibliographical references and index.
    ISBN 0-521-80021-8
    1. Labor policy – China.   I. Title.   II. Series.
HD8736.5 .F73   2001
331′.0951 – dc21

                                                                           2001025463

ISBN   0 521 80021 8   hardback

Contents

Contents

List of Tables

List of Acronyms

ACLC	All-China Labor Congress
BSA	Bureau of Social Affairs
CAL	Chinese Association of Labor
CBHRC	Chinese Business History Research Center
CCI	capital construction investment
CCP	Chinese Communist Party
CESI	China Economic Statistics Institute
EWC	Employee Welfare Committee
FFYP	First Five-Year Plan
FMC	Factory Management Conference
GLF	Great Leap Forward
GLU	General Labor Union
GMA	Guangzhou Municipal Archives
GMD	Guomindang (Nationalist Party)
GMU	Guangdong Mechanics Union
GPA	Guangdong Provincial Archives
GPIC	Guangdong Provincial Industrial Corporation
LCAC	Labor-Capital Arbitration Committee
LCCC	Labor-Capital Consultative Conference
MEA	Ministry of Economic Affairs
MPC	Municipal Party Committee
MSA	Ministry of Social Affairs
NGC	Naval Garrison Command
NRC	National Resources Commission
PLA	People's Liberation Army
PRC	People's Republic of China
RMB	*renminbi* (unit of currency)
SASS	Shanghai Academy of Social Sciences

List of Acronyms

SGC	Shenxin General Corporation
SMA	Shanghai Municipal Archives
SMPC	Shanghai Municipal Party Committee
SOE	state-owned enterprise

Preface

The Chinese Communist Party's (CCP) ongoing efforts to reduce state sector employment might be called the "third rail" of contemporary Chinese politics. Like their counterparts in the United States for whom social security reform is a politically perilous endeavor, officials in China who are dismantling the state sector are tampering with a highly charged social welfare institution upon which many millions of urban Chinese depend. Despite the risks involved, in the 1990s the Chinese government undertook a comprehensive reform of the state sector, in part because of the enormous financial burdens caused by the provision of enterprise welfare services to state workers.[1] Today, the ranks of state enterprise employees, which once reached 100 million in the 1990s, are declining by five million to six million per year.[2] Those who leave state sector employment, voluntarily or otherwise, stand to lose benefits that previous generations of full-time state workers enjoyed as part of membership in a "work unit" (*danwei*): free or low-cost housing, medical insurance, meals, educational and cultural resources, and other collective benefits that state enterprise managers in the past were expected to provide. Retirees from the state sector also depend upon their former places of employment for pensions and medical care, as government agencies struggle to take on such functions as social security and health care administration. Rising unemployment, declining social services, and the inability of some

---

[1] Edward S. Steinfeld, *Forging Reform in China: The Fate of State-Owned Industry* (New York: Cambridge University Press, 1998); Nicholas R. Lardy, *China's Unfinished Economic Revolution* (Washington, DC: Brookings Institution, 1998); Barry Naughton, *Growing Out of the Plan: Chinese Economic Reform, 1978–1993* (New York: Cambridge University Press, 1995).

[2] "China Aims to Keep Urban Unemployment Below 3.5 Percent," FBIS-CHI-2000-0307 via World News Connection.

enterprises to meet payroll and pension distributions have brought a remarkable number of labor protests, involving an estimated 3.6 million participants in 1998.[3]

The *danwei* has served as far more than just a social welfare institution for the Chinese state. The work unit structure once facilitated the CCP's goal of mobilizing and monitoring urban society at the most basic of levels. Before the industrial reforms of the 1980s, urban residents depended upon their workplace for access to daily necessities such as food and clothing (largely through ration coupons). Dependence upon one's workplace, a state enterprise, clearly entailed dependence upon the officials who acted as one's direct supervisors. Today, what one author has termed the "de-danweiization" of enterprises through economic reforms is bringing significant loosening of political controls over the workforce.[4] The process of dismantling critical work unit functions continues, and some time will pass before any alternative pattern of workforce organization might emerge in Chinese industry. This rather cautious observation highlights a more important theoretical point, which is that institutions take time, often considerable amounts of time, to "set" as durable norms and rules around which behavior is governed.

This book steps back from present discussions of state enterprise reform and "de-danweiization" to look into the past, to see how the *danwei* was created as the all-encompassing social and political institution that it became in Chinese industry.[5] As will become clear in the chapters that follow, the formation of the *danwei* in industry was a process, not an event. Moreover, what we now call the *danwei* was not a single institution but was comprised of distinct institutions or rules and norms for how workers would be hired, organized, and compensated. These "labor management institutions," as I call them, emerged at different times and exerted their influence on subsequent factory politics and the process of industrial *danwei* formation. In fact, labor management institutions that were formed prior to the revolution of 1949 influenced the

---

[3] Feng Chen, "Subsistence Crises, Managerial Corruption, and Labour Protests in China," *The China Journal* 44 (July 2000): 41. Reports on labor protests by state workers and retirees can be found in John Pomfret, "Miners' Riot: A Symbol of China's New Discontent," *Washington Post*, April 5, 2000, A1; "AFP: PRC Police, Steel Workers Clash Over Unpaid Wages," FBIS-CHI-2000-0516 via World News Connection.

[4] You Ji, *China's Enterprise Reform: Changing State/Society Relations after Mao* (New York: Routledge, 1998), 23–8.

[5] The central focus of this book is on labor management institutions within industrial units, although the *danwei* pattern of employment extends to commercial enterprises; educational, medical, and research institutions; and government offices.

structure of the welfare state that emerged under the CCP in the 1950s. This was a welfare state whose benefits were heavily concentrated within the state workforce and delivered through the workplace. The CCP also inherited, rather than formulated, a wage policy that favored seniority and narrow differences between the highest- and lowest-paid workers. These and other workplace institutions may have facilitated the CCP's quest to expand industry and to control the labor force, but they also in some ways constrained what was possible even during a period of rapid social and political transformation. Just as today's reformers in China confront the legacies of a centrally planned, state socialist economy, so too did the CCP in the 1950s face a set of institutional constraints on what was possible as it sought to remake the industrial sector and China's industrial working class.

The analysis that follows raises certain questions about our understanding of the *danwei*'s formation, the Chinese revolution of 1949 in urban areas, and the nature of political change in postrevolutionary settings. Through a narrative of factory-level changes in some of China's most important industrial enterprises, the chapters trace the emergence of particular workplace institutions at identifiable moments in roughly the middle third of twentieth-century China. It was over a 30- to 40-year period ending in the early 1960s that institutions formed and converged within Chinese factories to create what would become known as the *danwei* organizational structure within industry.

It is fitting that a book about institutional formation and change amid revolution and other crises is itself the product of a long-term process involving uncertainties, breakthroughs, transformations, setbacks, rewards, losses, triumphs, and other assorted episodes along the way. Unlike institutions, however, books ultimately stop evolving and are sent to the printing press. As I reflect back on all those who have furthered the process by which this book came into being, it is difficult to know where to start.

This book in an earlier incarnation was a Ph.D. dissertation submitted for a doctorate in Political Science at the University of California, Berkeley. It is appropriate to begin by acknowledging the organizations and individuals that supported the initial research effort that began in the mid-1990s. The Committee on Scholarly Communication with China and the Chiang Ching-kuo Foundation provided doctoral dissertation fellowships, and the Institute for East Asian Studies at Berkeley helped me establish invaluable contacts with academies and researchers in Shanghai. For my research in Guangzhou, I gratefully acknowledge Professor Ming Chan for his introduction to contacts and organizations that furthered my research efforts. The Shanghai Academy of Social Sciences (SASS) Foreign Affairs Office and the Zhongshan University Department of History served as my host units in Shanghai and Guangzhou respectively. I received support from numerous individuals at both these institutions, but I wish to extend special thanks to Professor Huang Hanmin of the SASS Institute of Economics, to Li Yihai and Tian Guopei of the SASS Foreign Affairs Office, and to Dr. Zhang Zhongli, the President of SASS, for their interest in and support of my research. I am also indebted to Professor Chen Chunsheng of Zhongshan University for the enthusiasm and encouragement that he showed toward my project. Thanks also go to the directors and staff of the Shanghai Municipal Archives, the Chinese Business History Research Center at SASS, the Guangzhou Municipal Archives, and the Guangdong Provincial Archives. At various stages of this project, I was graciously hosted by the Academia Sinica Institute of Modern History in Taipei, and by the Universities Service Centre in Hong Kong.

I owe special thanks to the many individuals who have read various chapters from the dissertation and the numerous drafts that came out in the transition toward its publication as a book. These include Chris Ansell, Ming Chan, Calvin Chen, Neil Diamant, Neil Fligstein, Seth Harter, Hong Yung Lee, Andrea McElderry, Jon Marshall, Andrew Mertha, Gregory Noble, Mark Selden, Patricia Thornton, and Andrew Walder. At different stages of this project I have had conversations about this research project with several individuals whose suggestions have been both encouraging and insightful. These include Morris Linan Bian, Ellis Goldberg, Xiaobo Lü, Richard Snyder, and Wen-hsin Yeh. Finally, I owe the most thanks to Professor Elizabeth Perry for her countless contributions to this project and to my career as a scholar.

I also wish to acknowledge the many comments offered from faculty and discussants to whom I presented the findings of my research at several venues and departments in recent years. Special thanks go to the Center for Chinese Studies at the University of California, Berkeley; the Department of Political Science at the University of Louisville; the faculty of Lawrence University; and the Department of Political Science at the University of North Carolina. Conversations with colleagues at the National Bureau of Asian Research (NBR), especially Richard Ellings and William Abnett, helped further my understanding of state enterprises in China and where my work related to contemporary problems in China's industrial reform. It was in working on a separate research project for NBR that I had the fortune to draw upon the wisdom and experience of Professor Michel Oksenberg. He gave his constant encouragement and support as I pursued the publication of this book. His memory continues to serve as an inspiration to me and so many others in the China field.

I extend very special thanks to the two anonymous reviewers for Cambridge University Press who rendered invaluable advice and suggestions in their reports on the initial draft of the manuscript. At the Press, my sincere thanks go to Mary Child for her interest in the project, her helpful suggestions along the way, and her timely responses to my queries, no matter how trivial. The Modern China Series editor, Professor William Kirby, offered his encouragement throughout the process. Special thanks also go to Christine Dunn for first-rate work in copyediting the manuscript. I gratefully acknowledge assistance from Henry Lyon at the University of Louisville for his attention to detail as this manuscript went into the final stages of preparation. Dianne O'Regan did superb work on the index.

It wouldn't have been possible to conduct and complete this project and book without the support and companionship I've received over many years from Karen Frazier. During the challenging years of graduate studies and dissertation research, she accompanied me to Taiwan, where she worked as an English-language radio announcer, and to China, where she patiently edited the headlines of a decidedly upstart English-language newspaper. Most importantly, she has enthusiastically pulled up stakes and moved to the various locations that my academic career has taken us. Along the way, we were joined by Shelby, who has seen her father work on this book for much of her three years, and Trevor, who has suffered my ramblings about this book on too many predawn walks for a two-year-old Labrador retriever to endure.

1

Introduction

> *The Russian is a bad worker compared with workers of the advanced countries ... The task that the Soviet government must set the people in all its scope is – learn to work.*[1]
>
> Vladimir Ilyich Lenin, 1918

What Lenin said of Russian workers highlights an important but understudied problem of many states that seek to jump-start industrialization through the rapid mobilization of capital and labor: building new factories also requires new norms and rules governing the employment relationship of the people who are to work in factories. These norms and rules can be imposed by fiat, but they are almost always subject to informal negotiation among state officials, managers, and workers. Such informal negotiations take place internally within the firm, especially when unions and other independent associations are repressed or lack the authority to represent workers' interests. In many cases of state-led industrialization, it is within public enterprises that workers come face-to-face with officials of the regime.

This book examines how officials, workers, and managers created institutions of labor management to cope with the transformation of China's industrial sector, from the early stages of industrial development to the imposition of a centrally planned economy in the 1950s. Labor management institutions can be defined as the formal and informal rules and structures that regulate how workers are hired, paid, organized, and supervised.[2] A central pursuit of this book is to identify the conditions

---

[1] Quoted in Reinhard Bendix, *Work and Authority in Industry: Ideologies of Management in the Course of Industrialization* (New York: John Wiley & Sons, Inc., 1956), 206.
[2] Labor policy, in contrast to the firm-level decisions of labor management, refers to the laws and administrative rulings on hiring, wages, benefits, and other employment issues

under which critical labor management institutions emerged; who contributed to their formation and reproduction; and how they changed over time.

Thus, while this is a book about China, it is also a book about institutional change in revolutionary contexts. Readers less interested in the specifics of labor, industry, or politics in China will find throughout different chapters a number of theoretical observations regarding the emergence and design of important sociopolitical institutions that mediate relations between state and society. Empirically, the effort is less on demonstrating how institutions shaped behavior than on identifying and explaining their emergence and evolution. In recent years many comparative political scientists and sociologists have sought to explore the past in order to identify the mechanisms by which different actors might reproduce an institution or use it for different purposes, well after the initial conditions that gave rise to the institution have receded.[3] Certainly in China's revolutionary environment during the 1950s, we might expect that labor management institutions emerged rather quickly amid rapid industrialization, mass mobilization, and the organizational transformation associated with the introduction of a command economy. However, such postrevolutionary changes should be placed in the context of processes under way *prior to* the change in regimes. As the factory-level evidence in this book will illuminate, the evolution of the Chinese industrial workplace, a microlevel outcome, unfolded against the backdrop of broad processes: industrialization, state building, labor mobilization, and within the firm, the process of bureaucratization, or the imposition of rules and procedures regarding hiring, work, and pay. These processes were all well under way prior to 1949, and they accelerated dramatically during the 1950s. Given China's political context in the 1950s, the

---

that governments attempt to regulate. Labor management is a subset of enterprise management, which includes the tasks of marketing, cost accounting, financial planning, etc. In a command economy, labor policy and labor management are integrated with industrial management, the broader set of incentives and constraints that state officials impose on enterprises to meet macroeconomic targets.

[3] A central concern of historical institutionalism is identifying the mechanisms by which institutions are reproduced by different actors over time, after the initial causes of the institution have receded. Paul Pierson, "Increasing Returns, Path Dependence, and the Study of Politics," *American Political Science Review* vol. 94, no. 2 (June 2000): 251–67; Kathleen Thelen, "Historical Institutionalism in Comparative Politics," *Annual Review of Political Science* 2 (1999): 369–404; Kathleen Thelen and Sven Steinmo, "Historical Institutionalism in Comparative Politics," in *Structuring Politics: Historical Institutionalism in Comparative Analysis*, Sven Steinmo, Kathleen Thelen, and Frank Longstreth, eds. (New York: Cambridge University Press, 1992), 1–32.

evidence presented also raises questions about institutional continuities amid revolutions.

Tocqueville was among the first to note that the institutions of revolutionary states frequently bear the marks of their predecessors in the old regime. He observed of the French Revolution and its strongly centralized postrevolutionary state that institutions whose formative periods begin prior to revolutions can become instruments of control for the new regime. In speaking of the actions of France's postrevolutionary leaders, Tocqueville said, "though nothing was further from their intentions, they used the debris of the old order for building up the new."[4] Theda Skocpol's account of social revolutions also discusses this issue of transrevolutionary continuities by showing how revolutionary crises and legacies of the old regime "shaped and limited the efforts and achievements of the state-building revolutionary leaderships."[5] The chapters that follow suggest that the politics of revolutionary regimes might also be fruitfully explored as a process of engagement between particular sectors of the state and groups within society. While Skocpol's explanatory framework for the policies of revolutionary states pays attention to broad structures such as industrial capacity, the international strategic environment, and domestic social alliances that regimes have forged prior to revolutions, this focus comes at some expense to the study of society itself, where certain institutions might be found that exhibit surprising durability. Exploring the arenas of state and society and their interaction reveals how revolutionary states operate within the societies that they seek to transform. Joel Migdal characterized this engagement between parts of the state with groups and individuals in society as a "mutually transforming" process that highlights some of the constraints on state power and pays attention to how states can be embedded in institutions, a process that Migdal terms "the state in society."[6]

Another explanation for postrevolutionary continuities lies in Douglass North's emphasis on the interaction of new, formal institutions imposed by revolutionary states and older, "informal institutions." While

---

[4] Alexis de Tocqueville, *The Old Regime and the French Revolution*, trans. Stuart Gilbert (Garden City, NY: Doubleday Anchor Books, 1955), vii.

[5] Theda Skocpol, *States and Social Revolutions: A Comparative Analysis of France, Russia, and China* (New York: Cambridge University Press, 1979), 172.

[6] Joel S. Migdal, "The State in Society: An Approach to Struggles for Domination," in *State Power and Social Forces: Domination and Transformation in the Third World*, Joel S. Migdal, Atul Kohli, and Vivienne Shue, eds. (New York: Cambridge University Press, 1994), 23.

revolutionary regimes attempt to impose new institutions on society, North notes that

> Perhaps most important of all, the formal rules change, but the informal constraints do not. In consequence, there develops an ongoing tension between informal constraints and the new formal rules, as many are inconsistent with each other. The informal constraints had gradually evolved as extensions of previous formal rules. . . . Although a wholesale change in the formal rules may take place, at the same time there will be many informal constraints that have great survival tenacity because they still resolve basic exchange problems among the participants, be they social, political, or economic. The result over time tends to be a restructuring of the overall constraints – in both directions – to produce a new equilibrium that is far less revolutionary.[7]

For some students of Chinese politics and society in the 1950s, this observation may appear to confirm the obvious. Recent scholarship has shown how social institutions limited revolutionary change in certain cases, and how Communist policies and laws led to unintended consequences.[8] North's suggestion that social actors restructure new postrevolutionary institutions to produce something that is "far less revolutionary" seems quite plausible, but it could also be the case that the resulting equilibrium represents a significant and dramatic rupture with past practices and power relations. For example, in China the collectivization of industry and agriculture in the 1950s brought with them a set of seemingly new institutional arrangements through which the average citizen interacted with the state. Among these was the "work unit" or *danwei*, to which virtually all urban residents belonged by the 1950s.

Within China's industrial sector, employment in state enterprises by the early 1960s had the following general characteristics:

---

[7] Douglass C. North, *Institutions, Institutional Change and Economic Performance* (New York: Cambridge University Press, 1990), 91.

[8] This is a theme throughout Friedman, Pickowicz, and Selden's detailed study of village politics and society in a North China county from the 1930s to the 1960s. Edward Friedman, Paul G. Pickowicz, and Mark Selden, with Kay Ann Johnson, *Chinese Village, Socialist State* (New Haven, CT: Yale University Press, 1991). For an analysis of the unintended consequences of the PRC's 1950 Marriage Law, see Neil J. Diamant, *Revolutionizing the Family: Politics, Love, and Divorce in Urban and Rural China, 1949–1968* (Berkeley, CA: University of California Press, 2000).

- Employees and managers viewed the workplace as a source of cradle-to-grave welfare benefits, including but not limited to housing, food, health care, pensions, insurance, child care, primary education, cultural activities, and more.
- Membership in this enterprise community was considered more or less permanent, and access to it was tightly restricted. Labor mobility even within the state sector was rare.
- New employees were assigned to state enterprises through comprehensive state labor allocation plans, and new workers generally underwent an apprenticeship before attaining the complete benefits of state employment.
- In theory, wage determination was based on a national wage scale that offered higher pay as a worker acquired greater technical skills. However, by the early 1960s this had evolved into a de facto seniority wage system, in which differences in pay reflected the sequence of entry into the state labor force.
- As physically walled compounds, work units were literally compartmentalized from the outside world, though the state had a number of "ports of entry" to them. Enterprises were the primary units of political communication and participation, with frequent meetings and political movements or "campaigns" that attempted to mobilize the workforce to raise production or to attack political targets.
- At the individual level, enterprises exerted political controls through a "dossier" system in which personnel departments maintained individual employee files that recorded extensive personal data – including political transgressions.
- The enterprise branch committee of the Communist Party exercised authority over labor issues, personnel appointments, and at times even day-to-day administrative matters. Party committees could also dictate to managers and factory directors how they should resolve broader questions such as the use of incentive bonuses and overtime pay.
- Labor supervisors served as critical intermediaries between enterprise directors and workers by using their dual powers as administrative and political authorities at the basic level. Expressions of personal and political loyalty by workers to their supervisors could strongly influence decisions on which workers would be approved for promotions or wage increases.

Many of these characteristics of the Chinese work unit are readily observed outside of China. For example, it is not difficult to find firms and industries in which private and public employers distribute extensive nonwage benefits to employees – by custom, by law, or by the preferences of particular company owners.[9] State control over the

[9] Stuart D. Brandes, *American Welfare Capitalism, 1880–1940* (Chicago: University of Chicago Press, 1976); Andrew Gordon, *The Evolution of Labor Relations in Japan: Heavy Industry, 1853–1955* (Cambridge, MA: Harvard University Press, 1985).

allocation of labor and wages are defining features of the "command economy" of state socialism. Likewise, seniority wages are found throughout developing and advanced industrial economies, be they socialist or market in name.[10] The use of political commissars or party committees to supervise the actions of employees and employers was prevalent throughout the former Soviet Union and Eastern Europe.[11] "Foreman's empires" are common to many economies in the early stages of industrialization, and they have persisted to different degrees in some industries.[12] The question is not why Chinese state enterprises developed features found elsewhere, but when, and why each of these elements emerged in China, how they changed over time, and how these labor management institutions reflected power relations between workers and the state.

EXPLAINING FACTORY INSTITUTIONS IN CHINA

Some discussions of the emergence of the *danwei* in China rely on a functionalist logic in which it is argued that the CCP imposed the work unit structure on factories and other basic units after 1949 in order to exert its domination of Chinese society. As Tianjin Shi remarks, "To ensure its control, the government developed a unique political structure – the work unit (*danwei*) – to help the authorities control the general populace in Chinese society."[13] Martin Whyte and William Parish's classic study of urban China interpreted the *danwei*, together with the CCP's highly intrusive pattern of urban household organization, as a result of the Communist regime's undertaking to rid Chinese cities of various social maladies in the 1950s. For a rural-based revolutionary movement

---

[10] Michael Burawoy, *The Politics of Production: Factory Regimes Under Capitalism and Socialism* (London: Verso Press, 1985); Charles F. Sabel, *Work and Politics: The Division of Labor in Industry* (New York: Cambridge University Press, 1982).

[11] Joseph S. Berliner, *Factory and Manager in the USSR* (Cambridge, MA: Harvard University Press, 1957).

[12] Bendix, *Work and Authority in Industry*, 53–8; Daniel Nelson, *Managers and Workers: Origins of the Twentieth-Century Factory System in the United States, 1880–1920*, 2nd ed. (Madison, WI: University of Wisconsin Press, 1995), 35–55; Sanford M. Jacoby, *Employing Bureaucracy: Managers, Unions, and the Transformation of Work in American Industry, 1900–1945* (New York: Columbia University Press, 1985); Nelson Lichtenstein, "The Man in the Middle: A Social History of Automobile Industry Foremen," in *On the Line: Essays in the History of Auto Work*, Nelson Lichtenstein and Stephen Meyer, eds. (Urbana, IL: University of Illinois Press, 1989), 153–89.

[13] Tianjin Shi, *Political Participation in Beijing* (Cambridge, MA: Harvard University Press, 1997), 13.

to transform the highly suspect manners and mores of city residents and workers, "everyone was to be organized from the ground up."[14]

By far the most influential work on shop floor politics in China, however, is Andrew Walder's *Communist Neo-Traditionalism*.[15] Walder argued that factories under Leninist regimes generated distinct forms of political control and worker dependency. In China, workers were both highly dependent on their enterprises for basic necessities and deeply divided between political activists and those more passively oriented who pursued material rewards through personalized ties with supervisors. In state enterprises during the Maoist era, employees could obtain basic living needs primarily and sometimes exclusively from their enterprise, by negotiating a dense set of political networks that included one's labor supervisor as a key node of exchange. In addition, because of the tight restrictions on job switching, state workers in China did not have an "exit" option in which they could readily seek employment elsewhere.[16]

Among the objections raised by Walder's critics was his claim that the pattern of labor relations that emerged during the 1950s in China's factories represented an abrupt break with the past.[17] As Walder argued, "Even if China's prerevolution labor traditions were unique, it would be difficult to find historical continuities in the face of the sweeping and systematic changes of the 1950s."[18] After enumerating the rapid changes during the 1950s in ownership and employment from small-scale, handicraft production to large-scale, modern factory production, Walder concluded that "the new Chinese regime literally created, almost from scratch, a new tradition of labor relations."[19] Unintended consequences did arise from this process of transformation, especially patron-client ties between supervisors and workers that undermined the regime's ideological goals. Furthermore, as Walder noted, the general pattern of shop floor relations remained relatively durable despite several changes in industrial and labor policy in subsequent years.[20] Other critics of Walder

[14] Martin King Whyte and William L. Parish, *Urban Life in Contemporary China* (Chicago: University of Chicago Press, 1984), 22.

[15] Andrew G. Walder, *Communist Neo-Traditionalism: Work and Authority in Chinese Industry* (Berkeley, CA: University of California Press, 1986).

[16] Ibid., 11–17.

[17] Deborah Davis, "Patrons and Clients in Chinese Industry," *Modern China* vol. 14, no. 4 (1988): 495–7; Elizabeth J. Perry, "State and Society in Contemporary China," *World Politics* vol. 41, no. 4 (1989): 579–91.

[18] Walder, *Communist Neo-Traditionalism*, 32.

[19] Ibid., 34.   [20] Ibid., 9.

questioned the validity of his argument that state industrial workers in China were enmeshed in dependent, patron-client relationships, and the extent to which this relationship characterized state-society relations in China more generally.[21] My purpose is not to challenge the characteristics of the factory regime that Walder vividly portrayed and analyzed, but to ask the question of where many of its institutional features came from.

If it is true that institutional formation takes place over a number of years or even several decades, then it is worth exploring the sequence in which various labor management institutions found in the work unit came together. In what ways did Nationalist Party rule (1927–49) contribute to the formation of the industrial work unit in the People's Republic of China (PRC)? How much did workers in state enterprises influence the process of institutional formation? Did the sequence in which certain labor management institutions formed create constraints on future choices of the Communist regime? To what extent did political and economic crises of the mid-twentieth century drive the process of institutional formation and change within the industrial workplace? It might be the case that the transformations of the 1950s displaced existing labor management institutions, as Walder's analysis suggests. Thanks in large part to the opening of many new documents in the archives in China containing reports by various party and government agencies, we can better assess these questions in ways that previous scholarly efforts could not.

Other discussions, dealing with industrial reform in China, generally treat labor management institutions of state industrial enterprises as a by-product or structural necessity of the "command economy" of comprehensive national plans in which state enterprises served as the key link in China's strategy of rapid industrialization. The "socialist transformation of industry" that ended in 1957 extinguished the private sector and consolidated state control over China's small but important industrial base. Under the command economy, state enterprises generated capital by receiving low-priced raw materials and other inputs and selling their output to state marketing agencies for a profit, which was then submitted to state planners for investment in other industrial facilities and

---

[21] Brantly Womack, "Transfigured Community: Neo-Traditionalism and Work Unit Socialism in China," *China Quarterly* 126 (1991): 313–32; Marc Blecher, "Communist Neo-Traditionalism: Work and Authority in Chinese Industry," *Pacific Affairs* vol. 60, no. 4 (1987–88): 657–9.

projects. This industrialization strategy entailed strict controls over the rate of growth of the state workforce, which numbered about 24.5 million in 1957.[22] Viewed from this perspective, the rapid mobilization of investment capital, state controls on factor inputs and prices, and an emphasis on heavy industry necessitated particular enterprise-level institutions to hire, train, organize, compensate, and mobilize China's workforce. In short, labor management institutions emerged from macroeconomic policy.[23]

The formation of firm-level labor institutions that would later be known collectively as the work unit pattern of employment is surely associated with the commands and controls of the centrally planned economy. However, this rather straightforward explanation for institutional outcomes in China's factories must account for the fact that certain labor management institutions closely resembling those of the socialist work unit predated the arrival of the command economy. Several scholars have identified practices and ideas within various social settings in the 1930s and 1940s that bear close resemblance to the organizational patterns and ethos of the socialist-era work unit.[24] Workers received broad benefits from their enterprises before 1949, and managers in pre-1949 China sought to create self-enclosed communities that would facilitate their control of the workforce.[25] As striking as these observations might seem, any presumed continuities between pre- and postrevolutionary workforce organization remain largely implied, and less carefully explained.

One potential explanation for any observed continuities might make reference to the importance of culture and the shared understandings that inform relations between employers and employees in an industrial

---

[22] State Statistical Bureau, *Zhongguo tongji nianjian, 1998* (China Statistical Yearbook, 1998) (Beijing: Zhongguo tongji chubanshe, 1998), 130.

[23] Justin Yifu Lin, Fang Cai, Zhou Li, *The China Miracle: Development Strategy and Economic Reform* (Hong Kong: Chinese University Press, 1996), 19–58; Barry Naughton, "*Danwei*: The Economic Foundations of a Unique Institution," in *Danwei: The Changing Chinese Workplace in Historical and Comparative Perspective*, Xiaobo Lü and Elizabeth J. Perry, eds. (Armonk, NY: M.E. Sharpe, 1997), 169–94.

[24] Xiaobo Lü, "Minor Public Economy: The Revolutionary Origins of the *Danwei*," in *Danwei*, Xiaobo Lü and Elizabeth J. Perry, eds., 21–41; Elizabeth J. Perry, "From Native Place to Workplace: Labor Origins and Outcomes of China's *Danwei* System," in *Danwei*, Lü and Perry, eds., 42–59; Wen-hsin Yeh, "The Republican Origins of the *Danwei*: The Case of Shanghai's Bank of China," in *Danwei*, Lü and Perry, eds., 60–88.

[25] Wen-hsin Yeh, "Corporate Space, Communal Time: Everyday Life in Shanghai's Bank of China," *American Historical Review* 99 (February 1995): 97–122.

setting. Labor management, as a general category, is bound up in the complexities of China's relationship to the outside world and the dialectic of Chinese "backwardness" and Western modernity.[26] The concept is used in Chinese sources (*laodong guanli*), but it was borrowed from Western personnel management theories that flourished in the first decades of the twentieth century. Western and Japanese systems of labor management have been subjects of much discussion and emulation in China since the introduction of market reforms in industry in the early 1980s. Indeed, Chinese factory directors and state officials have historically scrutinized foreign methods of organizing industrial labor. In the 1920s, capitalist factory owners tried to introduce the methods of scientific management associated with Frederick Taylor. In the 1950s, CCP officials enthusiastically copied the organization of industrial work in the Soviet Union. In discussions of this issue during any decade, one is hard pressed to find in Chinese sources any mention of a "Chinese employment system" or a "Chinese management system." Given the criticism that officials and others in China have heaped upon Chinese factory managers for their handling of labor issues, it would appear that such authors might regard the very notion of a "Chinese management system" as an oxymoron. Yet foreign observers, more often than not viewing China through the lenses of modernity and tradition – or at least with an eye for how distinct Chinese society and culture is from their own – have usually argued that Chinese factories do have readily identifiable forms and values by which workers are hired, paid, organized, and supervised. The institutional elements that made up labor management in China have changed over time. Visitors to Chinese factories in the 1920s and 1930s generally deplored their employment practices, in which dictatorial shop floor bosses, unsafe working conditions, and brutal exploitation of rural migrants were the norm.[27] During the 1960s and 1970s, the handful of foreign observers and industrial specialists who visited

---

[26] In the PRC, official scholarship has treated labor and factory management in pre-1949 Chinese businesses as the outgrowth of imperialism and capitalism. Since the 1980s, however, PRC scholars have suggested the importance of Chinese cultural influences on how business and commerce evolved in China. See Tim Wright, "'The Spiritual Heritage of Chinese Capitalism': Recent Trends in the Historiography of Chinese Enterprise Management," *The Australian Journal of Chinese Affairs* 19/20 (1988): 185–214.

[27] Various international groups sponsored investigations of factories in China during the 1920s and 1930s, especially in Shanghai. For a summary of how the International Labour Organization and others viewed labor issues and called for reform, see Robin Porter, *Industrial Reform in Modern China* (Armonk, NY: M.E. Sharpe, 1994).

Chinese factories had a very different impression that was generally positive (as their official hosts made sure), but like their predecessors in presocialist China, these authors were struck by the vivid contrasts between Chinese factories and industrial labor management in their own societies.[28] These observers and others who have followed during the 1980s and 1990s have argued that the characteristics of employment in Chinese factories are not easily grouped with those patterns found in the West, Japan, or the former Soviet bloc.[29]

Given the salience of foreign influences on China's industrial development, specifically from Western and Soviet methods of industrial management, it is important to capture how individuals within the Chinese factory modified the institutional blueprints from these sources with their own norms and practices. In an otherwise largely structural analysis of authority relations in Chinese factories, Walder suggested that the degree to which the CCP surpassed its Soviet counterpart in pursuing the moral cultivation of the workforce through normative appeals and mass mobilization could have derived from Chinese traditions of statecraft and authority.[30] This point raises a critical question about the cultural embeddedness of institutions.

A few observations are in order at this point regarding the treatment of culture as a category of explanation in this book. First, if institutions include unwritten "conventions and codes of behavior" as well as formal rules that guide behavior, then such unwritten rules, or what North calls "informal institutions" cannot be neatly differentiated from what someone else might call a cultural norm.[31] In fact, one might hypothesize that informal institutions influence the operation of formal institutions and the probability that the people holding such "conventions and codes" will accept formal institutions. Chinese enterprise managers borrowed heavily at different times from Western and Soviet models of labor management, and such models underwent substantial modification

---

[28] Charles Hoffman, *The Chinese Worker* (Albany, NY: State University of New York Press, 1974); Barry M. Richman, *Industrial Society in Communist China* (New York: Random House, 1969).

[29] John Child, *Management in China During the Age of Reform* (New York: Cambridge University Press, 1994); Gail E. Henderson and Myron S. Cohen, *The Chinese Hospital: A Socialist Work Unit* (New Haven, CT: Yale University Press, 1984); Fox Butterfield, *China, Alive in the Bitter Sea* (New York: Times Books, 1982); Richman, *Industrial Society*.

[30] Walder, *Communist Neo-Traditionalism*, 121–2.

[31] North, *Institutions, Institutional Change*, 4.

in the context of the Chinese factory. This suggests at least some role for informal codes and practices, provided that they can be isolated and analyzed independent of other potential causes such as prices, technology, etc. Second, beliefs and practices vary widely across time and territory, especially in the case of China. To take one example from this book, the provision of broad nonwage benefits to employees appears to be an enduring practice under several different regimes and political economies. One possible source is the elite expression of paternalism, deriving from the Confucian ideal of benevolence toward subordinates.[32] However, welfare provision to employees cannot be uniformly charted across the history of Chinese industry, nor across different industrial sectors. The practice is obviously more deeply rooted and its manifestations more extensive in the state sector than the nonstate sector. To understand this variation in the strength of institutions requires a historical perspective to discern precisely when practices and norms were established, where they were distributed, and why they seemed to persist. Third, the people involved in the process of institutional creation adopt cultural symbols and referents to make their cases: "Treat the factory as a family," we will hear a naval officer and shipyard director say in Chapter 3, when he is laying out his rationale for the establishment of comprehensive enterprise-based welfare provision in 1947. "It's a face-losing situation to pay one person more money and another person less money," a shipyard official told me in an interview in 1995 when he was explaining the current difficulties in implementing new wage guidelines among employees. These remarks are not presented here to show that people use culture to cloak their genuine motives, though some may read them that way. These statements also illustrate how individuals might present and interpret institutions. People who were involved in the creation of workplace institutions in China held preferences and expressed them through cultural referents (family, face). If institutions shape preferences and define interests, then it is important to ask the question of

---

[32] Research on the business organization and management of enterprises in Taiwan, Hong Kong, and among overseas Chinese communities suggests that firm managers and owners share paternalistic and other consistent beliefs and preferences that influence firm management and operations. S. Gordon Redding, *The Spirit of Chinese Capitalism* (New York: Walter de Gruyter, 1990); Richard Whitley, *Business Systems in East Asia: Firms, Markets and Societies* (London: Sage Publications, 1992); Gary G. Hamilton and Nicole Woolsey Biggart, "Market, Culture, and Authority: A Comparative Analysis of Management and Organization in the Far East," *American Journal of Sociology* 94 (1988): S52–S94; Siu-Lun Wong, *Emigrant Entrepreneurs: Shanghai Industrialists in Hong Kong* (New York: Oxford University Press, 1988).

how existing preferences interact with newer, formal institutions, particularly institutions imposed by state officials in a revolutionary context.

The importance of political variables in explaining labor management institutions in China or any other country may seem obvious, until one considers that economic or cultural explanations carry a great deal of importance in the literature on labor management. The substantial body of work on Japan's industrial employment institutions, for example, can be grouped around those who view lifetime employment and seniority wages as primarily cultural manifestations and those who see the same phenomena as the result of skilled labor shortages and other economic variables.[33] Andrew Gordon's alternative, firm-level perspective on Japanese labor management institutions shows that state officials, managers, workers, and their unions negotiated the terms of industrial employment over a period of several decades before and during the Second World War.[34] Postwar labor institutions remained in place to influence labor organization during the U.S. Occupation period and beyond. Linda Weiss furthers Gordon's argument with her state-centered, geopolitical explanation for the Japanese employment system.[35] The comparative historical analysis of employment patterns suggests that conflicts over labor management unfold at varying rates, bringing divergent outcomes depending upon various political coalitions within and external to the factory.[36]

POLITICAL REGIMES AND WORKPLACE REGIMES IN CHINA

The emergence and evolution of labor management institutions in China are inseparable from the process of state building. As in other late

---

[33] James Abegglen, *The Japanese Factory: Aspects of its Social Organization* (Glencoe, IL: The Free Press, 1958); Robert E. Cole, *Japanese Blue Collar: The Changing Tradition* (Berkeley, CA: University of California Press, 1971); Ronald Dore, *British Factory – Japanese Factory* (Berkeley, CA: University of California Press, 1973); Koji Taira, *Economic Development and the Labor Market in Japan* (New York: Columbia University Press, 1970).

[34] Gordon, *The Evolution of Labor Relations in Japan*; Andrew Gordon, "Conditions for the Disappearance of the Japanese Working-Class Movement," in *Putting Class In its Place: Worker Identities in East Asia*, Elizabeth J. Perry, ed. (Berkeley, CA: Institute of East Asian Studies, 1996), 11–52.

[35] Linda Weiss, "War, the State, and the Origins of the Japanese Employment System," *Politics & Society* vol. 21, no. 3 (September 1993): 325–54.

[36] Sanford M. Jacoby, ed., *Masters to Managers: Historical and Comparative Perspectives on American Employers* (New York: Columbia University Press, 1991).

developers, state officials sought to mobilize investment capital for industrialization and to create a base of industrial workers. In pursuing the
latter goal, state officials designed labor policies and firm-level labor
management institutions. Such institutions reflected competing aims of
state officials to mobilize workers for political as well as production purposes. In China, the processes of state building and industrialization were
disrupted and transformed beginning in the late 1930s by the crises of
foreign invasion, hyperinflation, civil war, regime collapse, and revolution. Both the Nationalist and Communist regimes, despite their obvious
contrasts in ideology and organizational effectiveness, took measures
often in crisis environments to administer the industrial sector and its
workforce. Both attempted to make inroads into the Chinese labor force
by controlling union organizations and their leaders, and by placing constraints on enterprise managers and owners. Imposed from above, state
solutions to the problems of workforce organization and mobilization
did not always take shape in their intended form and function. The preferences of workers and managers substantially altered such institutional
designs of the state. In short, the labor management institutions of political regimes did not translate neatly into workplace regimes within the
factory.

Chapters 2 and 3 analyze the emergence of factory-level labor
management institutions during the Nationalist (*Guomindang* [GMD])
regime. Most accounts, scholarly and otherwise, have characterized the
GMD as a factionalized, corruption-ridden party-state that essentially
collapsed under the pressures of economic crisis and Communist insur-
gency during the late 1940s.[37] The debate over the failings of the GMD
and its relative autonomy from social forces is an old one, but there is
little question that in the industrial sector at least, the GMD developed
an impressive set of state plans and mechanisms to coordinate enterprises through state ownership. The most important such government
institution was the National Resources Commission (NRC), which
operated over one hundred heavily capitalized enterprises employing
172,000 people by the mid-1940s and continued to be important in the

---

[37] Lloyd Eastman, *The Abortive Revolution: China Under Nationalist Rule, 1927–1937*
(Cambridge, MA: Harvard University Press, 1974); Hung-mao Tien, *Government and
Politics in Kuomintang China, 1927–1937* (Stanford: Stanford University Press, 1972). For
a recent treatment that puts the Nationalist regime in a compelling theoretical framework emphasizing institution building under serious internal and external challenges,
see Julia Strauss, *Strong Institutions in Weak Polities: State Building in Republican China,
1927–1940* (New York: Oxford University Press, 1998).

development of Taiwan's economy after 1949.[38] During the War of Resistance Against Japan (1937–45), officials at arsenals and heavy industrial plants provided wide-ranging welfare services to employees in order to cope with labor turnover and soaring inflation.[39] This enterprise welfare system was a response to wartime emergencies as much as the result of a coherent Nationalist labor policy. Following the Japanese surrender in 1945, the Nationalist government undermined whatever social welfare policy it envisioned with a disastrous economic policy that dramatically intensified hyperinflation. It was its failure to contain prices that condemned the government in the eyes of many urban residents and workers.[40]

Even before the crises of foreign invasion, civil war, and hyperinflation, managers at some enterprises in the 1920s and 1930s attempted to take control of the labor process through the rationalization of enterprise administration. Taylorist principles of scientific management gave rise to much discussion among Chinese managers during the 1920s and 1930s. Concurrent with this impulse to bring scientific management to the labor and production process was a preference for "enterprise communities" in which communal and paternalistic norms were injected into personnel departments and employee training protocols. This dialectic of rationalization and personalization of the employment relationship continued into the 1950s as the CCP attempted to introduce Soviet labor management practices (which were heavily informed by Lenin's open admiration for Taylor and scientific management). In this and other respects, the effort to rationalize factory labor management in the 1930s looked and sounded much like similar efforts that the Communist regime would undertake two decades later. As Wen-hsin Yeh concludes from her analysis of the corporate community of white collar employees and managers at the Bank of China in Shanghai in the 1930s and 1940s, "many of the features that characterized the socialist *danwei* were prefigured in a pre-Communist urban setting." Among such features were collective living arrangements and an enterprise culture that emphasized the

---

[38] William C. Kirby, "Continuity and Change in Modern China: Economic Planning on the Mainland and on Taiwan, 1943–1958," *The Australian Journal of Chinese Affairs* 24 (July 1990): 128.

[39] Morris Linan Bian, "Development of Institutions of Social Service and Industrial Welfare in State Enterprises in China, 1937–1945" (Paper presented at the annual meeting of the Association for Asian Studies, 1998).

[40] Suzanne Pepper, *Civil War in China: The Political Struggle, 1945–1949* (Berkeley, CA: University of California Press, 1978), 129–31.

personal and moral cultivation of employees.[41] Yeh also notes the important shift from a largely patriarchal and hierarchical pattern of authority to a community bound together by wartime patriotism – a point that
suggests some relationship between external crises and changes in
enterprise labor management institutions.

Of course, the CCP over the 1950s and 1960s attempted in far more
explicit ways to transform the organization of work, through material
and ideological means. Creating new factories meant creating a new class
of industrial workers, whose ranks would expand from roughly 3 million
in 1949 to 7.5 million by 1957, and much more rapidly thereafter.[42] This
vast undertaking began in large and medium enterprises immediately
after the CCP's takeover of China's industrial centers in 1949. While the
Soviet Union and its factory organization heavily influenced how the
CCP would pursue industrialization in China, certain party leaders also
drew upon their personal experiences in the pre-1949 labor movement
in cities such as Shanghai. Early PRC labor policy, including enterprise-
based medical care, disability insurance, and retirement pensions, Elizabeth Perry has argued, sprang from legislation authored in the early
1950s by high-ranking CCP cadres who had many years of experience in
union organizing and leadership. Some of these figures also had direct
knowledge of work in an earlier era of urban craft guilds that distributed
exclusive benefits and jobs to their members. Foremost among this group
was Li Lisan, whose government portfolio in the early 1950s included
labor policy, and Chen Yun, a former skilled worker in Shanghai whose
contribution to industrial policy and state planning would span several
decades.[43] As Perry observes, "It was these individuals who formulated
policies that turned state enterprises into institutions remarkably reminiscent of the artisan's native-place guild."[44]

Yet CCP leaders in the late 1940s and early 1950s also pursued the
formation of a modern socialist enterprise, and with it a vision of the
factory and work organization that represented a conscious break from
the "feudal" past and its traditions. Here the exemplar was the Soviet
Union and its impressively modern industrial sector. Copying Soviet
labor management institutions extended to the translation of hundreds
of books and articles on Soviet methods of workforce organization and

[41] Wen-hsin Yeh, "Republican Origins," 63–73.
[42] State Statistical Bureau, *Zhongguo laodong gongzi tongji ziliao, 1949–1985* (China Labor and Wage Statistical Materials, 1949–1985) (Beijing: Zhongguo tongji chubanshe, 1987), 83.
[43] Perry, "From Native Place to Workplace," 44–7.
[44] Ibid., 44.

mobilization. As Deborah Kaple has shown, the CCP translated (literally and figuratively), ideas from Soviet texts that were written during a radical phase of party-led mobilization and production campaigns between 1946 and 1950.[45] "High Stalinism," a departure from earlier Soviet management practices, called for the dominance of party committees over administrators within enterprises; party-led mobilization of industrial workers through socialist competitions and other mass campaigns; party-led efforts to propagandize and educate the industrial workforce; and the use of military terminology, martial rhetoric, and patriotism to achieve economic goals.[46] High Stalinism emerged from efforts to bring about a rapid postwar recovery to the Soviet economy and to preserve a place for party committees at local and enterprise levels. It also clearly bore the stamp of Stalin at the height of his personal supremacy and power over the Soviet system.

As is evident from Kaple's observations, China adopted more than a single "Soviet model." There was the model of High Stalinism, with its crash production drives and close supervision by party committees. There was also the Soviet model from earlier Five-Year Plans of the 1930s, encapsulated in one-man management, which concentrated authority at each level of administration within a single figure who was to be responsible for that unit's fulfillment of the production plan. One-man management in effect imposed a strict hierarchical and bureaucratic order over enterprises that was antithetical to the mobilizational impulses of High Stalinism. (Soviet theorists in the late 1940s got around this problem by designating a role for the party committee to guarantee implementation of central government directives.[47]) To carry out one-man management, Chinese enterprises during the early 1950s enacted the production-territorial system, a hierarchical or line reporting arrangement in which orders flowed from the factory director's office downward to workshops (*chejian*), intermediate work sections (*gongduan*), and to basic-level production teams (*shengchan xiaozu*). At each level, a director or section chief had sole authority to enforce orders issued from the higher level. As Chapters 5 and 6 demonstrate, one-man management proved to be a short-lived affair in Chinese factories, though the production-territorial structure remained in place. When translated into the institutional context of Chinese workplaces, both one-man management and High Stalinist principles underwent considerable

---

[45] Deborah A. Kaple, *Dream of A Red Factory: The Legacy of High Stalinism in China* (New York: Oxford University Press, 1994), 11–18.
[46] Ibid., 7–9.   [47] Ibid., 45.

modification.[48] The command economy imposed a set of labor management institutions on factory floors in China that contradicted many of
the preexisting formal and informal rules of labor management. As managers and workers adapted to the new rules, they also altered them in
discernible ways.

In 1957 the CCP undertook to transform industrial management
through a decentralization of administrative powers that would culminate in the Great Leap Forward (GLF). Many thousands of state
enterprises, which had previously submitted all profits to the central
government and had bargained for investment and labor resources from
the center, suddenly in late 1957 were transferred to provincial and
municipal governments. (While the central government formally retained
rights to most enterprise profits, fiscal relations were adjusted so that local
governments could tap a portion of enterprise profits.) Within enterprises, party committee dominance quickly followed the decentralization
of enterprise control in 1957. In effect, the ideas that the CCP had drawn
from High Stalinism – party committee dominance of administrative
matters, mass mobilization of the workforce through recruitment of
activists, and others – were far more influential and more completely
implemented within Chinese factories after 1957 than before. Chapter 7
discusses these and other changes in the late 1950s and early 1960s.

THE EMPIRICAL APPROACH

The chapters that follow present as much as possible of the existing and
available historical records of selected factories in China. The intent is
to enliven the analysis of labor management institutions within enterprises by documenting how real people devised, fought over, and compromised on various rules about hiring, pay, and the assignment of
benefits. The use of a microlevel approach to illuminate various battles
over labor management institutions raises the question of representa-
tiveness and the ability to generalize whatever findings emerge from the
factory cases. After all, I am examining a period in which Chinese industry expanded significantly, with many thousands of new enterprises
coming on line, particularly as state investment poured into the industrial sector in the 1950s. Enterprises with relatively long histories dating
from the 1920s or 1930s constitute a special group. If these enterprises

---

[48] For a recent discussion of the downfall of one-man management in China, see You,
China's Enterprise Reform, 35–7.

were unimportant in the story of China's economic development and in the eyes of state officials, a research focus on such factories might present a problem. However, in certain cities, especially the coastal cities of China, older enterprises were very significant in both economic and political terms. During the First Five-Year Plan (FFYP), while over 40 percent of state industrial investment went toward the establishment and expansion of about 200 new industrial facilities that used Soviet technical advice and machinery imports, only about 30 percent or less of China's industrial output came from these new or reconstructed plants.[49] In other words, older factories and mines, many of them "inherited" from the Nationalist regime, produced an estimated two-thirds of the current output during the 1953–7 period – when the value of industrial output rose from 10.7 billion yuan in 1952 to 34.3 billion yuan in 1957.[50] Rawski noted that the investment bias toward newer enterprises forced managers in older factories to make do with existing capital equipment and technology, which brought rapid gains in productivity.[51] Older enterprises and their workers were also important politically as the carriers of institutions that existed before the command economy. The process of institutional innovation and change was contentious within these older enterprises.

My attention here is less with the notion of segmentation of Chinese industrial workers into various categories of full-time employment in the core state sector versus collective and handicraft production units. The idea of "segmentation," or the stratification of industrial workers into privileged cores and underprivileged peripheries, has been a dominant theme of the labor relations literature. Scholars have attributed multiple causes to this differentiation of workers and working conditions across sectors or within particular industries, including the deleterious effects of market development, asymmetries in the distribution of technology, and long-term patterns of conflict between workers and owners.[52] It is

---

[49] Thomas G. Rawski, *China's Transition to Industrialism: Producer Goods and Economic Development in the Twentieth Century* (Ann Arbor, MI: University of Michigan Press, 1980), 29.
[50] Ibid., 34–5. [51] Ibid., 78–9.
[52] For the United States, see David M. Gordon, Richard Edwards, and Michael Reich, *Segmented Work, Divided Workers: The Historical Transformation of Labor in the United States* (New York: Cambridge University Press, 1982); Richard Edwards, *Contested Terrain: The Transformation of the Workplace in America* (New York: Basic Books, 1979); Michael Burawoy, *Manufacturing Consent: Changes in the Labor Process under Monopoly Capitalism* (Chicago: University of Chicago Press, 1979). For Western Europe, see Sabel, *Work and Politics*; Suzanne Berger and Michael J. Piore, *Dualism and Discontinuity in Industrial Societies* (New York: Cambridge University Press, 1980).

well established that workers outside the state sector did not enjoy the same level of housing provision, health care, and other benefits associated with work-unit employment in the formal state sector. Because my theoretical concern is with the evolution of institutional forms of industrial labor management, and because China's industrial sector was absorbed into state administration during the period under consideration, a focus on enterprises that eventually became part of the core state sector is warranted.

Before the FFYP, and even more so in the 1930s and 1940s, industry in China was limited to a handful of cities and regions: Shanghai, the center of intensive foreign and private industrial investment; Manchuria (including the cities of Shenyang, Dalian, and Harbin), the center of heavy industry and Japanese military control during the 1930s and the war; Chongqing, the wartime capital, which along with the surrounding province of Sichuan and others saw rapid industrial growth under Nationalist government coordination; and finally, a group of cities such as Tianjin, Guangzhou, Wuhan, and possibly Beijing, where large-scale industrial units were the exception rather than the rule (unless they were foreign owned) and small-scale production units predominated. The task of tracing institutional processes within factories might reveal considerable variation among these centers of industry, particularly given foreign ownership. To simplify the analysis and still offer the microlevel detail of particular factory cases, I have chosen a strategy of a paired comparison between two industries in two of these industrial centers: the textile and shipbuilding industries in the urban centers of Guangzhou and Shanghai.

While both of these sectors date from China's early industrialization, clear differences in technology and production would lead us to predict that their labor management practices would also differ substantially. The generally high-skilled work involved in the production of ships, for example, suggests that labor management would be arranged so as to retain relatively scarce skilled workers. In the textile industry, however, the form of labor management might reflect the more labor-intensive, less-skilled production process. In China, both industries were important for generating revenues for the state, but the textile industry by the First World War was dominated by private ownership, both domestic and foreign. Shipbuilding in China, particularly for large ocean-going vessels, has often involved state ownership, with administration by industrial ministries, if not the military.

The cities of Guangzhou and Shanghai have been important coastal centers for commerce and foreign trade since the nineteenth century, and in the twentieth century they have stood as the core sites of both economic development and political conflict in their respective regions – the Pearl River Delta and the lower Yangzi River Valley. In both cities, workers organized and became a viable political force during the 1920s, at the same time that Nationalist and Communist party leaders clashed with regional warlords and with each other. However, these two cities in what is generally regarded as Southern China have historic differences in industrial organization that would make it reasonable to expect some differences in the evolutionary paths of labor management institutions. For example, industry in Shanghai was far more developed than that of Guangzhou during the period under study. At the enterprise level, the scale of Shanghai factories during the first two-thirds of the twentieth century far exceeded those of Guangzhou. Also, foreign-owned factories were very important economically and politically in Shanghai, but in Guangzhou the foreign sector was, thanks to nearby Hong Kong, minimal. For these reasons, one might be justified in predicting at least some differences in the workplace institutions that took shape and evolved during the different regime phases under consideration.

Each of the following chapters traces out changes in the labor management institutions within the particular factories in question, and to some degree within production units more generally in Shanghai and Guangzhou. Concurrently, each chapter explores changes in state controls over firm-level labor management. Chapter 2 thus begins with a general overview of industrial production in Shanghai and Guangzhou during the 1920s and 1930s, then traces institutional formation in the workplaces of these cities. Chapter 3 does the same, with greater attention to records that are available from historical archives in China and from the factories themselves, during the postwar Nationalist regime. Chapter 4 analyzes the regime transition and reconstruction phase of the early 1950s, relying on evidence from Communist Party archives that offers fresh insight into how the CCP administered urban areas more generally in this period. Chapters 5 and 6 turn to a rich body of evidence on how state officials, factory managers, and workers informally bargained over the new workplace institutions of state socialism. Here again, the investigation benefits from a wide array of archival material filed under various state and party departments. Chapter 7 analyzes changes in workplace institutions during the late 1950s. The discussion of that turbulent period and its aftermath is supplemented by general reports on industrial labor management in the two cities and conflicts that arose from efforts to impose economic retrenchment on enterprise investment and labor. The concluding chapter discusses in general terms the process of institutional formation and change within enterprises during China's transition to socialism, with some observations about contemporary labor institutions within the four enterprise cases.

2

Labor Management and
Its Opponents, 1927–1937

IN the spring of 1933, a group of researchers from the China Economic Statistics Institute (CESI), with the backing of the Nationalist government, set out to conduct China's first comprehensive industrial census. The motivation for the census, as laid out in the preface of the eventual report published in 1937, was explicit: accurate industrial statistics were an indispensable element of national defense.[1] The author of the preface noted that during the European War (World War I), the governments of several Western nations including the United States had established wartime industrial management boards that among other things conducted national censuses to measure industrial capacity. The census report's publication in 1937 ironically foreshadowed China's own wartime mobilization against Japan, and the study represents one part of the Nationalist government's broader state-building effort in the 1930s.

The census-taking process and the obstacles that the CESI researchers encountered in their 1933–4 survey census reveals something of the limits of central government power in relation to local officialdom. For example, Shanghai authorities refused to grant permission to the census takers to carry out their survey, a stance that posed obvious problems for the research effort because a large percentage of China's industrial base was located there. According to the author of the census report, the Shanghai municipal government's Bureau of Industry (*gongbu ju*) refused to grant permission for the census to be taken within the city's factories on the grounds that CESI was a national, not a local government entity. Shanghai's Bureau of Industry even enlisted the support of

---

[1] Liu Dajun, ed., *Zhongguo gongye diaocha baogao* (Report on Industrial Survey of China) (Nanjing: Jingji tongji yanjiusuo, 1937), 1:1–2.

police precincts in the city to intervene should CESI researchers attempt to undertake the survey.[2] The dispute was ultimately resolved and the survey proceeded in Shanghai after a local organization, the National Goods Advisory Institute, received permission to survey "national goods" factories (*guohuo gongchang*), while other Shanghai factories were handled by CESI representatives. (The census report does not enumerate the number of enterprises that each institution surveyed under this research-sharing arrangement.) In the northern city of Tianjin, local authorities also initially resisted the census takers and ultimately reached an accommodation that split the research effort between CESI and Tianjin's Nankai University. Another center of industry, the northeastern provinces of Manchuria seized by Japan in 1931, were obviously not included in the industrial census.

China's first industrial census offers another nuanced view of the limits of state power by the actual scope of what officials sought to regulate as "factories." Excluded from the census were any production units that did not meet the standards for being classified as factories under the 1929 Factory Law. That law had two central criteria for enterprises to meet before they could be considered as factories for regulatory purposes: 1) the use of mechanized power in production, and 2) the employment of over thirty workers. Enterprises not meeting both these criteria were not considered factories, and therefore remained exempt from state regulations laid out in the Factory Law. By these standards, and with the exclusion of Manchuria as well as national mints and arsenals in China proper, the census takers found that China had 2,435 factories under Chinese ownership employing 435,257 workers.[3] Thus slightly over half of China's industrial workforce actually worked in what were legally considered factories. Other estimates put the number of industrial workers in Chinese-owned enterprises (ex-Manchuria) in 1933 at between 738,029 and 783,200.[4] Moreover, in keeping with the Factory Law, the census did not take into account the significant and sizable handicraft production sector, which not only employed 12.13 million (a figure that does include

---

[2] Ibid., 1:10. [3] Ibid., 1:9.

[4] Albert Feuerwerker, *Economic Trends in the Republic of China, 1912–1949*, Michigan Papers in Chinese Studies 31 (Ann Arbor, MI: Center for Chinese Studies, 1977), 18–21. Feuerwerker cites the figure of 783,200 from Liu Dazhong and Ye Gongjia, *The Economy of the Chinese Mainland: National Income and Economic Development, 1933–1959* (Princeton: Princeton University Press, 1965), 142–3; 425–8; the figure of 738,029 comes from Wu Baosan, *Zhongguo guomin suode yijiusansan nian* (China's National Income, 1933) (Shanghai: Zhonghua, 1947), 1:64ff, 70–1.

Manchuria) but also accounted for over two-thirds of the value added in the entire manufacturing sector in 1933.[5]

China's 1933–4 industrial census serves as a useful point of departure to analyze how the expansion and limits of state power influenced the development of labor institutions within industrial enterprises. A central task of this book is to identify how state officials sought to impose rules regarding the hiring, pay, benefits, and political participation of industrial workers, and to assess how factory managers and workers modified or even rejected such rules. During the prewar "Nanjing decade" of 1927–37, no one group in this formulation – state officials, factory managers, or industrial workers – had the resources or power to impose a uniform set of rules on China's scattered and loosely organized industrial sector. Just as the forms of manufacturing units in China during this period were extremely diverse, ranging from sole proprietorships engaged in handicrafts to foreign-invested factories with several thousand employees, so too did rules and norms regarding everyday labor practices vary widely. In such an environment of highly differentiated forms of production, there were multiple answers to the questions of how laborers might be recruited and dismissed, how wages would be determined and subsequently adjusted, and which (if any) forms of nonwage benefits workers might receive. Upon closer observation of particular enterprise cases, it becomes clear that several formal and informal labor management institutions at the factory level existed alongside one another, and no coherent set of institutions emerged to displace existing practices.

Many studies have described the enigmatic (or indeed, failed) state-building project of the Nationalist government in the Nanjing decade.[6] Some of these studies have pursued the question of government intervention in the commercial and industrial sectors, but few offer perspectives from the factory level.[7] This chapter, focusing as it does on

---

[5] Feuerwerker, *Economic Trends*, 27.

[6] Tien, *Government and Politics in Kuomintang China*; Eastman, *The Abortive Revolution*; Strauss, *Strong Institutions in Weak Polities*. At the county level, an expanded state presence was nevertheless undermined when the Nationalist government collected taxes through intermediaries. See Susan Mann, *Local Merchants and the Chinese Bureaucracy, 1750–1950* (Stanford, CA: Stanford University Press, 1987), 171–99; Prasenjit Duara, *Culture, Power, and the State: Rural North China, 1900–1942* (Stanford, CA: Stanford University Press, 1988), 58–85.

[7] In banking and industry, for example, business owners were subject to extensive tax levies and forms of extortion. At the same time, they managed to defend their interests and in some cases undermine government policy. See Parks Coble, Jr., *The Shanghai Capitalists*

employment institutions in particular factories and cities during the Nanjing decade, provides only limited evidence toward the broader question of Nationalist government autonomy and power. However, an interesting picture of the Nationalist regime emerges as one proceeds through the historical record on industrial management. From a macroeconomic and fiscal perspective, only a small amount of the Nationalist regime's tax revenues came from the industrial sector, nor were significant portions of government expenditures directed toward industrial investment. Some might argue that this relative distance between officialdom and the industrial sector is one source of China's robust industrial growth between 1912 and 1936, estimated at 8.1 percent yearly.[8] State intervention in the industrial sector, though not apparent from tax and investment data, did take a number of less obvious forms.

THE MODERNIZATION OF LABOR MANAGEMENT

Convergent with the Nationalist regime's state building during the Nanjing decade was an effort to develop large-scale systems of factory production, in both public and private enterprises. This process, often understood as a "secular" (e.g., apolitical) evolution toward larger forms of industrial production, resulted in frequent conflicts over the organization of labor. Such conflicts presented state officials and other political entrepreneurs with opportunities to participate in the design of institutions that attempted to resolve labor disputes. As scholars of industrialization and the organization of production in the West have argued, it is not the case that factory forms of production inevitably and invariably have replaced the workshop-handicraft sector.[9] Frequently the two undergo expansion and contraction at the same time. From the perspective of employment institutions, it is interesting to observe how

and the Nationalist Government, 1927–1937 (Cambridge, MA: Harvard University Press, 1986); Sherman Cochran, *Big Business in China: Sino-Foreign Rivalry in the Cigarette Industry, 1890–1930* (Cambridge, MA: Harvard University Press, 1980); Joseph Fewsmith, *Party, State, and Local Elites in Republican China: Merchant Organizations and Politics in Shanghai, 1890–1930* (Honolulu: University of Hawaii Press, 1985); Richard C. Bush, *The Politics of Cotton Textiles in Guomindang China, 1927–1937* (New York: Garland Publishing, 1982).

[8] Thomas G. Rawski, *Economic Growth in Prewar China* (Berkeley, CA: University of California Press, 1989), 69–70.

[9] Charles Sabel and Jonathan Zeitlin, "Historical Alternatives to Mass Production: Politics, Markets and Technology in Nineteenth Century Industrialization," *Past and Present* 108 (August 1985): 133–76.

the workshop-handicraft sector influenced the evolution of workplace norms and rules in the factory or modern production sector. Modern forms of industrial production (factories) acquired traits from "traditional" production units.

In many factories with modern technology and Western-trained industrial engineers, professional managers sought to control the labor process throughout the 1930s. Such reforms were inspired by a global trend in industrial management, a movement begun in the United States and most often associated with the ideas of Frederick Taylor. The set of principles known as scientific management spread rapidly throughout the industrialized world in the first two decades of the twentieth century, and they were widely acclaimed in both the West and the Soviet Union in the 1920s. Factory managers in China, especially in its most cosmopolitan and capitalist city of Shanghai, sought to overhaul employment practices by replacing "feudal" personal ties between workers and "masters" with the professional codes of personnel departments and efficiency standards.

Several studies during the 1920s and 1930s generally concluded that the failure to create a modern labor management system in Chinese factories lay with the incompetence of its enterprise managers. The prominent social scientist Xianting Fang (H.D. Fong) argued that factory "administration," such as it was, lacked both technical knowledge and a sense of proper conduct in business. "Cut-throat competition" hurt both industry and wages.[10] New factories shamelessly poached away workers by offering higher wages, a practice Fang attributed to the fact that "there is no recognized code of business ethics, much less an established convention."[11] On the other hand, firms that had been operating with a well-trained workforce soon lost business to upstart factories that produced at lower prices with lower-paid labor. Fang could not quantify the rate of labor turnover, but he did note how labor contractors, with a superior knowledge of wage rates, would recruit a group of workers to follow him or her off to another factory in pursuit of higher wages. In the professional and trade journals of the period, Chinese managers of the largest factories viewed contracting and other practices associated with what they called the "foreman system" (*gongtou zhi*) as "backward," "feudalistic," and most importantly, inefficient and ineffective by the standards

---

[10] Xianting Fang (H.D. Fong), *Industrial Organization in China* (Tianjin: Nankai Institute of Economics, Nankai University, 1937), 7.

[11] Ibid., 37.

of modern scientific management.[12] In fact, one of the biggest obstacles to gaining such control was the autonomy of labor contractors. Much of the history of early labor management in China can be understood as the effort by both state officials in the public sector and capitalists in the private sector to sidestep the intermediary labor contractor and establish direct hiring and supervision of the workforce.

Shipbuilding and Textiles

The two industries from which much of the evidence in this study is drawn, shipbuilding and textiles, are both prominent in the early stages of industrial development in many countries. Moreover, both sectors draw upon preindustrial forms of employment. While new production technologies such as power lathes and spindles bring advances in productivity, many "early-modern" factories rely on skills found in pre-existing occupations, such as forging and carpentry. However, textile mills generally use technology that relies on a new class of workers rather than those who produce yarn and cloth using traditional or handicraft methods. Tending a set of spindles and power looms were jobs that, given a relatively short training period, could be taught to new hires with little if any previous experience in a manufacturing trade. In industries such as textiles where technology produced new occupations, factory managers encountered the problem of gathering pools of workers who could be trained to do the tedious tasks demanded by the new machines. Mill owners and engineers turned to labor recruiters and other intermediaries to find a steady supply of untrained workers, such as peasants and child laborers, who it was thought could be broken in as mill hands and disciplined in the rhythms of mechanized factory production.

In heavy or capital-intensive industries such as shipbuilding, the age-old skills of carpentry, forging, metalworking, and others were critical components of production. Hence, factory managers frequently turned to local guilds for supplies of skilled labor. Because guilds controlled the training and pay of these workers according to the relevant trade, factory managers' efforts to impose their own training and wage regimes frequently met resistance from guild leaders. In China, at least, shipyard owners and other industries requiring skilled labor tended to delegate

---

[12] Wu Zhixin, "Zhongguo baogongzhi zhi xianyou xingtai" (Present Patterns of the Chinese Contract Labor System), *Laogong yuekan* vol. 5, no. 8 (August 1, 1936): 1–6.

entire production contracts to guild leaders or other intermediaries who had access to workers with the needed skills. The production process peculiar to shipyards almost demanded some form of contracting for skilled labor. Shipbuilding required the production of various parts of a vessel and its assembly in a drydock. Because each vessel was designed and built to the specifications of customers, shipbuilding (unlike automobile production) was not an industry that permitted the use of continuous production assembly lines. Because of this, shipyard managers would invariably turn over specific aspects of a ship's construction to an independent contractor who would deploy a team of painters, for example, to complete a job on the ship's hull. Such a contractor, therefore, had extensive controls over the workforce and the pace of production, owning the tools and materials and in a sense, the labor of the workers. If the organization of production and technology tended to influence different forms of workforce organization over the course of industrialization, regional dispersion of production and technology created in turn different local patterns of workforce organization in China.

Shanghai and Guangzhou

The CESI census had surveyed 2,435 factories in 1933–4, but the report also provided data from several cities on the number of production units that did not qualify for the survey as formal factories under the Factory Law definition. Thus, it was reported that Shanghai had 3,485 industrial enterprises that were capitalized at 190.8 million yuan and employed 245,948 workers. The capitalization of Guangzhou's 1,104 enterprises was put at 13 million yuan, by contrast, and these enterprises employed 32,131 workers. The value of output in Shanghai was estimated at 727.7 million yuan, or more than seven times the value of output in Guangzhou enterprises.[13] The figure for Guangzhou's industrial employment is probably an undercount, reflecting different criteria for what qualified as industrial (factory) employment as opposed to workshop and handicraft employment. A 1932 census put Guangzhou's total workforce at 293,046, but a substantial portion of these were employed in nonindustrial sectors such as construction, transportation, and service sector trades. Moreover, high-employment sectors such as "knitting

---

[13] Liu, *Zhongguo gongye diaocha*, 3:8, 3:11, 3:326, 3:328.

and garment" (44,250 workers) and other textile-related sectors (12,000 workers) would have included large portions of handicraft or nonfactory forms of employment.[14] The wide variation in estimates of Guangzhou's industrial workforce – 32,000 versus over 200,000 – thus demonstrated the different meanings attached to who counted (literally) as a "worker": only those who worked in production units of a certain size or, in addition, those engaged in small workshop and handicraft production.

Another important distinction existed between Shanghai and Guangzhou that is more difficult to discern from these absolute figures on employment and factories. The organization of labor in large manufacturing facilities, which were far more numerous in Shanghai, required some intermediate level of supervision over workers. While it was normal for enterprise owners to directly supervise workers in small-scale enterprises that were the norm in China at this time, larger factories employing over 100 workers required intermediaries or perhaps professional staff, not only to supervise and coordinate production activities but in many cases, to recruit, train, compensate, and discipline workers in the routines of factory production. In the factories in which the CESI census was conducted, investigators counted the number of "low-level staff and foremen" in selected factories of different industries in several cities. Although the data are far from complete, they illustrate the positive correlation between factory size and number of labor supervisors. In Guangzhou, a lack of large factories and the prominence of workshop production ruled out the need for supervisors. The typical worker had a direct relationship with the employer-owner. But in Shanghai, larger factories meant a greater reliance on such an intermediate layer of supervisors. For example, in the machine manufacturing and repair sector, eighty-four Shanghai factories reported 478 supervisors and 4,747 workers (including 1,614 apprentices). On the other hand, the four Guangzhou machine workshops in the survey reported just three supervisors and 152 workers.[15] In the cotton-weaving sector, seventy-four Shanghai mills in the survey reported a total of 1,357 supervisors who oversaw 8,845 workers. In Guangzhou's thirty-seven weaving workshops, the survey found only four supervisors among a labor force of 2,122. In the cotton-spinning mills in Shanghai, there were 1,618 supervisors over-

---

[14] Ming K. Chan, "Labor and Empire: The Chinese Labor Movement in the Canton Delta, 1895–1927" (Ph.D. diss., Stanford University, 1975), 81–8.
[15] Liu, *Zhongguo gongye diaocha*, 2:246–8.

seeing 55,292 workers.[16] (Guangzhou had no cotton-spinning mills in the early 1930s.)

Given the highly differentiated manufacturing sectors in Guangzhou and Shanghai, how did labor management institutions reflect this diversity? It is not the case that particular institutional patterns can be neatly distinguished across regions or across enterprises varying in scale, ownership, or sector. Indeed, different solutions to the problems of labor management can be found, sometimes in conflict, within the same enterprise. Yet it is possible to identify certain formal and informal employment institutions from a rich array of sources on laborers and enterprises from the 1920s and 1930s.

Guilds and Apprentices

Membership in guilds was a common feature of employment in the workshop sector of many trades. In Guangzhou and Shanghai, guild rules governed the terms and treatment of apprentices during their training.[17] Guild membership also reinforced the relationships of authority between superior and subordinate. Knowledge of the trade and place in a cultural and economic hierarchy gave workshop masters power over their apprentices. Trade guilds had an array of quasi-religious rituals and ceremonies, and each had its own patron deity. "Honoring the master" was an important component of the guild ceremony. This solidified the status and roles of master and disciple and reinforced patrimonial authority.[18]

In part as a result of guild dominance of particular trades, apprentices were especially common in occupations that demanded more complex technical skills, such as machine building and metalworking. In Shanghai's small machine shops and foundries during the 1920s and

---

[16] Ibid., 2:269–70. The figures for cotton-spinning mills include those that engaged in both spinning and weaving at the same mill.

[17] Chan, "Labor and Empire," 104; Jean Chesneaux, *The Chinese Labor Movement, 1919–1927*, trans. H. M. Wright (Stanford, CA: Stanford University Press, 1968), 113–14.

[18] Shanghai Academy of Social Sciences, Institute of Economics, ed., *Rongjia qiye shiliao* (Historical Materials on the Rong Family Enterprises) (Shanghai: Shanghai renmin chubanshe, 1980), 1:138–9 (hereafter cited as SASS Economics Institute, *Rongjia qiye*); Chinese Academy of Social Sciences, Institute of Economics, ed., *Shanghai minzu jiqi gongye* (Shanghai's Domestic Machine Industry) (Beijing: Zhongguo shehui kexue yuan, 1966), 2:813 (hereafter cited as CASS Economics Institute, *Shanghai minzu jiqi*); Elizabeth J. Perry, *Shanghai on Strike: The Politics of Shanghai Labor* (Stanford, CA: Stanford University Press, 1993), 35.

1930s, apprentices made up an estimated 70 to 80 percent of all workers.[19] The CESI survey in 1933–4 found that in the machine manufacturing and repair industry in Guangzhou, where employment averaged 14.2 workers per establishment, 42 percent of workers were registered as "juvenile labor" (*tonggong*), a term that suggests they were also apprentices.[20]

Recruitment to apprenticeships in Chinese workshops relied on connections to the home village of the workshop owner. In Shanghai, shop owners recruited apprentices to the machine and shipbuilding trades by drawing upon ties to their home villages in southern Jiangsu province.[21] After the completion of their training period, apprentices frequently went into business themselves as workshop owners. The masters of Shanghai's machine industry "lane factories" (*longtang gongchang*) were "hammer-pinchers" (*nie langtou*), those formerly employed in handicraft shops or in large machine plants and shipyards.[22]

Workshops in Guangzhou were filled with apprentices who were at least one generation removed from agricultural pursuits. An investigation of Guangzhou workers in the early 1930s found that only 15.2 percent of workers surveyed had a member of his or her immediate family engaged in agriculture.[23] Even if recruitment for such apprenticeships in the south did not rely on peasant labor, family and native-place ties remained important. The rubber trade of Guangzhou had several native-place "factions" based on the Guangdong county from which a worker hailed.[24] In an area in which single-surname villages were common, native place and kinship often overlapped. In one Guangzhou machine shop, all apprentices and workers bore the surname of Chen.[25]

---

[19] Zhu Bangxing, Hu Linge, and Xu Sheng, *Shanghai chanye yu Shanghai zhigong* (Industries and Employees in Shanghai) (Shanghai: Shanghai renmin chubanshe, 1984), 498; CASS Economics Institute, *Shanghai minzu jiqi*, 2:807–8.

[20] Liu Dajun, *Zhongguo gongye diaocha*, 3:325.

[21] Li Cishan, "Shanghai laodong zhuangkuang" (Shanghai Labor Conditions), *Xin qingnian* vol. 7, no. 6 (1920): 44.

[22] Chinese Communist Party, Shanghai Municipal Committee, Party History Research Office and Shanghai Municipal Labor Union, *Shanghai jiqiye gongren yundongshi* (The History of the Labor Movement of Shanghai Machinists) (Beijing: Zhongguo gongchandang dangshi chubanshe, 1991), 40 (hereafter cited as Party History Research Office, *Shanghai jiqiye gongren*).

[23] Chan, "Labor and Empire," 93.

[24] Guangzhou Municipal Labor Bureau, "Guangzhoushi laodong zhi" (The Guangzhou Labor Gazetteer), ch. 2, 10 (mimeo, n.d.).

[25] "Jiefang qian Guangzhoushi siying jiqi gongye gaikuang" (Background on Pre-Liberation Guangzhou's Private Sector Machine Industry), *Guangzhou wenshi ziliao* 23 (1981):89 (hereafter cited as "Jiefang qian Guangzhoushi jiqi gongye"). See also Guangzhou Municipal Labor Bureau, "Guangzhoushi laodong zhi," ch. 2, 9–10.

In workshops under the direction of a skilled worker or owner, the personal authority of the shop proprietor was the only labor management "institution" of any kind. Given the fluid nature of employment and production, owners could decide on short notice to halt production during a business downturn. At other times, especially at the end of the year, workshop owners tallied their accounts and cut back on their workforce if necessary. Guangzhou workshop owners exercised their patrimonial authority by dismissing employees in a symbolic ritual that was common by the late 1930s. On the second day of the New Year, the shop owner customarily banqueted employees. If slack business forced the owner to consider dismissing one or more workers, the bad news was delivered during the meal. The shop owner graciously heaped pieces of chicken into the bowl of those employees who were being released, with the words, "I wish you well in finding a better job." While politely conducted as a host serving an infrequently consumed meat dish to a guest, this exercise in symbolic power was clear to all. It put the authority of the workshop owner on display, and probably added insult to injury when an employee was given the dismissal notice before an assembled group of fellow workers at the holiday festival. In Guangzhou's workshop economy this practice was known as the "heartless chicken" (*wuqingji*). As many as 30,000 workers were let go this way during the New Year festivities in 1937.[26]

By controlling the distribution of particular skills and the knowledge to acquire those skills, guilds carved out a niche for themselves and their members in the first factories in China, especially those located in urban areas where guilds had a long history. Guild customs and culture, which had governed the conduct of owners in small-scale craft workshops, spread to the shop floors of the modern factory by way of the foreman-contractor.

Gangs and Contractors

The figure of the despotic shop floor supervisor stands out in nearly all accounts and descriptions of factories in China during the 1920s and 1930s. A foreman (or forewoman, in many cases) controlled virtually every aspect of a worker's employment: access to jobs, training, pay, promotion, leave time, dismissal, and very often housing and food. Traditional ties of loyalty and reciprocity such as kinship or guild

---

[26] Guangzhou Municipal Labor Bureau, "Guangzhoushi laodong zhi," ch. 2, 10.

membership cemented relations between workers and overseers. Factory managers and owners had little control over day-to-day production and minimal contact with workers. Scholars of Chinese labor history have described Chinese factories, especially those prior to 1949, as "fiefdoms" ruled by shop floor overseers.[27] The personalistic rule of shop floor supervisors indeed made production lines in China a "foreman's fiefdom."[28]

In the production departments of large mills in Shanghai, employees were bound to overseers through patron-client ties. Gift giving and other rites of respect to one's overseer were critical in attaining a factory job and in keeping it.[29] The line supervisors, called "Number Ones," had important powers. Foremost among these was their ability to protect a mill hand from the threat of layoffs and dismissals, though this came under pressure in the 1930s during the recession in the textile industry.[30] Another important power was the ability to assign a worker to a more desirable post, one that might entail less physical exertion and the same or better pay than another work post.

One of the most important ways that less-skilled workers in textile mills and other labor-intensive industries were tied to their overseers was through common membership in gangs and secret societies. To survive in the alien and threatening environment of the city, Chinese workers sought patronage and protection from the extensive networks of urban gangs. For the average mill operative lacking the technical skills of a craft worker, such protection and financial support were even more critical than guild membership. As was the case with craft workers, whose loyalty to their masters was reinforced through guild rites and ceremony,

[27] Perry, *Shanghai on Strike*, 138; Gail Hershatter, *The Workers of Tianjin, 1900–1949* (Stanford, CA: Stanford University Press, 1986), 142.
[28] Terms such as "shop floor supervisors," "foremen," "overseers," and "factory bosses" used in this and subsequent chapters refer to those individuals who directly supervise production and workers in manufacturing units. This definition excludes office staff and engineers, whose contact with workers is minimal, although they might have had significant power over labor issues under some circumstances.
[29] Emily Honig, *Sisters and Strangers: Women in the Shanghai Cotton Mills, 1919–1949* (Stanford, CA: Stanford University Press, 1986), 84–7.
[30] Foremen were also pivotal in labor management in the Soviet textile industry of the 1920s during the New Economic Policy. A similar system of patronage evolved because of a labor shortage and the need to train textile workers. Shop floor supervisors were at the center of the recruitment and training process. Chris Ward, *Russia's Cotton Workers and the New Economic Policy: Shop Floor Culture and State Policy, 1921–1929* (New York: Cambridge University Press, 1990).

semiskilled and unskilled textile mill workers paid homage to their over-seers as both bosses and gang elders.[31] Whether their patron in the gang hierarchy was actually their immediate factory floor supervisor or not, the resources available from these patrons – and in many cases sheer coercion – made gang membership all but universal. As one Tianjin mill worker quoted by Hershatter remarked, "You *had* to join."[32]

Textile mill bosses had controlled entrance to the mill workforce since the establishment of the first mills, both foreign and Chinese, during the late nineteenth century and early twentieth century. Shared native place with a labor supervisor was critical for access to a mill job. During the 1920s, hiring in Chinese mills in Shanghai came under the control of labor racketeers, and an informal recruitment system using rural net-works evolved into a semislave trade in the bonded labor of young peasant women. Labor recruiters for Shanghai's mills searched impov-erished rural villages, especially those north of the Yangzi River in Jiangsu province, for poor peasant families compelled to broker their daughters into an "apprenticeship" with a contractor. Once apprenticed in this way, the women worked essentially unpaid for several years under the direct and abusive rule of contractors, usually men.[33] In northern cities such as Tianjin or Beijing, apprentices accounted for about 75 percent and in some cases the entire workforce in carpet factories and weaving mills.[34]

The expansion of textile production during the 1920s and the estab-lishment of apprenticeship programs at many mills only intensified the practice of contract labor. These factory apprenticeships were an effort to recruit a stable and loyal workforce, avoiding the problem of cliques of workers loyal to a labor boss. In practice, company apprenticeships created opportunities for racketeering, as independent recruiters would deliver large pools of young peasant women to the mill.[35] Admission to mill apprenticeships remained under the control of forewomen and foremen with gang connections.[36] This system of labor contracting in textile mills and its spread to both foreign and domestic cotton mills during the 1930s has been documented in detail by Emily Honig. By 1937, the estimated number of workers under the contract system was put at between 70,000 and 80,000, up considerably from a

---

[31] Perry, *Shanghai on Strike*, 50–1.   [32] Hershatter, *Workers of Tianjin*, 172.
[33] Honig, *Sisters and Strangers*, 94–114.
[34] Chesneaux, *Chinese Labor Movement*, 55–6.
[35] Honig, *Sisters and Strangers*, 119.   [36] Hershatter, *Workers of Tianjin*, 150.

different survey in 1932 that found approximately 10,000 contract workers.[37]

The Green Gang was the notorious organization that dominated Shanghai's labor rackets by the 1930s. The Green Gang had engaged in labor racketeering since the early 1920s, well before the Nationalist regime's establishment,[38] but during the 1930s the gang's powers expanded into the control of Shanghai's seven largest trade unions and the local government. Jiang Jieshi (Chiang Kai-shek) first used gang connections and sheer coercion to repress left-wing labor unions; after this method of control met with mixed success by 1929, the stage was set for a closer alliance between Nationalist officials in Shanghai and Green Gang leader Du Yuesheng.[39]

NATIONALIST LABOR POLICY AND ENTERPRISE CASES

The Nationalist Party pushed through a series of labor legislation in the late 1920s and early 1930s before Jiang consolidated his power over the party in 1932. These labor laws were closely modeled on policies advocated by social reformers, bureaucrats, and labor parties in Japan and the West. The laws contained specific codes governing factory employment and labor organization, and on paper, appeared progressive. The Factory Law of 1929 (which as noted, applied only to enterprises with more than 30 employees) prohibited the employment of children under age fourteen, set the working day at eight hours, and stipulated conditions for factory operations beyond eight hours. The law mandated overtime wages, safety provisions, and guidelines for an employer's provision of employee medical expenses. To resolve disputes and to suggest improvements in enterprise safety and employee welfare, the law called for Factory Councils to be established in all enterprises above a certain size. Enterprise management was also required to keep detailed records on personnel, including native place, hours, pay level, skills, efficiency, rewards, and penalties, and to submit these records once every six months to the municipal government. The 1929 Labor Union Law was

---

[37] Honig, *Sisters and Strangers*, 126.

[38] Li, "Shanghai laodong zhuangkuang," 10–11.

[39] Brian G. Martin, *The Shanghai Green Gang: Politics and Organized Crime, 1919–1937* (Berkeley, CA: University of California Press, 1996), 168–72; Perry, *Shanghai on Strike*, 88–103; Edward Hammond, "Organized Labor in Shanghai, 1927–1937" (Ph.D. diss., University of California, Berkeley, 1978), 71.

more overt in its assertion of state control over union organization. While the law gave workers the right to organize industrial and trade unions across districts, all such unions were subject to approval and administrative authority of the provincial or municipal government. The 1930 Labor Dispute Resolution Law also gave municipal officials a direct hand in labor disputes by stipulating mediation and arbitration boards composed of the conflicting parties and city officials.[40] Yet these legal initiatives were only important to the degree that central and local government officials had the will or the resources to enforce them. Neither Chinese nor foreign enterprises paid much heed to any of this legislation.[41] In Shanghai, enforcement of the union law was a thinly disguised ruse for Green Gang intervention in labor relations.

The alliance between gangsters and the Nationalist regime formed with the purge of Communist-union leaders in 1927 and the subsequent "reorganization" of unions under the Nationalist government. In Shanghai, Nationalist control over labor was tantamount to Green Gang dominance of the labor market and local unions. By the early 1930s many leading union politicians and local government officials had joined the Green Gang. The Green Gang's dominance of labor markets, exercised at the grassroots through contractors and foremen, expanded dramatically during the 1930s as a result of its ties with local officialdom in Shanghai.[42] The Green Gang controlled not only labor recruitment at the factory level but also the city's official labor union and its administrative units that oversaw labor issues. By the mid-1930s, Green Gang members filled all five seats on the standing committee of the Shanghai General Labor Union (GLU) and headed three of four departments at the Bureau of Social Affairs (BSA).[43] Du and the Green Gang intervened in major strikes in Shanghai in the 1930s and acted as the Nationalist regime's de facto institution of labor control. Fang Xianting noted of Shanghai in 1937 that "official unions were reduced to organizations which closely resembled their 'feudal' predecessor, the labor contract system."[44]

Officials in the Nationalist government gave their enthusiastic support to scientific management and rational administration of government and

[40] English translations of these laws can be found in U.S. Department of State, *Internal Affairs of China, 1930–1939*, 893.504/76, 82.
[41] Fang, *Industrial Organization in China*, 63–6.
[42] Honig, *Sisters and Strangers*, 121–4.
[43] Martin, *Green Gang*, 170; Perry, *Shanghai on Strike*, 100.
[44] Cited in Hammond, "Organized Labor in Shanghai, 1927–1937," 244.

many other areas including industry.[45] Yet by dispensing political patronage to organized crime groups such as the Shanghai Green Gang, regime officials clearly undermined such rationalization efforts. Moreover, the regime's close integration with the Green Gang did not necessarily stifle labor protest during the 1930s, because Du Yuesheng and other gang leaders could just as easily organize strikes as suppress them. The Nationalist government's informal alliance with gangs and their networks that extended to factory floors through labor supervisors created an important legacy. By turning to the Green Gang to repress a left-wing labor movement in 1927, the Nationalist government's ability to regulate shop-floor relations was heavily compromised. Labor intermediaries, whether associated with the Green Gang or other less notorious forms of control over Shanghai's industrial workforce, maintained their autonomy as "masters of the shop floor."

In sum, paternalistic authority relations found in apprenticeships, guilds, and other institutions existed in uneasy tension with projects by factory managers and state officials to rationalize and standardize a formal set of rules that would govern factory employment in the modern sector. As personnel departments and factory managers paid closer attention to the problems of recruiting and retaining a reliable workforce, they came into sharper conflict with the norms and rules held by employees and many of the overseers who supervised them. The following enterprise cases from Shanghai and Guangzhou trace this conflictual process – and the Nationalist state's pivotal role in it.

The Jiangnan Shipyard

The Jiangnan Shipyard, situated on the northern edge of the Huangpu River as it traverses through Shanghai's southern districts, holds the mantle of being "Shanghai's first factory." This claim to fame is established somewhat indirectly, because it was actually the Jiangnan Arsenal that the Qing dynasty provincial governor Li Hongzhang first established in 1865. The shipyard did not come into operation as an entity separate from the arsenal until 1905. (The arsenal was later renamed the Shanghai Munitions Factory in 1917, and it was shut down permanently following the Japanese attack on Shanghai in 1932.) The growth of the Jiangnan Shipyard from the Jiangnan Arsenal is interesting from the

---

[45] Strauss, *Strong Institutions in Weak Polities*, 182–4.

standpoint of labor management institutions because the two entities had very different histories in this respect.

Management during the late nineteenth century at the Jiangnan Arsenal exercised far more direct control over the workforce than would be the case in the first three decades of the twentieth century at the shipyard. Arsenal management set rigid pay and work guidelines for its foreign technicians and Chinese workers. The arsenal's workforce consisted of full-time laborers, who were paid directly by the company. Management set the hours of work, at six days a week and eight hours a day. To control the movement of the workforce in and out of the arsenal, officials provided housing within the compound to its 1,500 employees.[46] Employees who had previous experience as forgers and carpenters in foreign enterprises in Hong Kong filled the ranks of the workforce, including their apprentices.

This pattern of direct managerial control over the arsenal workforce stood in marked contrast to labor organization at the shipyard when it was established in 1905. That year, Qing officials appointed a British naval technician named R.B. Morgan as chief engineer.[47] Morgan, who had directed operations at a British-owned shipyard in Shanghai, introduced a system of internal contracting that had been in use at his former employer. This arrangement suited the Jiangnan Shipyard's emphasis on civilian rather than exclusively military production. Morgan dismissed virtually all the original workers who had been at the shipyard division of the Jiangnan Arsenal and replaced them with a labor force of contract workers.[48] Internal contracting permitted management to tap quickly the labor power of seven to eight thousand workers when orders grew brisk for ship repair and production, as they did during and after the First World War.[49]

The network of independent labor contractors who had provided Morgan with teams of skilled workers at the British shipyard now offered him the same services at the Jiangnan Shipyard. These labor contractors were none other than the masters of Shanghai's metalworking, forging, woodworking, and other guilds. With the active support of guild leaders, shipyard engineers developed an elaborate subcontracting system that tapped the pools of trained forgers, casters, molders, caulkers, riveters,

---

[46] Shanghai Academy of Social Sciences, Institute of Economics, *Jiangnan zaochuanchang changshi* (Factory History of the Jiangnan Shipyard) (Shanghai: Shanghai shehui kexue yuan, 1983), 89–91. (Hereafter SASS Economics Institute, *Jiangnan changshi*.)

[47] Ibid., 98.   [48] Ibid., 100.   [49] Ibid., 109.

carpenters, and a host of other occupations needed in the construction and repair of vessels. Management retained about 30 percent of the workforce as full-time employees paid on an hourly wage basis – these were the most critical jobs of lathe operators, fitters, and coppersmiths. All other tasks were given over to contractors and their respective guilds. Forgers and casters, job titles that had been classified as full time under the previous management, were placed under contract employment in 1918.[50]

Native-place ties and guild membership remained strong within the Jiangnan Shipyard workforce. A worker's native place almost always denoted a particular occupation at the shipyard. Coppersmiths and fitters came from the coastal city of Ningbo; forgers and boilermakers were from farther inland in Wuxi; and carpenters hailed from Guangdong province. The relatively less-skilled riveters were closer to home, from the Pudong area east of Shanghai and from Subei, a region of Jiangsu province north of the Yangzi River whose inhabitants were the target of strong regional discrimination by self-styled "native" residents of Shang-hai.[51] Each of these occupations was under the firm control of guilds or "clubs," the leaders of which profited handsomely from their monopoly over an artisanal task. Casters, who came from Ningbo, had to pay their guild leaders 10 yuan as initiation fees, and an additional 1 yuan per month during their first year of work. A painter had to be a member of the "Tea Society" to obtain work on a contract team, for which the con-tractor deducted 1 fen (1 cent of a Chinese yuan) per day.[52]

Different occupations at the shipyard had different contract arrange-ments. Teams of carpenters and painters, for example, labored under a single contract boss and could be mobilized for work at any of the ship-yards in the city, not simply at the Jiangnan yard. Workers whose skills involved them in "hull labor," such as riveters, were enmeshed in an elab-orate hierarchy of contractors and subcontractors, at the top of which sat a contractor with close ties to management. Riveters accounted for about

---

[50] Ibid., 147–8.

[51] Jiangnan Shipyard, Factory History Archives, Series 27. These are a series of oral his-tories collected in the early 1960s, when factory historians conducted hundreds of interviews with veteran workers, managers, and retirees about the shipyard before "liberation." Written summaries of these recollections are held at the Jiangnan Ship-yard's Factory History Research Office.

[52] Shanghai Jiangnan Shipyard Labor Movement History Group, *Shanghai Jiangnan zaochuanchang gongren yundongshi* (The History of the Labor Movement at the Shang-hai Jiangnan Shipyard) (Beijing: Zhonggong dangshi chubanshe, 1995), 45.

half of all contract laborers.[53] In shipbuilding and other industries, the power of labor bosses stemmed from both guild membership and their ability to retain a team of several dozen workers who could be deployed in an ad hoc contracting arrangement.

This is not to say that workers had a special affinity for the contract system. Several times in the mid-1920s, Jiangnan Shipyard workers made demands for the abolition of contract work, but each time they succeeded in winning only empty promises from management. During the citywide general strikes in Shanghai in the 1920s, forgers and casters at the shipyard raised demands to abolish the contract system in their departments. In 1927, Shanghai workers, under the direction of Communist Party labor leaders, participated in three attempts to seize the powers of municipal government through armed force. Some Jiangnan Shipyard employees engaged in these clashes, which ended in defeat in April 1927 when the Nationalists violently suppressed the left-wing labor leadership.[54]

Despite their mutual suspicions, Nationalist officials and Jiangnan Shipyard workers found themselves both opposed to labor contracting. When the Nationalist government took control of the shipyard in 1927, officials quickly sought to undermine the contracting system. The shipyard's director, Ma Deji, was a specialist in naval engineering who had studied at the Massachusetts Institute of Technology. Under him were a cohort of naval technicians, many of whom had also undergone training in the United States. The new administration sought to overhaul what it perceived as outmoded "feudalistic" personnel practices at the shipyard.[55] Ma Deji and the Navy administrators established a new Labor Inspection Department (*kaogongke*) that had the power to hire full-time production workers and to control them with a new set of disciplinary codes.[56] The Labor Inspection Department adopted rules to prevent absenteeism and idleness on the job, and to curb attempts by workers to organize unofficial meetings. Naval officials hired a staff of inspectors (*jianchayuan*) who patrolled workshops and levied fines on workers as well as their foremen-supervisors. Full-time workers now had to log their hours through a card-punching clock. Workers wore numbered,

---

[53] SASS Economics Institute, *Jiangnan changshi*, 150.
[54] Shanghai Jiangnan Shipyard Labor Movement History Group, *Jiangnan zaochuanchang gongren yundongshi*, 102–8.
[55] SASS Economics Institute, *Jiangnan changshi*, 203.
[56] Ibid., 205.

color-coded work cards that allowed inspectors to identify the workshop to which the laborer belonged. Employees who were discovered outside their designated workshops without permission received fines or wage deductions.[57] For full-time employees, Nationalist officials provided a range of welfare measures, such as meals and housing as well as a jointly funded pension plan, in an effort to lessen workers' dependence on guild patrons.

Naval officials at the shipyard further threatened the power of foremen-contractors by breaking their monopoly on technical training. Ordinary semiskilled contract workers relied on their boss for work and wages, but apprentices in the skilled trades also relied on him for learning the valuable technical knowledge that would determine their future livelihood. Ma and the Nationalist Party administration undercut this practice by setting up a technical institute at the shipyard in 1928.[58] This enrolled several hundred apprentices in classroom as well as factory training for three to four years, thus guaranteeing the shipyard a ready source of skilled labor, because graduates of the school had to work there for at least three years before taking their skills elsewhere.[59] Director Ma, according to a factory official at the time, established the apprentice training institute specifically to increase his power vis-à-vis foremen.[60] Besides the apprentice institute, management also established a school for workers, with subsidized books and tuition, and dormitories for the three hundred enrollees.[61] For all workers, management reduced the work day from nine to eight hours, and provided overtime pay for work on Sundays. Under a savings plan set up in 1935, shipyard officials matched each deposit of a worker's daily wage with the equivalent of two days' pay added to the account. The accumulated sum was to be distributed to a worker who had fulfilled five years of service at the shipyard.[62]

Shipyard workers appear to have supported such moves to abolish their dependence on contractors, and many temporary or contract workers demanded that management classify them as full-time employees. Representatives from a newly constituted "official" union

[57] Jiangnan Shipyard, Factory History Archives, Series 17; SASS Economics Institute, *Jiangnan changshi*, 214–15.
[58] Jiangnan Shipyard, Factory History Archives, Series 17.
[59] SASS Economics Institute, *Jiangnan changshi*, 207–8.
[60] Jiangnan Shipyard, Factory History Archives, Series 27.
[61] SASS Economics Institute, *Jiangnan changshi*, 214.
[62] Ibid.

established after the purge of Communist Party sympathizers in 1927 made demands to abolish the contract system and replace it with full-time or hourly work schedules for all employees. When shipyard management gave forgers full-time status, workers in other departments raised demands to grant them full-time employment as well.[63] Casting department workers, carpenters, painters, and semiskilled hull workers all made such demands. Ultimately, management reasoned that finances permitted the more skilled operatives in the casting and forging departments to go on the full-time hourly work plan, but the assemblers, carpenters, and painters, who were relatively less skilled and not needed full time, would remain as contract labor.[64] Given the rivalry between contractors and management over these reforms, this compromise may have been political as much as it was financial.

The effects of these new measures, however, were limited. Between 60 and 75 percent of the workforce remained under some form of contract work and were therefore under the same system that offered no protection against the paternalistic authority of contracting bosses.[65] Management also did little to alter the authority relationships in the shipyard, because it simply deputized many contractors as "labor affairs staff" (*gongwuyuan*) and gave them power to tap workers for jobs that demanded overtime.[66] "In those days, a worker around a labor boss was like a mouse who sees a cat," noted one worker in a post-1949 interview.[67] It is also clear that shipyard workers, while welcoming the more stable employment offered by hourly work, intensely opposed the new regime of rules and inspection enforced by a professional staff.[68] Furthermore, labor management reforms did little to improve the shipyard's efficiency or other performance indicators. The proliferation of staff and new departments raised costs and brought long delays in ship

[63] Ibid., 215–16.

[64] Ibid., 206–7; Jiangnan Shipyard, Factory History Archives, Series 17.

[65] Jiangnan Shipyard, Factory History Archives, Series 27. Some workers put the figure at 1,200 to 1,300 out of 5,000 as full-time workers, while elsewhere others estimated 1,000 out of 3,000 (SASS Economics Institute, *Jiangnan changshi*, 205).

[66] Jiangnan Shipyard, Factory History Archives, Series 17; SASS Economics Institute, *Jiangnan changshi*, 215.

[67] Jiangnan Shipyard, Factory History Archives, Series 17; SASS Economics Institute, *Jiangnan changshi*, 216.

[68] SASS Economics Institute, *Jiangnan changshi*, 205. The number of sections rose from 5 to 12, and another 240 staff members (*zhineng renyuan*) were added to the original staff of over 100. The total staff pay rose from 85,130 yuan in 1922 to over 200,000 yuan by 1928–33, or about 4 to 5 percent of the shipyard's total wage bill (Ibid., 206).

construction and repairs. Customers who suffered production delays on their orders called the Jiangnan Shipyard the "Naval *yamen*"[69] (after the local administrators of the Qing dynasty).

Contractors, as less powerful foremen or otherwise, still exerted considerable authority and could quickly bring their workers off the job, as the evidence suggests in several confrontations with inspectors and police. Workers resented new provisions to conduct body searches and inspect their toolboxes for stolen goods. In 1928 and 1929, simmering resentment broke out into open clashes as misunderstandings invariably arose between staff inspectors and armed police on the one hand and workers and their masters on the other. Several scuffles between police and workers led to brief work stoppages that forced Ma Deji and other top factory officials to mediate. When police guards beat up a foreman, a full-scale strike followed in which workers made demands to abolish the new workshop inspection system, to disarm factory police, and to fire the director of the police detachment.[70] After management consented to the second of these demands, foremen-contractors persuaded workers to return to the job.

The Western-trained naval officials who sought to place themselves in a direct administrative relationship to the workforce also pursued new ways of organizing the workforce for political participation. They introduced a new union system that coopted nascent left-wing unions and provided nominal representation for both staff and production workers. Shortly after the Nationalist administration took control of the shipyard in April 1927, officials set up a party-dominated staff union and a Congress of Production Representatives (*shengchan daibiao dahui*) for workers. Perhaps as an effort to mollify foremen-contractors, or to separate them from workers, union rules stipulated that supervisors were to be included in the staff union (*zhiyuan hui*).[71] This division into staff and worker unions, according to participants, was at the wish of both sides, but also at the urging of management.[72] Still, GMD officials could not control the outcome of union elections, or its proposals. In the election process, every ten workers elected one representative, who in turn voted

[69] Ibid., 205.
[70] Jiangnan Shipyard, Factory History Archives, Series 17.
[71] Ibid.
[72] Jiangnan Shipyard, Factory History Archives, Series 27; SASS Economics Institute, *Jiangnan changshi*, 213.

for members to an Executive Committee and a Board of Directors. Many of these representatives had been involved in "red unions" in 1926–7. In February 1928, the new board members advocated an eight-hour workday and improvements in benefits, plus half-pay on holidays. In 1929, when the union opposed the firing of three workers, Nationalist Navy officials arrested two board members who denounced the action, but officials in Nanjing forced their release when union leaders petitioned in the capital.[73]

Despite the presence of political officials, the unions had no rigid ideological qualifications for employees to become party members. As one electrician recalled, a Nationalist Party cadre came to his workshop and simply handed out membership cards to workers, which was tantamount to their joining the party.[74] The GMD Naval Political Department (*haijun zhengzhi bu*) also dispatched officials to the shipyard to serve as "advisers" to the unions. Among them was Ye Baoduan, who directed the armed police guard battalion at the shipyard and exerted strong control over the union councils.[75] Participants say that despite Ye's considerable powers, elected labor representatives made frequent demands for his dismissal. Having a high-placed regime official such as Ye at the enterprise could also be a benefit. When production was halted after Japanese troops attacked Shanghai on January 28, 1932, Nationalist officials intended to close the Jiangnan Shipyard indefinitely because of sluggish business. But in May, Ye led union representatives to Nanjing to petition the Department of the Navy to resume production at the shipyard. The mission was a success and the plant reopened.[76]

The case of the Jiangnan Shipyard illustrates an ongoing tension within one of China's largest industrial facilities between a project to impose modern forms of legal-rational authority on a workforce that had been governed under institutions emphasizing personal authority and reciprocity between guild masters and their trainees. If this was the case in one of the most modernized state-owned production facilities in Shanghai during the 1920s and 1930s, what of efforts to reform labor management in the largely privately owned cotton-textiles sector?

---

[73] Jiangnan Shipyard, Factory History Archives, Series 17; SASS Economics Institute, *Jiangnan changshi*, 213.
[74] Jiangnan Shipyard, Factory History Archives, Series 26.
[75] SASS Economics Institute, *Jiangnan changshi*, 214.
[76] Ibid., 218.

The Shenxin Corporation

If the Jiangnan Shipyard garners the distinction of being Shanghai's first factory, the founder of the Shenxin Corporation, Rong Zongjing, is known in local lore as Shanghai's first capitalist. Rong and his family established corporate structures to manage several flour mills and cotton-spinning mills that Rong built or acquired during the first two decades of the twentieth century. By 1931, Shenxin operated a total of nine cotton mills, seven of them in Shanghai. The management of Shenxin, and Rong's sons in particular, undertook extensive efforts to develop professional personnel departments in the Shenxin mills starting in the late 1920s.[77]

At the Shenxin Number Two Mill, for example, the Rongs shut down the factory in the summer of 1927 and dismissed all employees from the factory director down to production workers. When the mill reopened several months later, the Rongs brought in a cohort of professional managers and engineers, including a factory director who had studied in Japan and technicians who had gained managerial experience in Japanese-owned spinning mills. The new management recruited apprentices from towns in neighboring provinces and reregistered old workers at reduced wages.[78] A new personnel department had full authority to recruit, fire, and punish workers. Yet the personnel department was hardly the model of modern management envisioned in the professional journals of the era. Indeed, it turned out that the director of the personnel department was one Huang Longhua, described by the mill's workers decades later as a "big-time gangster" who ruled over production workers with an iron fist.[79]

The Shenxin Number Two Mill's compromised transformation of labor management was hardly exceptional within the Shenxin group of enterprises. The Shenxin Number Nine Mill, which the Rongs acquired in 1931, soon attained notoriety for its dominance of labor contractors and harsh work conditions. Unlike labor contracting in the Jiangnan Shipyard, which at least involved some reciprocity in the relationships between guild-patrons and apprentice-clients, almost all labor contracting in textile mills was coercive and highly exploitative. Thus, at Shenxin

---

[77] Xu Weiyong and Huang Hanmin, *Rongjia qiye fazhanshi* (History of the Development of Rong Family Enterprises) (Beijing: Renmin chubanshe, 1985), 75–82.
[78] SASS Economics Institute, *Rongjia qiye*, 1:335–6.
[79] Ibid., 1:332.

Nine, it seemed that the worst of both the contracting system and the newer company-supervisor program prevailed. The apprentice system, under which about 1,200 of 3,000 employees worked, was run by labor contractors with gang connections.[80] In addition, there were, as an article from a workers' magazine in 1938 put it, "hundreds of supervisors all over the place. There [were] engineers, examiners, inspectors, overseers, assistant overseers, instructors, checkers, supervisors" who constantly patrolled the shop floor.[81] In the late 1930s Shenxin Number Nine had a reputation among Shanghai mill workers as the harshest working environment in the city.[82]

The weak capacity of private factory owners and managers in Shanghai to gain direct control over their workforce was also on display at the cotton mill that is to be the focus of subsequent chapters, Shenxin Number Six. The Shenxin Corporation purchased this mill from an ailing domestic competitor in the fall of 1931, a period of difficult economic times for Shanghai's export-dependent textile industry. When word spread among cotton mill workers in the area that the eminent capitalist Rong Zongjing had acquired the mill from a domestic competitor, Rong found himself caught up in labor, local, and national politics. Some two thousand employees of the nearby Japanese-owned Tongxing Number Two Cotton Mill (some of whom had been laid off, others of whom had spurned their Japanese employers) went to Rong and the Shanghai municipal authorities to demand employment at the Rong family's newly acquired mill. Negotiations ensued among Rong, Nationalist Party labor leaders, the Shanghai Bureau of Social Affairs, and the nationalist Resist Japan Society (*Kangri hui*). The parties struck a deal in early November. Rong not only agreed to hire the workers away from their Japanese employers but also resolved to pay them full wages, even though his mill would not be operational for another month.[83] The hiring of so many workers from the Japanese mill, combined with those who were already there, bloated the size of the workforce so that it was second only to the largest Chinese-owned mill in Shanghai, Shenxin Number Nine.

At Shenxin Number Six, the Rongs sought to overhaul labor management, this time by transferring rules and staff from the adjacent

[80] Ibid., 1:575–80.
[81] Cited in Honig, *Sisters and Strangers*, 179–80.
[82] Zhu, Hu, and Xu, *Shanghai chanye yu zhigong*, 34.
[83] Chinese Business History Research Center, Shanghai Academy of Social Sciences, Institute of Economics, Archive Series R20–5. (Hereafter CBHRC.)

Shenxin Number Five Mill that had been in operation since 1925.[84] Labor management changes included the use of labor inspection engineers (*kaogongshi*) to supervise the labor force and to mediate labor disputes. Curiously, Shenxin Number Six never used contract labor.[85] Although managers at this mill apparently avoided dependence on labor contractors, this did not mean that the personnel department achieved direct control over the labor force. Instead, shop floor supervisors retained the power to hire and allocate workers.[86] Such supervisors were usually older and more experienced women mill workers who were critical intermediaries for those seeking jobs. It is revealing that during the 1930s the Shenxin Number Six workforce hailed from villages and counties in the provinces of Sichuan and Hunan as well as from the town of Wuxi. Because the mill's chief engineers and department directors came from these two provinces, and the Rong family was based in Wuxi, these shared native-place patterns among management, labor supervisors, and production workers suggest that labor recruitment at Shenxin Number Six may have been relatively freer from Green Gang control than was the case at other mills within the same corporation.

This contrast of professionally trained factory directors apparently compromising with or yielding to the coercive powers of shop floor supervisors recalls a similar pattern found in the Jiangnan Shipyard. Why did factory owners and managers, in both public and private enterprises, apparently consent to highly personalized forms of shop floor rule that were so antithetical to the principles of scientific management? Perhaps factory owners and managers faced a labor market shortage and thus reluctantly turned to shop floor supervisors to fulfill the shortfall in available factory hands. If this was the case, the existing and plentiful historical record on the development of industry in China is relatively silent on labor turnover problems, particularly in comparison to other cases of late industrialization, such as Japan, where turnover was acute. The record more subtly reveals that Shanghai factory managers did at times face a tight labor market, but one that had been made so by

[84] Chinese Communist Party, Shanghai Municipal Committee, Party History Research Office and Shanghai Municipal Labor Union, *Shanghai disanshiyi mianfangzhichang gongren yundongshi* (The History of the Labor Movement at the Shanghai Number Thirty-One Cotton Spinning and Weaving Mill) (Beijing: Zhonggong dangshi chubanshe, 1991), 67. (Hereafter SMPC, *Shanghai disanshiyi mianfangzhichang.*)

[85] Author's interview, Factory Director's Office and Personnel Department, Shanghai Number Thirty-One Mill, January 14, 1995.

[86] SMPC, *Shanghai disanshiyi mianfangzhichang*, 24–5.

guilds and contracting networks with ties to gangs. Furthermore, with the supremacy of the Green Gang in Shanghai and its expansion into Shanghai's government and trade unions after 1932, prominent enterprises such as those in the Shenxin group could scarcely exercise autonomy over the highly politicized issue of labor.

During the early 1930s, Nationalist government officials intervened in the textile industry in other, less direct ways that also influenced labor management at the mills. The depression forced the closure of many mills and left thousands of workers unemployed. Nationalist officials sought to revive the textile industry, which had been severely affected by high raw-materials costs and low prices. These officials harshly criticized management of privately owned cotton mills, including those in the Shenxin group, for poor management that resulted in high production costs, large debts, and low-quality goods.[87] In 1934, the Ministry of Industry conducted a thorough investigation of the Shenxin Corporation, detailing each mill's employment structure, wages, and production costs. A report concluded that all Shenxin mills fell below productivity and efficiency standards of mills run by Japanese or British companies. Nationwide, officials called for large-scale reductions in the workforce, but admitted the difficulty in doing so without causing widespread unemployment.[88] The government eventually placed four of the Shanghai mills under the control of a bank consortium.[89] With pressure from the government to make the mills more efficient, the Rongs attempted to lower wages and dismiss workers. At Shenxin Number Six, management cut back 21 percent of the workforce between 1931 and 1935.[90] In November 1933, Shenxin Number Six managers cut daily wages by 0.2 yuan, or almost 50 percent of total wages for some workers. There were scattered protests, but apparently to no effect.[91] The mill escaped being placed under state control by the bank consortium in 1934, but the depression forced the mill to close temporarily in July 1935. It reopened later that year when the cotton harvest improved and cotton prices stabilized.[92] In an unstable economic environment, unemployment was a threat both to

---

[87] SASS Economics Institute, *Rongjia qiye*, 1:424–6.
[88] CBHRC, R03-2. This file contains the journal *Shenxin xitong qiye shiliao* (Historical Materials on the Shenxin Enterprise System) vol. 2, no. 2 (November 1956).
[89] SASS Economics Institute, *Rongjia qiye*, 1:442–5; 467.
[90] CBHRC, Series R03-4, containing *Shenxin xitong qiye shiliao* (Historical Materials on the Shenxin Enterprise System) vol. 7, no. 1 (March 1957).
[91] SMPC, *Shanghai disanshiyi mianfangzhichang*, 71.
[92] Ibid.

workers and to the contractors who made their living providing large pools of labor to Shanghai mills.

The Rongs and other Chinese cotton-mill owners therefore faced a serious dilemma in the 1930s: on the one hand, they had to show state officials from the Ministry of Industry that they would take the steps necessary to raise productivity and bring their mills up to international standards, or risk what amounted to nationalization. But to reduce excessive costs, they had to lay off employees and eventually take control of the training and hiring process themselves – actions that workers, contractors, the Green Gang, and, by implication, local authorities in Shanghai all opposed.

Similar efforts by management at the Shenxin mills and the Jiangnan Shipyard to introduce formal employment practices brought few substantive changes in the authority relations between workers and their overseers. While managers and office staff appear to have established new controls over hiring and wage distribution, in practice the details of such items were left largely to the shop floor supervisor to carry out. Although the reforms reduced management's reliance on different forms of contracting – whether subcontracting production or farming out the task of labor recruitment – office staff had no more authority over factory workers than before. If factory shop floors in Shanghai and other commercial and industrial centers can be called "foreman's fiefdoms," the industrial census of 1933–4 shows that in other areas of China where factories were far less concentrated and much smaller in scale, labor intermediaries were far less prevalent. This observation is easily attributable to scale – fewer employees in smaller enterprises could be directly supervised by the owner. Another important distinction for cities such as Guangzhou with largely workshop forms of production is that local officials, not capitalists, were the ones who spearheaded industrialization efforts. In creating an industrial sector, such officials also had to fabricate an industrial working class from the ranks of the workshop and handicraft sectors.

Provincial Government and Industrial Development in Guangzhou

Industrial development in Guangdong province, and in many other regions of China, had been hampered by decades of military conflict among rival warlords in the 1910s and 1920s. By the 1930s, the militarist Chen Jitang controlled much of the province and its capital, Guangzhou.

Chen had been appointed as the region's supreme military commander by the Nationalist government, but in fact he paid lip service to the Nanjing regime and in 1931 declared outright independence. During the first half of the decade, Chen embarked on an industrialization project for the province (and succeeded, it should be noted, in amassing a vast sum of personal wealth). The Guangdong Provincial Development Department (*jiansheting*) built and operated a dozen industrial enterprises during this time. Chen Jitang's minister in charge of industry, Lin Yungai, headed the Development Department and was a strong proponent of public ownership of industry: "Because of the administrative powers of government, whether one talks about labor relations, personnel, finance, production, or markets, [state ownership] has numerous advantages," Lin contended.[93] He believed that officially managed industry, when compared to private management, was both more "beneficial" (*bianli*) and capable of more rapid growth.[94] Lin admitted that the province's arsenal, mint, and cement plant had poor performance records, but administrative mismanagement lay not with public ownership. Rather, the shortcomings in these enterprises reflected the problem of what Lin called the "human factor" (*ren fangmian*). The key to successful industrial development, Lin believed, lay in the recruitment of talented personnel. "If able personnel (*deren*) are selected to run provincial industries, not only will the past problem of officially-run industry vanish, but it will be a great opportunity to promote people's livelihood and private industry." It would also "promote among the citizenry a new faith in publicly owned industry."[95] In the past, provincial government officials had forced enterprise directors to hire friends and relatives, but Lin would curb this practice by giving factory directors at the provincial enterprises the authority to hire those they believed most capable and experienced.[96] Under Lin's direction, the Provincial Development Department in the 1930s built and operated a cement plant, six sugar mills, a fertilizer plant, chemical factory, paper mill, and beverage plant. The provincial government also took over the Guangzhou Electric Plant from a group of private owners, and in 1934, brought the first large-scale textile mill to the province.

Located on the south bank of the Pearl River in Guangzhou, the Guangdong Textile Mill was a diversified manufacturing facility that

[93] Fu Zechu, *Zhanqian Guangdong zhi gongye* (Industry in Prewar Guangdong) (Nanjing: Zhongyang rixingshe, 1947), 2.
[94] Ibid.   [95] Ibid.   [96] Ibid., 9.

produced silk, hemp, and wool products in addition to cotton goods. The cotton-spinning and weaving departments accounted for most of the output of the mill's approximately two thousand workers.[97] With 20,000 spindles, the Guangdong Textile Mill remained far smaller than the scale of most of Shanghai's cotton mills, which averaged around 35,000 spindles. Lin acquired foreign technology and brought in foreign technicians to operate and maintain the machinery.[98] Factory managers, who had official ranks within the Development Department, recruited local technicians as well from around Guangdong province. These "common" technicians received further training at the mill. To prevent such trainees from abandoning the facility after acquiring new skills, managers imposed a rule that required departing technicians to pay back all subsidies they had received.[99] Mill officials also set up an apprentice program for production-line workers and provided them with dorms, dining halls, and medical facilities. Workers received subsidies for family funerals and weddings, as well as for recuperation following an injury. Managers concerned about absenteeism drew up a list of detailed rules on how and when absences would be permitted, and with what consequences for wage deductions or firing if a worker accumulated excessive absences. The mill's staff had a separate set of rules for taking leave, slightly more lenient than those set for production workers.[100] Not much evidence exists regarding the mill's wage structure, except that workers were divided into those on hourly systems and those on piece rates.[101] Likewise, the historical record from the 1930s offers no clues about the social composition of the mill's workforce or how employees actually responded to the various inducements and constraints from management. Still, just as in Shanghai's large-scale production facilities in textiles and shipbuilding, factory managers and personnel departments sought to impose a modern vision of workforce organization.

This is not to say that opponents of modern labor management were insignificant in Guangzhou or Guangdong province. Indeed, Guangdong

---

[97] Huang Zengzhang, "Minguo shiqi Guangdong shengying gongye gaikuang" (Overview of Guangdong's Provincial-Owned Industry in the Republican Period), *Guangdong shizhi* 2 (1989): 17–18; "Guangdong fangzhichang zhi yuanqi ji qi jianglai" (The Origins of the Guangdong Textile Mill and Its Future), *Xiandai shengchan zazhi* (1934): 1. (Hereafter "Origins of the Guangdong Textile Mill.")

[98] Fu, *Zhanqian Guangdong zhi gongye*, 4; Guangzhou Municipal Archives, Series 130, *Gongbao* (Public Report) 277. (Hereafter GMA.)

[99] "Origins of the Guangdong Textile Mill," 2.

[100] GMA, Series 136, Public Report 286.

[101] Ibid.

artisans enjoyed a rich guild tradition, and guild masters, similar to their counterparts in Shanghai, adapted to modern forms of factory production. At the Shijing Arsenal, which employed over two thousand workers in the 1930s, artisans replicated the craft workshop and its traditions on the shop floor. Enterprise directors, who as political appointees had little technical knowledge, relied on craft masters to run machines and train workers in their operation. True to their artisan background, the craftsmen closely guarded the secrets of their trade, often concealing technical manuals and blueprints so that their valuable skills could not be acquired by others. Because of the plant-specific nature of the skills, the techniques that workers learned from the arsenal's masters were not easily transferred to other factories and workshops in the city. When a skilled employee could not readily find work outside the arsenal because of these plant-specific skills, a sense of mutual dependence and patron-client ties developed between workers and their overseers. Knowing the consequences of dismissal, it was all the more important for a worker to be on good relations with the shop floor boss.[102]

Still, the nature of the work skills that curbed turnover at the arsenal remained exceptions to the rule in Guangzhou and its surrounding labor market. The elaborate intraregional guild network that extended throughout the Pearl River Delta's cities and towns meant that the prospective factory manager had few resources to induce a skilled worker to commit to a life of factory employment if the alternative of workshop employment was preferable. This pattern was visible in Guangzhou's machinery industry, where production remained small-scale. In the 250 machine manufacturing and repair yards in the city, shop owners made contracts with larger plants to do short-term production on individual orders. When such orders increased, a shop owner would draw upon a pool of labor and rent tools to fulfill the order. This arrangement was called a "roofless factory" (*tongtian chang*).[103] This pattern of industrial organization was also reflected in Guangzhou's privately owned shipyards, which employed some 2,000 workers, including machinists and boilermakers who directly serviced the shipbuilding enterprises. During the 1928 to 1936 period, considered a golden age for the machine and shipbuilding industry, fluid labor markets helped to weaken previous patterns of employment in which native-place and

---

[102] Wu Weipu, "Guangdong bingqi zhizaochang gailue" (Outline of the Guangdong Arsenal), *Guangdong wenshi ziliao* 9 (1963): 24.
[103] "Jiefang qian Guangzhoushi jiqi gongye," 105.

kinship ties closely demarcated occupations. The expansion in production orders caused these small-scale manufactories to attract skilled labor from all reaches of the Pearl River Delta.[104]

Machine shops and shipyards in Guangzhou were headed by a skilled craftsman who had received training through work in other establishments.[105] Former machine shop employees moved into and out of the ranks of ownership depending on the demand for machinery repairs and production.[106] The number of machine manufacturing and repair shops in Guangzhou rose from 177 in 1932 to over 250 in 1936.[107] Guangzhou's weaving and knitting trades, similar to its metalworking and machine manufacturing sector, were dominated by small-scale craft workshops and a handful of larger establishments employing a few dozen workers. In the 1920s, knitting became a staple of the textile industry, with production characterized by small workshops with little if any mechanization. The knitting workforce consisted largely of rural women, who carried out production on a short-term basis with temporary work contracts and piece rates.[108] During the 1920s, the knitting of socks and stockings flourished as a cottage industry that utilized a hand-powered machine. A "master" who knew how to operate the machine would offer a week-long tutorial in its use, after which the prospective knitter could lease or buy the simple technology and then earn money as an independent producer. It was estimated that a diligent knitter could earn up to 30 yuan a month.[109]

Labor markets in Guangzhou prior to 1937 may have been more fluid than those in Shanghai, but they were hardly free of control. A labor organization known as the Guangdong Mechanics Union (GMU) exercised considerable power in Guangzhou by the 1920s. The GMU set out to establish control over the scattered workshop labor force, and it

---

[104] Huang Xihui, "Guangzhou jindai siying chuanbo xiuzaoye" (The Modern History of Guangzhou's Private Sector Ship Repair and Construction Industry), *Guangdong wenshi ziliao* 61 (1990): 245. (Hereafter cited as Huang, "Guangzhou chuanbo xiuzaoye.")

[105] "Jiefang qian Guangzhoushi jiqi gongye," 104–5; Huang, "Guangzhou chuanbo xiuzaoye," 248.

[106] Contact with foreign technology allowed the craft workshop owners to "transfer technology" by copying the design of imported machines for use in their own workshops. "Jiefang qian Guangzhoushi jiqi gongye," 104–5.

[107] Ibid., 102.

[108] Zhang Qi and Chen Guokang, "Guangzhou zhenzhiye" (Guangzhou's Knitting Industry), *Guangzhou wenshi ziliao* 36 (1986): 71.

[109] Ibid., 80–1.

operated like a "macro-guild" that weakened the position of employers. Officially established in 1922, the GMU was preceded by several "Labor Mutual Aid clubs" that acted as a bargaining agent with owners of small machine shops in the early 1920s. These clubs were the creation of a staff member at the privately owned Xietonghe machine factory named Li Dexuan, a reputed anarchist who had close ties with local secret societies as well. With Li's broad powers, about 70 percent of mechanics in the city joined his union. The GMU collected about 5 percent of each worker's monthly pay, and was known to use extortion and other tactics.[110] The Municipal General Labor Union (*zonggonghui*), like its counterpart in Shanghai, employed gang violence to control independent labor activity. It had investigation teams designed specifically to compel workers to pay union fees. The Guangzhou GLU also could deduct various fees and expenses from workers' wages.[111] The GMU and the GLU maintained a tight grip over labor activity, especially after the "Canton Commune" of December 1927, when a detachment of left-wing Nationalist troops mutinied and together with Communist leaders seized the municipal administration. The GMU and the GLU aided in the violent suppression of the short-lived commune.

Still, despite such efforts by the GMU and GLU to restrict the access of Guangzhou employers to the labor market, there was little to prevent a craftperson who had fulfilled guild requirements from becoming an independent producer or shop proprietor. As evidenced by the expansion in these production units during the prewar period, it was common for apprentices over time to move up into the ranks of shop owners.

The tension between a formal means of control through administrative staff and an informal rule through patrimonial overseers stands out as a persistent theme in the evolution of factory labor institutions, in China and elsewhere. The "foreman's empire," as shop floors in American factories in the first two decades of the twentieth century have been called, reflects more generally a strategy by management to control factory workers through the despotic authority of a supervisor who rules through coercion and intimidation.[112] Prominent during the early stages of industrial development in many countries, such shop floor despotism has given way to more formalized means of employment through personnel departments or other structures that allow owners or professional

---

[110] "Jiefang qian Guangzhoushi jiqi gongye," 87–8.
[111] GMA, Series 92–121; "Jiefang qian Guangzhoushi jiqi gongye," 89.
[112] Nelson, *Managers and Workers*, 35–55.

managers more direct control over the workforce.[113] This transformation has taken place during discernible historical periods, often in conjunction with changes in capitalist economies; the emergence of labor movements and trade unions; and intervention by the state. Through different means, involving formal and informal settlements as well as varying degrees of political conflict and violence, workers, factory owners, and state officials established new forms of governance at the shop floor level.

In China, Japanese-owned textile mills in Shanghai appear to have first confronted labor contractors and their autonomy by setting up personnel offices and training programs for production workers and technicians. Chinese mill owners in Shanghai quickly followed suit.[114] It is interesting to note that Japanese-owned mills in Shanghai and other cities achieved relatively greater success in reforming labor management practices, but such changes brought numerous strikes. Labor stoppages were especially frequent at the mills owned by the Naga Wata Kaisha company, and arose largely in reaction to the company's managerial reforms of the mid-1920s.[115] After Japanese companies purchased several textile mills in Tianjin in 1936, initiatives by management to recruit workers without going through contractors and shop floor supervisors failed to make much headway. Hiring via foremen, as Hershatter notes, "was impervious to Japanese attempts to rationalize it away."[116] Even in those mills that did establish personnel departments, shop floor bosses or local strongmen retained control of access to labor markets.[117]

The foreman's fiefdom was not an inevitable form of workforce organization in China, nor one for which Chinese managers or workers expressed strong preferences. Managers could and did gain more direct control of workers under certain conditions, as seen in a few scattered instances in this chapter. The Jiangnan Shipyard, as a naval facility under Nationalist government control, underwent certain limited reforms in management that brought some groups of workers under the control of management. Yet the Nationalist regime also unwittingly legitimized the rule of shop floor bosses in its efforts to extirpate independent labor

---

[113] Jacoby, *Employing Bureaucracy*; Edwards, *Contested Terrain*; Burawoy, *Manufacturing Consent*.

[114] Xu and Huang, *Rongjia qiye fazhanshi*, 75–8; Honig, *Sisters and Strangers*, 79–81.

[115] Martin W. Frazier "Mobilizing a Movement: Cotton Mill Foremen in the Shanghai Strikes of 1925," *Republican China* vol. 20, no. 1 (November 1994): 6.

[116] Hershatter, *Workers of Tianjin*, 143.

[117] Honig, *Sisters and Strangers*, 129.

unions and to control them through state sponsorship. Moreover, as its administration of the industrial sector grew, the state could not easily withdraw from shop floor labor issues. The Nationalist regime needed shop floor supervisors to de-mobilize workers, yet at the same time the regime sought to destroy supervisors' powers in its quest to establish direct administrative controls over production. In the 1930s the first traces appeared of an ambiguous web of authority relations among the Chinese state, industrial workers, and those appointed to control them.

Envisioning an Industrial Future

At another cotton mill under the ownership of the Shenxin Corporation, managers had apparently discovered one way of undercutting the power of shop floor supervisors during the 1930s. Xue Mingjian, Shenxin's specialist on personnel management, claimed that he had established a new way of managing workers at the company's Number Three Mill located, not coincidentally, some sixty miles out of Shanghai, in Wuxi. When a group of technical students enrolled at a nearby institute visited the mill in early 1937, they were deeply impressed by what they saw. Xue had created a "labor self-rule district" (*laodong zizhiqu*). The textile institute trainees expressed wonder and admiration for the self-sufficient nature of this enterprise community, in which employees owned and operated schools, hospitals, cooperatives, dining halls, recreation facilities, gardens, and livestock pastures. A hospital provided free health care and a staff of full-time doctors. "The spirit of self-rule and self-respect are everywhere," the visitors noted in their report. They said of the dormitories that housed over 2,000 workers and staff: "They're no less tidy than the barracks of the National Military Academy!" The members of this community also ran a labor-dispute resolution committee, a labor insurance system, and their own courts.[118]

Xue Mingjian had set up this "labor self-rule district" in the early 1930s, convinced that it was the best form of labor management for Chinese industry. There was an ancestral shrine, whose tablets recorded lineages and praised both distant ancestors and workers who had lived out their days in the community. Workers had built the village in the early 1930s and received prominent status in the temple's lineage records.

---

[118] Ding Yisheng, "Mingbu xuchuan zhi shenxin laogong zizhiqu" (The Well-deserved Reputation of the Shenxin Labor Self-rule District), *Wuxi zazhi* 22 (February 1937): 15–24. In CBHRC, Series R-03-2.

Employees' children had special priority in the allocation of dormitory space. The mill's slogan, authored by Xue, was, "Improve the lives of citizens; cultivate good workers."[119] Xue, who labeled this labor management style as "labor kindness" (*huigong*), had somewhat less than altruistic motives in setting up this industrial utopia. He was convinced that this factory campus, because it isolated workers from "external influences," would prevent labor disputes. In 1932 he argued that all factories in China should have cafeterias, meeting rooms, and dorms, reasoning that "usually it's best to completely sever [workers] from the outside world, and not permit their coming and going."[120] The mill's factory union was under Nationalist Party supervision, and party cadres based in Wuxi set up a social services center in the factory compound in order to give workers "organizational abilities, to increase their knowledge, improve their discipline, and assist the area in its complete self-rule." The Nationalist Party branch in Wuxi and mill management jointly operated a tea house and a reading room on the factory grounds.[121] In 1937 Xue wrote that the result of his "labor project" (*laodong shiye*) had been to eliminate labor-management "misunderstandings," as well as strikes.[122] Xue also claimed to have resolved the problem of recruitment by setting up a training institute from which the mill could draw new workers.

By technical measures, the experiment had been a success. According to Xue, productivity at the mill increased 25 percent between 1931 and 1936, and production costs dropped 35 percent between 1933 and 1936. A significant portion of this production cost decline came in the form of the wage bill, which fell between 25 and 30 percent.[123] "[China's] social organization greatly emphasizes the family system," Xue noted, "so in our labor practices, the influence of the family is very deep."[124] Xue's inspiration for this undertaking may appear to have been Confucian and paternalistic in some respects, but he credited these achievements in organization and production to a very different source: Henry Ford. "The fact that it is possible to improve skills and reduce labor, and still increase

[119] Ibid., 16.

[120] SASS Economics Institute, *Rongjia qiye fazhanshi*, 1:584.

[121] Ding, "Shenxin laogong zizhiqu."

[122] Xue Mingjian, "Gongchang zhuzhong laogong shiye yu benshen zhi guanxi" (Factory Emphasizes the Connection Between Labor Institutions and Self-Interest), *Wuxi zazhi* 22 (Feb. 1937): 31. In CBHRC, Series R-03-2.

[123] SASS Economics Institute, *Rongjia qiye fazhanshi*, 1:582.

[124] Xue, "Gongchang laogong," 25.

output," Xue wrote, "has its clearest example in the factories of America's Ford Motor Company."[125]

Whatever the source of Xue's vision of "labor kindness," his ideas did fit comfortably with Confucian values of loyalty and reciprocity between superiors and subordinates. As Wen-hsin Yeh has shown in her account of white-collar employees at the Shanghai branch of the Bank of China, paternalism and welfare provision had strong roots in some commercial enterprises as well.[126] The aspirations of Xue Mingjian and others to create a benevolent form of capitalism in which employers and workers subordinated their interests to the pursuit of social harmony proved utopian indeed. Enthusiastic reportage and visionary accounts of what industrial and commercial society might be like failed to match reality for the vast majority of urban employees in China during the 1930s. Yet the provision of goods and services to employees directly from their enterprises, and efforts to isolate workers in self-sufficient enterprise communities, did become nearly universal management norms in China's state sector during the 1950s. The organization of urban residents into work units during the latter decade shares several obvious qualities with Xue's industrial experiment in "labor self-rule." Most notable of these, besides the distribution of housing, food, and other daily necessities, was the isolation of workers from the "outside world" and the effort to control their "coming and going." What brought some of the institutional arrangements from Shenxin Number Three, an admittedly isolated example in China's highly diversified industrial landscape of the 1930s, into broader and nearly universal practice by the late 1950s? To get at this question first requires a closer look at the Nationalist regime labor policy during its wartime mobilization and its ultimate collapse after the war.

[125] SASS Economics Institute, *Rongjia qiye fazhanshi*, 1:582.
[126] Yeh, "Corporate Space, Communal Time."

3

Welfare and Wages in Wartime

AS much as Xue Mingjian trumpeted the benefits of "labor kind-ness" in his creation of an enterprise welfare community at the Shenxin Number Three Mill in Wuxi, only a handful of other factories pursued Xue's strategy to fuse scientific management with Confucian benevolence. A few large-scale enterprises in Shanghai under British, Japanese, and Chinese ownership – such as the plants operated by the British American Tobacco Company, Naga Wata Textile Corporation, the Nanyang Brothers Tobacco Company, and the Commercial Press – did offer employees limited nonwage benefits.[1] In the thousands of small manufacturing workshops in Chinese cities, owners at times extended certain benefits to apprentices and employees. Even labor contractors were nominally responsible for providing workers with housing, food, and clothing. However, the fact that owners and managers of large fac-tories housed workers in a primitive factory dormitory or offered simple meals in a dining hall – fees for which were commonly deducted from a worker's pay – should not be overemphasized as the "sprouts" that even-tually grew into the work-unit structure of the 1950s. In most cases in the 1930s, managerial provision of housing and food simply helped to ease the inconvenience of journeying back and forth from a distant dwelling for meals and rest. Such examples of nonwage benefits were qualitatively different from the kind of enterprise welfare measures that became stan-dard practice in large state-owned enterprises by the late 1940s. Without the crises of war and economic collapse in the 1940s, it is likely that enter-prise communities of the kind found in Xue Mingjian's Wuxi mill would have remained exceptional. The dramatic shift from the limited man-

[1] Porter, *Industrial Reform*, 23.

agerial paternalism of the 1930s to the conception of the enterprise as the focal point for the delivery of employee housing, health care, education and training, retirement pensions, and other goods began with the emergency measures that the Nationalist government undertook during the War of Resistance.

In July of 1937, Japanese Imperial forces based in Northeast China precipitated an all-out war against China that soon led to the seizure and occupation of the centers of Chinese industry and commerce, such as Beijing, Tianjin, Shanghai, Nanjing, and Guangzhou. Nationalist government forces retreated to the interior provinces of China, transporting the seat of government as well as any industrial equipment they could from coastal cities. In its wartime capital of Chongqing, the Nationalist regime continued its industrialization program under state planning agencies. The war, while posing obvious threats to the existence of the state, gave government officials emergency controls over much of what remained of Chinese industry. A number of scholars have noted the Nationalist government's adoption of centralized command and control over the wartime economy during the 1940s.[2] The industrial base in east and central China that had been transferred to southwest China came more directly under the auspices of the NRC, a powerful bureaucratic entity that would coordinate industrial planning and policy during the late 1930s and 1940s. By 1943, China's industrial sector amounted to 3,758 factories with 241,662 workers, according to the Ministry of Economic Affairs. State-owned enterprises, numbering 656, now accounted for 69 percent of total capitalization.[3] The state's presence in the most critical parts of the industrial sector, outside of military arsenals, was concentrated in enterprises belonging to the NRC. The NRC administered 103 factories, mines, and electric plants with 160,000 workers and 12,000 staff by 1944.[4] As the Nationalist regime undertook a broader role in the management and coordination of China's industrial sector, it also developed a coherent set of policies for managing workers within state and even nonstate factories.

[2] Kirby, "Continuity and Change," 121–41; Lloyd E. Eastman, "Nationalist China during the Sino-Japanese War, 1937–1945," in *The Cambridge History of China*, vol. 13, Republican China, Part 2, John K. Fairbank and Albert Feuerwerker, eds. (New York: Cambridge University Press, 1990), 547–608.

[3] Feuerwerker, *Economic Trends*, 19.

[4] Kirby, "Continuity and Change," 128.

WARTIME LABOR POLICY

Nationalist labor policy during the war years was in large part driven by the challenges of spiraling inflation and labor turnover. Official cost-of-living indexes for industrial workers, if fixed at 100 in 1937, rose to nearly 144,000 by 1945 in Chongqing.[5] To cope with inflation and labor turnover, the Nationalist government ordered managers of all enterprises to provide employees with extensive nonwage benefits. The Ministry of Economic Affairs enacted new regulations during the late 1930s ordering factory managers to build dining halls, dormitories, schools, medical clinics, and consumer cooperatives. The same regulations mandated strict controls over prices and wages through the use of official indexes.[6] The delivery of consumer goods and services to industrial employees obviously served the goal of controlling prices and wages – if workers did not have to purchase basic consumer goods, there was a greater chance of gaining control over inflation. Such employee welfare measures were to be financed through different channels depending on whether the factory was publicly or privately owned. State-owned enterprises could apply to the bureaucratic ministry that supervised them for finances, whereas privately owned factories, with government approval, could go to state-owned banks for loans.[7]

Labor legislation, generally a dead letter since its passage in the late 1920s and early 1930s, underwent major revisions in the early 1940s. The wartime cooperation of the Ministry of Economic Affairs, the Ministry of Social Affairs, the Military Affairs Bureau, and the State General Mobilization Conference led to new controls over wages, benefits, and union organization. With skilled labor in very short supply, especially for critical sectors associated with military production, the GMD industrial and defense bureaucracy attempted to curb labor turnover by both legal decree and by sealing off factories into self-sufficient compounds.[8] The Ministry of Economics issued regulations in the late 1930s prohibiting factories from hiring workers who already had other jobs. The Ministry of Social Affairs (MSA) and its Labor Bureau regulated wages starting in the early 1940s, overseeing the critical tasks of curtailing labor

---

[5] *Tongji yuebao* (Statistical Monthly), 117/118 (May–June 1947): 92–3.
[6] Ministry of Economics Archives, Institute of Modern History, Academia Sinica, Taipei, Taiwan, Series 18-22-90. (Hereafter MEA.)
[7] Ibid.
[8] Bian, "Development of Institutions of Social Service and Industrial Welfare."

turnover and determining wage indexes that were linked to commodity prices.[9] The government attempted to control skilled labor in the cities of Chongqing, Kunming, and Chengdu through further decrees in April 1942.[10] The Chinese Association of Labor (CAL), a semiofficial national union, cooperated with the MSA to write and enforce policies to control union activity, wage levels, and the movement of skilled labor.[11]

It was not simply that Nationalist government officials administering arsenals and other critical production facilities in Southwest China and elsewhere felt that labor turnover meant lost investment in human capital. Meeting records of the Munitions Office (*binggong shu*) dating from the summer of 1939 are quite explicit about the malicious influences of the "environment" outside the factory walls, as Xue Mingjian had been in Wuxi a few years earlier. Workers were so difficult to manage, the Munitions Office observed, because they "come from different provinces, have different habits, and reside in scattered places." It was essential, therefore, that factories offer dwellings for workers and their family members. Though it was a costly proposition for enterprise administrators, the Munitions Office felt that within factory compounds, workers and staff would be tightly organized through the "militarization of employee life" (*zhigong shenghuo junduihua*) and through the use of the traditional Chinese household registration system (*baojia*). "In this way a factory without differences becomes a family, each other's personal lives can be mutually investigated, and the allure of the outside world will not be able to intrude."[12]

Outside Southwest China, Nationalist government policy reached the Guangdong provincial government, which operated in remote regions of the province during the war. Guangdong officials also called for Welfare Societies to be set up in large enterprises.[13] Welfare Societies were to build and manage dining halls, dormitories, family living quarters, hospitals and clinics, educational facilities, baths, hair salons, child care centers, laundry and tailoring facilities, libraries, recreation clubs, athletic

---

[9] U.S. Department of State, *Internal Affairs of China, 1945–1949*, 893.504/130.

[10] Editorial Committee, *Zhongguo jindai bingqi gongye dang'an shiliao* (Archival Materials on the Defense Industry of Modern China) (Beijing: Bingqi gongye chubanshe, 1993), 3:814–16, 960–1; "Wartime Labor Conditions in China," U.S. Department of State, *Internal Affairs of China, 1945–1949*, 893.504/130.

[11] U.S. Department of State, *Internal Affairs of China, 1945–1949*, 893.504/130; Pepper, *Civil War in China*, 98.

[12] Editorial Committee, *Zhongguo jindai bingqi*, 3:960–1.

[13] Guangdong Provincial Archives, Series 19-1-7. (Hereafter GPA.)

facilities, legal services, and "other undertakings related to the welfare of employees." The regulations stated that, in principle, all of these services should be free of charge to employees. Factory-based unions were to establish and operate the Welfare Societies, and local government officials had the power to supervise the societies. Later known as Employee Welfare Committees (EWCs), the societies spread rapidly in public enterprises in the province after the war. The welfare measures were by law funded in part through enterprise capital, and in part by taking a percentage of the monthly payroll and annual profits for investment in EWC operations.[14]

In coastal cities occupied and administered through the Japanese military authorities, most factory production ceased during the war. However, in a few cases such as Shanghai's Jiangnan Shipyard, the Occupation authorities maintained production for strategic concerns. During the eight-year rule of the Japanese military followed by a "puppet" or collaborationist Chinese regime, wartime shortages and spiraling inflation forced managers of those enterprises still operating to expand the provision of basic services to workers. At the Jiangnan Shipyard, which the Mitsubishi Corporation ran during the Occupation, Japanese managers distributed allotments of rice and coal in addition to wages.[15] Such measures were necessary in many factories because of soaring inflation rates, which were generally higher in occupied cities such as Shanghai than in the interior.[16]

Wartime inflation brought about a lasting impact on Shanghai's wage structure that would persist well into the 1950s. Inflation among China's largest concentration of workers created a pattern in which inter-industry wage differentials "compressed" dramatically by 1946, as did intrafirm or occupational wage differences. In other words, wages varied little across industries or across jobs. Christopher Howe has observed that all branches of the textile industry saw a rapid rise in wage levels relative to other industries, while real wages also rose considerably for workers in many Shanghai industries between 1936 and 1946 (three- and fourfold in some cases).[17] Howe attributed this phenomenon to the fact that inflationary conditions generally cause average wages to rise (as

---

[14] Ibid.

[15] Jiangnan Shipyard, Factory History Archives, Series 27.

[16] *Tongji yuebao* (Statistical Monthly), 117/118 (May–June 1947): 92–3.

[17] Christopher Howe, *Wage Patterns and Wage Policy in Modern China, 1919–1972* (New York: Cambridge University Press, 1973), 22–7.

labor organizations demand living wages for their workers), while the same conditions erode wage differentials between the lowest and highest paid workers. The latter tends to occur as official measures to cope with price-wage spirals affect the highest wage earners most directly by putting caps on their wage levels.[18] Intraindustry wage spans between unskilled and skilled workers in Shanghai declined to a ratio of only 1 to 1.5. (In the machinery industry, the wage differential across jobs was 1 to 1.09 and in cotton spinning, 1 to 1.36.)[19] Nationalist government wage policy after the war, which essentially continued the practice of indexing wages to soaring prices, would maintain and even intensify this phenomenon of wage compression.

Recent investigations of the CCP's administration of base areas during the War of Resistance Against Japan have revealed a similar pattern of enterprises operating as closed, self-sufficient units that provided employees with basic necessities, including housing. Xiaobo Lü has shown how the "free supply system" (*gongji zhi*) was the result of wartime exigencies that forced the CCP's scattered commercial, industrial, and administrative units to provide for themselves and their employees.[20] Indeed, official texts in contemporary China trace the labor policies of the 1950s to the free supply system, which is now derided as the principal source of "egalitarian thinking" that has caused employees to expect free housing, medical care, and a range of benefits regardless of skill level or job performance.[21] Thus, while it was the policy of both the Nationalist and Communist parties during the war years to encourage enterprises to provide welfare measures to employees, it is important to note that similar policies emerged from different circumstances. While Nationalist-government production facilities were concerned with sealing off workers into factory compounds where they could be more easily managed and controlled through militaristic organization, for CCP officials in base areas one goal was to introduce more civilian forms of organization into military enterprises. A report by the Military Production Department of the 18th Group Army Headquarters in 1942 expressed satisfaction that the thirty-four factories it ran in the Hebei-Shandong-Henan border area were now in effect moving away from a

---

[18] Ibid., 26.
[19] Ibid., 17–19 (Tables 5 and 6).
[20] Lü, "Minor Public Economy."
[21] Li Weiyi, *Zhongguo gongzi zhidu* (China's Wage System) (Beijing: Zhongguo laodong chubanshe, 1991), 10.

military provision system in which workers received the same compensation and benefits (including housing allowances) as troops. Military officials were pleased that they had established a wage system that rewarded greater skill with higher pay, including a piece-rate system to induce greater productivity. They continued to provide subsidies for food and clothing, given the soaring prices in the area, but these factories did not provide housing for their workers.[22]

ENTERPRISE WELFARE PROVISION IN POSTWAR CHINA

The Nationalist government emerged from the war as the owner and operator of most of China's important industries, and with the NRC as the bureaucratic and technocratic core of industrial planning. NRC enterprises numbered 291 factories and mines with 223,770 employees by 1947.[23] The rapid expansion of state ownership of industry during the war also resulted in a more coherent labor management policy for state enterprises than was the case before 1937. Shortly after the Japanese surrender, the labor management practices of Nationalist-controlled factories in the interior drew the attention of American consular officials. Julian Friedman, a Shanghai-based official who visited factories in Chongqing in early 1946, observed that several chemical plants, textile mills, and steel mills appeared to be "communities in themselves." Management in these state-run factories provided a range of welfare measures to workers, because the distribution of such services from the factory was far less expensive than if employers had to pay workers at wage rates that would enable them to obtain basic goods on their own. Friedman suspected a more sinister motive behind what he called "the compound system." He argued that it "subjected the workers to regimentation. . . . Such matters as hours of sleep, type of food, visits outside the factory grounds, recreation, education, and political activities were controlled by management and, in some cases, the Kuomintang." The aim, he suggested, was "to make the worker as dependent on the employer and, in cases of grievances, on the Kuomintang as possible." Friedman concluded that the compound system "must be considered a serious obstacle to the development of democracy in China." Not only did this system of labor management discourage individualism, participation, and other correlates of democratic development that American

[22] Editorial Committee, *Zhongguo jindai bingqi*, 4:66–86.
[23] Feuerwerker, *Economic Trends*, 24.

observers felt important, but it also "encouraged, unwittingly, secret and underground activity among the workers."[24]

When the Nationalist government returned to cities following the Japanese surrender, it took ownership of many large-scale enterprises and public utilities, along with factories formerly owned by Japanese corporations. The "compound system" that characterized the largest factories in the interior would have been impossible to duplicate in every enterprise in coastal cities such as Shanghai and Guangzhou. Still, the controls practiced during the war laid a foundation for central and local officials in these two cities after 1945.

One of the most significant steps was the decision in April 1946 to require all employers to pay workers based on their 1936 earnings, which were then multiplied by a cost-of-living index published monthly.[25] As the index ascended to new heights each month, so did wages. Hyperinflation continued at an accelerated rate in 1946 and skyrocketed in 1947–8 to proportions rivaled by only a few other episodes in global economic history. While Howe's data on wage differentials before 1949 take into account the inflationary episodes only to the end of 1946, the effects of hyperinflation ultimately made wages worthless in comparison to actual goods and services that could be obtained from the enterprise. Interindustry "wage compression" and narrow occupational wage spans found in Shanghai, Guangzhou, and Chongqing up to 1946 carried over into the early 1950s, and were an obvious and frequently discussed problem among CCP labor and industrial officials.[26] In 1950, average wages in the textile and tobacco sectors were 22 to 26 percent higher than those in the machine-making sector and 30 percent higher than those in iron and steel enterprises.[27] Little wonder that CCP officials who took over China's industrial centers in 1949 would complain frequently of wage "inversions" in which unskilled workers in some industries earned more than technicians in others. Another legacy of late 1940s hyperinflation, directly related to these wage distortions, was the provision of nonwage benefits directly through the enterprise.

Statistics on the spread of welfare measures in the final years of the war and in the early postwar period show a steady expansion (see Table 1). The increase in the number of enterprises (industrial and otherwise) offering some form of employee welfare provision rose from 2,813 in 1944 to 10,890 in 1947, which included nearly 549,000 employees. Of

---

[24] U.S. Department of State, *Internal Affairs of China, 1945–1949*, 893.504/2–2846.
[25] Pepper, *Civil War in China*, 100–1.   [26] Howe, *Wage Patterns*, 46–7.   [27] Ibid.

Table 1. *Expansion of Enterprise Welfare Units, 1944–1947*

	Late 1944	Late 1945	Late 1946	June 1947
All Units with Welfare Measures	2,813	5,585	7,598	10,890
Number of Factories	558	973	1,082	1,354
Number of Employees (all units)	–	343,656	393,057	548,588
Employee Welfare Committees	79	110	161	213
Employee Welfare Societies	56	99	157	214
Union Welfare Committees	–	14	52	95
Worker Welfare Societies	33	106	139	180
Worker Welfare Committees	n/a	n/a	n/a	15

Source: Xu Kan, ed., *Zhonghua minguo tongji nianjian* (Republic of China Statistical Year-book) (Nanjing: Zhonghua minguo tongjiju, 1948), 382–4.

these units, the number of factories with welfare programs increased from 558 in 1944 to 1,354 in 1947. (The number of industrial workers is not specified.) This expansion, particularly for factories, should be placed in context. First, the figures represent a fraction of the roughly one million technicians and production workers employed in factories with over ten employees (the 1947 survey did not include smaller production units).[28] Moreover, of the 717 industrial, administrative, and commercial enterprises that had established official welfare committees or cooperatives within their units by mid-1947, 401 of these were factories or mines. (Another official survey from late 1947 put China's total industrial sector at 11,877 privately owned industrial units and 454 state-owned factories.)[29] Many of these factory welfare organizations were found in the interior: fifty-eight in Shaanxi province, forty-nine in Sichuan province, forty-one in Jiangxi province, thirty-nine in Shanxi province, and thirty in Chongqing municipality. Formal welfare committees were to be found in only twelve Shanghai factories and five Guangzhou factories by mid-1947.[30]

[28] Xu Kan, ed., *Zhonghua minguo tongji nianjian* (Republic of China Statistical Yearbook) (Nanjing: Zhonghua minguo tongjiju, 1948), 379.
[29] *Tongji yuebao* (Statistical Monthly), 123/124 (November/December 1947): 40.
[30] Xu, *Zhonghua minguo tongji nianjian*, 384.

Evidence from reports by provincial administrators in Guangdong province, however, suggest that enterprise welfare provision expanded rapidly after 1947. The province's Division of Social Affairs (*shehui chu*) reported in April 1948 that seventy-four public and private enterprises had organized "employee welfare projects" (*zhigong fuli shiye*). These represented every large-scale enterprise in the province, including several salt mines, coal mines, steel mills, machine plants, several rubber factories, a tobacco processing plant, and Guangzhou's largest industrial employers: the Guangzhou Electric Company, the Guangzhou Cement Plant, the Guangzhou Waterworks, the Guangzhou Ice Plant, and the Guangdong Textile Mill.[31] The Guangdong Provincial Industrial Corporation (GPIC) funneled millions, soon billions, of yuan toward these enterprises in order to comply with welfare policies and to keep pace with the rise in price levels.

It is difficult to gauge the expansion or possible contraction of such welfare committees in the final months leading up to the Communist victory and occupation of Shanghai and Guangzhou in 1949. Ultimately, the halting of production at hundreds of enterprises brought the suspension of employee welfare measures. But as the discussion of evidence from particular enterprises in the following sections demonstrates, the norm of enterprise welfare provision to employees had been well established as an institution by the time of the CCP takeover of the two cities in 1949. In fact, labor unrest caused in part by the closure of factories was one of the most immediate and difficult challenges for CCP administrators in urban areas in the 1949–52 political transition. (This period is the focus of Chapter 4.) The new municipal officials had to curb the excesses of nonwage expenditures by private and public factory managers in order to jump-start industrial production and raise productivity. While the new regime was committed to a socialist agenda to provide a greater share of the nation's wealth to industrial workers, the Nationalist regime had, wittingly or not, laid the foundation for the provision of enterprise-based welfare measures.

Guangdong Textile Mill

The GPIC, a department of the provincial government, managed between fifteen and twenty factories during the 1940s, including the Guangdong Textile Mill. As public employees, managers were

[31] GPA, Series 19-1-212.

accountable directly to the local government. They submitted hundreds of pages of reports each year to the GPIC (*Guangdongsheng shiye gongsi*, literally "project corporation"). The director of the mill was accountable to and appointed by the GPIC. The provincial government, through the GPIC, had the power to approve the factory director's selections of division and section heads.[32] Officials in the GPIC had extensive training and experience in industry, and they appointed those with similar qualifications to operate the company's factories. Li Juyang, the director of the mill in 1946, had been an official in the provincial government's Development Department (*jiansheting*) and had graduated from the Philadelphia Textile Institute in the United States. Xiao Guofan, who took over as mill director in late 1946, had worked as an arsenal director in Hunan in the 1930s, later to become the manager of the Hunan Provincial Number One Cotton Mill.[33] Xiao's fellow provincial, the chief engineer of the Guangdong Textile Mill, had been an official in Hubei's provincial government.

Management at the mill retained close control over recruitment, training, job allocations, and dismissals. A Labor Affairs Department kept meticulous personnel records on all employees down to the lowliest apprentice. Managers recorded a worker's job title, salary level, native place, marital status, current address and long-term address, educational background, the names of all family members including grandparents, the date the worker entered the factory, the name of the individual who had recruited them, the name of a guarantor, and the respective addresses and occupations of these two individuals. For the majority of the over 1,000 employees who worked at the mill in 1948, the recruiter and the guarantor were staff members or fellow workers at the mill.[34] Huang Jinsheng, the Labor Affairs Department's assistant director, recruited many of these employees, and only rarely in the employment records do "shift leaders" (*lingzu*) appear as either guarantors or recruiters.[35] All of the mill's hirings of skilled workers and technicians had to be reported to the GPIC.[36] The Guangdong Textile Mill, also with GPIC encouragement, set up an apprentice program in 1948 "to cultivate textile skills among women workers." Under the program, recruits would undergo a six-month training period, then be transferred to work in specific departments.[37] These methods of recruitment, as seen by the formal use of

---

[32] GPA, Series 19-1-237.   [33] GMA, Series 32-11-94.   [34] GPA, Series 19-1-223.
[35] GPA, Series 19-2-32 through 19-2-37.   [36] GPA, Series 19-1-237.
[37] GPA, Series 19-1-226.

recruiters and guarantors, were not necessarily meant to overhaul the accepted practices for hiring and employment that existed before the war. Native-place ties remained an important component of finding work. The workforce at the Guangdong Textile Mill came largely from the eastern areas of Guangdong province, as well as from Taishan and Guangzhou. The staff hailed from Hunan province, as a result no doubt of their ties to factory director Xiao Guofan.[38]

The managers of the Guangdong Textile Mill codified an extensive set of punishments and incentives for workers. Employees could earn a bonus for "making contributions to production," or for preventing the occurrence of accidents and fires. Punishments were meted out for "loafing," unexcused absences, arriving at work late or leaving early (even by five minutes), or surreptitiously departing from one's work post during production hours. More serious actions such as refusing to obey orders, insulting staff, fighting, or damaging machinery were punishable by firing. Before starting a shift, each worker retrieved his or her nameplate from a board and entered the work site. An electric buzzer and red lights indicated when workers could leave their posts, at which time they returned their nameplates.[39]

The mill authorities placed a great deal of emphasis on holding meetings, for top-level staff as well as the front-line production workers. As an introduction to the "meeting system" (*huiyi zhidu*) stated, "This factory, in order to strengthen the collective leadership system, to establish a work style of correct democratic centralism (*minzhu jizhong*), to improve work, and to raise efficiency, should call various meetings on a scheduled or unscheduled, temporary, comprehensive, or partial basis, in order to decide all problems, and to advance work." Rules stipulated the precise times and duration of meetings for engineers, production teams, "All-Employee Workshop Conferences," and a Factory Management Committee.[40]

Nationalist Party cadres at the mill held meetings once a month over one or two days. The director of the mill's General Affairs Department had served as a Nationalist Party secretary in Fujian province and was the party's liaison at the Guangdong Textile Mill.[41] These party meetings were to last "no longer than three hours," in which the factory director would "make criticisms" in a summary report on production and the fulfillment of work tasks. He would also report on the "employees' ideological situation, work style, and the organization and discipline of

[38] GMA, Series 92-475.   [39] GPA, Series 19-1-223.   [40] Ibid.   [41] GPA, Series 19-1-226.

work." Guidelines told cadres how they ought to treat these meetings: "in their minds, place heavy emphasis on meetings, and don't treat them as a burden." During the meetings, all levels of staff were expected to be open-minded about improving their leadership work style, and to act "according to the opinion of the masses." Criticism and self-criticism were also encouraged: participants were told to bring to the meetings a "spirit of democratic centralism" and to "do one's utmost to debate and criticize the work and personnel at all levels during meetings."[42] The Nationalist Party branch in the factory was composed almost entirely of nonproduction workers: thirty-four out of the thirty-six party members were office staff. As a Communist Party report would admit in the early 1950s, "the role of [the factory's] Nationalist Party branch was minor."[43] Moreover, like most Guangzhou factories during the 1940s, the Guangdong Textile Mill had no Communist Party representation to speak of.

The GMU, on the other hand, made significant inroads at the textile mill. The GMU could claim as members many employees in the machinery and maintenance department, all males, as well as some women who worked in the spinning and weaving rooms. A strike in May 1946 at the Guangdong Textile Mill ensued over management's failure to raise wages sufficiently to keep pace with inflation. The GMU and its leader Li Dexuan were behind the strike, and according to management, used coercive tactics to keep workers away from the mill. In any event, mill workers did petition the provincial government on May 11, and walked off the job two days later. The rationale behind the strike was that workers at the mill had seen their incomes eroded drastically because of inflation as well as management's policy to deduct meal fees from wages. After such deductions were taken, the GMU argued, workers had insufficient income to buy daily necessities for themselves, much less to support families.[44] Mill Director Li countered that he had given out 40- and 50-percent wage increases to all employees during the previous months, with some as high as 90 percent. What was more, management pointed out, these increases were in compliance with government-mandated wage adjustments. If GPIC officials would give orders to raise wages again, factory management would comply. Otherwise, they were powerless to do anything independently. Because the walkout had occurred in the middle of negotiations between management and GMU officials representing workers, factory officials suspected that an "evil

[42] GPA, Series 19-1-223.   [43] GMA, Series 92-475.   [44] GMA, Series 10-247.

party" (*jiandang*) was involved. Mill management, labor leaders, and municipal officials ended the strike in late May, with a settlement that set limits on the amounts that management could deduct from wages for food costs.[45] While workers failed to gain any adjustments in pay, the GPIC did order mill management to raise wages continuously in the ensuing months. Such orders drew frequent objections from managers concerned about rising production costs.[46]

As a public enterprise, the Guangdong Textile Mill increasingly relied on the provincial government's coffers simply to meet its payroll. By November 1947, the mill's monthly wage bill actually exceeded the capital of the mill. The 877 employees received over 940 million yuan in wages, whereas the total capital was 726 million yuan. There are no specific monthly figures for welfare expenditures, a category separate from wages, but the mill did provide housing for 560 employees, a dining hall, family residences for twenty-five households, a medical clinic, showers, a legal advice center, a consumer's cooperative, a library, recreation club, and a hair salon. Schools for both employees and their children, a day care center, and a laundry and tailoring service were scheduled to be constructed.[47] For all of 1947, the mill reported 218 million yuan in welfare expenditures. Other enterprises run by the GPIC also reported levels of expenditures on wages and welfare measures in the hundreds of millions.

On paper, such welfare expenditures might look impressive, but the hyperinflationary conditions undermined even the provincial government-owned mill's ability to meet minimum standards such as providing meals to employees. Through the summer of 1948, the wage bill continued to rise, doubling from 9.4 billion yuan in April 1948 to 18.8 billion yuan in June 1948. When GPIC officials abolished the overquota bonus system in January 1949 for all its enterprises, mill management reported that productivity, as well as worker morale, had fallen sharply. Skilled workers were leaving for Hong Kong, and those who stayed suffered income reductions. The newly installed factory director Wu Yukun pleaded with GPIC that reintroducing the overquota system would lower production costs, allow for easier recruitment of skilled workers, and ease the tasks of management – "angry words [between staff and workers] and the violation of rules will decrease."[48] In September 1949, the Guangdong Textile Mill reported to GPIC that the mill's Employee Welfare

[45] GMA, Series 32-12-105.   [46] GPA, Series 19-1-233.
[47] GPA, Series 19-1-212.   [48] GPA, Series 19-1-28.

Association had drawn the blame of workers for providing such poor food that they would not continue to work unless there were improvements. (Curiously, the report makes no mention of a possible occupation of the city by the People's Liberation Army [PLA], which arrived in Guangzhou the following month.) Mill management said that "to prevent strikes and protect the welfare of all personnel" the mill's Welfare Association was to be abolished.[49]

Management at the Guangdong Textile Mill of the late 1940s adopted certain practices that resembled the norms of the Communist-era work unit that would emerge in the 1950s. The mill funded its welfare provision by relying on local government finances and ownership, and political party cadres expressed the intent at least of organizing employees and staff for ideological, as well as administrative, purposes. It is clear that hyperinflation, and to some degree turnover problems, had been the driving forces behind the mill's continuing practice of welfare provision. The Communist authorities in the early 1950s, as Chapter 4 illustrates, would continue to grapple with the inflation problem in part by restricting urban consumption and restoring the practice of enterprise welfare provision after its breakdown in 1949. Admittedly, the Guangdong Textile Mill and other GPIC enterprises were not representative of Guangzhou's predominantly small-scale industrial sector in the late 1940s. However, along with other public enterprises in the city, the mill constituted a critical segment of the industrial base from which the Communist regime would build in the 1950s.

Huangpu Naval Shipyard

More typical of Guangzhou's industrial base of small- and medium-size production units during the 1940s was the Huangpu Naval Shipyard, located down the Pearl River east of the city. The shipyard shared a large island with an important symbol of China's nationalist movement, the Whampoa Military Academy that had trained a generation of Nationalist and Communist Party leaders during the early 1920s. (*Huangpu* is the pinyin spelling of *Whampoa*.) The Huangpu Shipyard never established a stable employment system of any consequence during the 1940s, despite (or perhaps because of) its formal connection to the central government and status as a Nationalist Navy facility. While shipyard officials had some control over the recruitment of workers and wage and

---

[49] GPA, Series 19-1-212.

benefit distribution, they chose a strategy that emphasized temporary and short-term labor. Production and repairs at the Huangpu facility remained piecemeal throughout the 1940s. The financial situation at the shipyard floundered as funds from the central government shrank and management could hire only a small portion of workers as full-time employees. The total number of employees rose from only 79 in early 1947 (this included 23 naval officials, 32 workers, and 24 apprentices) to over 300 by the first half of 1948 as orders for repairs grew. But only sixty of these production workers were considered full-time, with the remainder employed on a temporary basis.[50]

Managers at this shipyard attempted to provide workers with nonwage benefits in the highly unpredictable economy of the late 1940s. Zhang Yu, the shipyard's director, set up simple housing facilities, such as an employees' dorm, some separate family dorms, and a small "western-style" building.[51] Zhang also offered subsidies and limited medical care facilities to workers and apprentices. Workers received two Chinese dollars, indexed for inflation, as living fees to purchase basic necessities. Each worker also received a company uniform, which served for more than its practical value, because wearing it meant free passage on Guangzhou's busses and ferries and other discounted services when workers made the journey into town. In 1948, shipyard management also started a "welfare farm" (*fuli nongchang*) in which employees raised crops and livestock for the factory community.[52]

Financial troubles continued to plague the shipyard in the late 1940s. Guangdong Provincial Secretary Song Ziwen (T.V. Soong) helped the shipyard gain contracts for several major repair jobs, and revenues increased with numerous minor repairs on vessels in the neighboring river port of Huangpu.[53] Shipyard Director Zhang gained a short-term cash infusion by selling two vessels left behind from the Japanese Occupation. This earned the shipyard over 200,000 Hong Kong dollars, which Zhang immediately began distributing to both full-time and temporary

---

[50] Author's interview, Huangpu Shipyard officials, May 3, 1995; Author's correspondence with Huangpu Shipyard official, May 16, 1995.

[51] Editorial Group for Historical Materials on China's Warship Industry Series, *Zhongguo jindai jianting gongye shiliaoji* (The Collection of Historical Materials on the Modern Chinese Warship Industry) (Shanghai: Renmin chubanshe, 1994), 526. (Hereafter cited as Warship Industry Group, *Jindai jianting*.) The new building managed to gain Nanjing's approval after it was named the "Chiang Kai-shek" building. Chiang stayed there in the summer of 1949.

[52] Author's interview, Huangpu Shipyard officials, May 3, 1995.

[53] Warship Industry Group, *Jindai jianting*, 526.

workers. These subsidies provided workers with valuable hard currency, but after that cash had been depleted, the shipyard suffered the fate of many of Guangzhou's shipyards and machinery workshops. In the second half of 1948, some two hundred of the three hundred Huangpu Shipyard workers went in search of employment elsewhere, many of them to Hong Kong.[54] By 1949, only sixty-eight production workers remained.[55] Among those who fled to Hong Kong was Zhang Yu, who for good reason suspected that his future with the Nationalist Navy would be a short one if he joined the government on Taiwan. Instead, he linked up with Communist Party representatives in Hong Kong and, by late 1949, announced his conversion to the CCP. Zhang returned in short order to the Huangpu Naval Shipyard, where he continued to direct its operations under the new regime.

Jiangnan Shipyard

In Shanghai, the repossession of the Jiangnan Shipyard by the Nationalist Navy following the Japanese surrender created a window of opportunity for management to resolve labor problems that had plagued the operation of the facility in the prewar period. During the war, Japanese officials had turned over administration of the shipyard to the Mitsubishi Corporation, whose four to five hundred Japanese managers operated through a form of subcontracting involving few full-time workers and as many as 10,000 production workers.[56] When Ma Deji and Nationalist Navy officials resumed control of the Jiangnan Shipyard in the late summer of 1945, they first expanded the proportion of professional staff far above prewar levels. Nonproduction personnel rose from 200 staff in 12 divisions to 456 staff members in 27 different departments. This expansion easily outpaced the growth in the number of full-time production workers, which rose from about three thousand in the prewar period to some four thousand after the war. Management also underwent "militarization" (*junhua*). Staff were divided into military officials, military assistants (*jun zuo*), and military subordinates (*jun shu*). Military officials had graduated from the Naval Officers School, while assistants had special training in finance or military provisions, and military subordinates were largely support staff and secretaries. All staff, including technicians and

---

[54] Ibid., 856.
[55] Author's correspondence with Huangpu Shipyard official, May 16, 1995.
[56] Jiangnan Shipyard, Factory History Archives, Series 27.

engineers, were given official naval titles and ranks, and they received pay according to military salary standards.[57] Among the newly expanded sections were the Police Affairs (*jingwu*) Office and the Labor Inspection Section, with staffs of forty-four and thirty-three respectively.[58]

With the professionalization, and militarization, of the shipyard's personnel offices, Ma Deji was able to achieve a long-sought goal of converting the entire workforce from contract to full-time labor. In the spring of 1946, he announced the abolition of the contract system: "The thing I am most dissatisfied with is the labor situation. At present we have over 5,000 workers, among whom contract-hourly laborers are the majority. Contract labor has various disadvantages. . . . Every project must have accurate records, but if we use contract labor, this will not happen." Subsequently, shipyard management gradually phased in all workers as official employees paid on an hourly basis directly from the company. However, rather than dismissing existing contractors, Ma Deji converted them to "labor affairs staff," just as he had done with ex-contractors in the 1930s.[59]

In a speech to the new "labor affairs staff" in 1946, Ma acknowledged their importance as the "backbone elements" of the shipyard, but pointed out how their monthly salary of 300 yuan nearly exceeded that of the shipyard's technicians and engineers. Ma told the contractors that he would pay them an incentive bonus for projects they completed ahead of schedule. Depending on the time that the foremen took to complete the project, they could receive 50 percent of the remaining wage bill for the unworked hours. If the assigned project went beyond the estimated schedule, however, Ma would pay no extra wages.[60] In doing this, Ma essentially reversed the incentive structure for the foremen – rather than overreporting the actual number of work hours as they had done in the past, they now could overestimate how long a project would take and then push workers to complete it as fast as possible.

The dependence of workers and factory officials on contractors, now titled as workshop directors and shift leaders, continued as in the prewar period. Occupational stratification based upon native place also carried over from the 1920s and 1930s. Full-time workers remained directly responsible to labor affairs staff or shift leaders, not to personnel

---

[57] Jiangnan Shipyard, Factory History Archives, Series 28.
[58] SASS Economics Institute, *Jiangnan changshi*, 286.
[59] Jiangnan Shipyard, Factory History Archives, Series 28.
[60] Ibid.

department staff or engineers. Line supervisors, whether former contractors or not, could determine a worker's pay, benefits, and dismissal
prospects. The foremen also maintained lucrative earnings because they
reported their subordinates' work hours to engineers in the departments.
By inflating the number of hours, or even the number of workers in a
given period of time, they could pocket the difference. Often the foremen
shared this surplus with engineers. Management calculated that in one
month the difference between the reported and actual amount of labor
used totaled over two thousand hours per week. In other words, the shipyard foremen together were taking in what amounted to more than the
combined daily wages of 250 workers, each day.[61]

Ma Deji also attempted to restructure wages at the shipyard so that
pay was attached to jobs rather than to individuals. He had introduced
a wage grade system for full-time workers during the 1930s. After 1945,
he instituted a "56-grade" wage system that assigned a numerical ranking
to all production workers, from technicians to "ordinary labor" (*cugong*),
with the lowest being grade 56 and the highest being grade 1. (Apprentices were ranked outside the "56-grade" scale, down to grade 95.) Each
job title or position had a particular range of grades corresponding
to different levels of pay. For example, the uppermost rungs, grades 1 to
14, were reserved for engineers and technicians, grades 15 to 27 for
workshop directors, and so on.[62] Despite the apparent skill criteria
encouraged by the wage grade system, however, wage adjustments, or
promotions up the wage ladder to higher rates of pay, remained in the
hands of workshop directors and shift leaders. This meant that wage
adjustments could be given out in a highly arbitrary fashion, based on a
worker's personal relations with the workshop director or shift leader.[63]
Even if they were not involved in contracting for unskilled temporary
labor, such supervisors still had extensive power over skilled workers by
being able to set a worker's wage grade and to make subsequent adjustments to it.

Ma also expanded welfare measures as part of a comprehensive goal
to combine scientific management with a harmonious family environment. Writing in the journal *New Navy Monthly* in 1946, Ma expressed
the prevailing view of officials at the shipyard:

---

[61] SASS Economics Institute, *Jiangnan changshi*, 290.
[62] Shanghai Municipal Archives, Series Q6-6-39, bk. 2. (Hereafter cited as SMA.)
[63] Author's interview, Jiangnan Shipyard History Research Office, December 26, 1994.

To transform the mind of the worker, to eradicate labor disputes, we must stress welfare. This will stabilize [workers'] livelihood, establish incentives, and stimulate their interest. It will make everyone view the factory as a family, to love what is public and get beyond the private.[64]

Naval officials running the shipyard argued that the central goal of efficiency could be attained through both a precise division of labor and a welfare policy for employees that integrated them with the workplace. The impersonalism and quantitative rule of scientific management were seemingly compatible with the paternalistic view of "factory as a family."

Yet the removal of the distinction between full-time and contract laborers and the idea of "factory as a family" did not mean that all workers were equal in the eyes of management. Ma and personnel officials reclassified each shipyard worker into one of several categories, corresponding to the degree of importance attached to the job: "permanent" labor (*guding gong, jiben gong*), "common reserve" labor (*changbei gong*), "temporary" labor (*linshi gong*), "common temporary" labor (*changlin gong*), and "provisional temporary" labor (*linlin gong*).[65] This arrangement allowed shipyard managers to retain a relatively large workforce without having to pay a costly wage bill that would have been the case if all workers were paid based on a set amount of hours.

Workers at the shipyard who remained classified as temporary labor demanded status as full-time employees and the accompanying benefits during the postwar period. In the summer of 1946, ship carpenters issued an appeal to management and the Shanghai BSA. They called on management to change the terms of their employment, from what they called a "mobile worker system" (*liudong gongren zhi*) to a "factory labor system" (*changgongzhi*). Using the government policy as the basis of their argument, the carpenters said their wages should be adjusted for inflation according to official standard of living indexes, as was the case at other shipyards. Calling themselves the "basic cells of the ship-

---

[64] *Xin haijun yuekan* (New Navy Monthly) 3 (September 1946): 43.

[65] The distinctions and their labels vary from source to source. Shanghai Jiangnan Shipyard Labor Movement History Group, *Jiangnan zaochuanchang gongren*, 22; SASS Economics Institute, *Jiangnan changshi*, 288; "Recollections of Jiangnan Shipyard Workers," Shen Wenxian. (This is a private collection of short biographies based on interviews with veteran workers in the early 1960s, made available to the author in 1994.)

building industry," the ship carpenters demanded benefits and policies for which full-time shipyard employees were eligible: medical benefits, compensation for accidents and death, sick leave, severance and retirement payments, pensions, paid holidays, and regular subsidies. The carpenters also demanded that workers who obeyed regulations could not be dismissed "without a detailed reason that is explained to him." If a factory rule had been violated, it must have already been issued by the departments and made public. Jiangnan Shipyard management declined to accept the demands of the carpenters. The BSA, in reply to the ship carpenters' petition, explained that the Jiangnan Shipyard's status as a military production facility meant that the BSA had no power to regulate labor matters there.[66]

It was soon after this petition that Ma Deji formally abolished the contract system, an action that reduced the size of the workforce and gave the remaining full-time employees wide-ranging benefits. The shipyard's Workers' Welfare Committee cooperated with management to convince the Nationalist government to increase funding to the enterprise and to improve the standard of living for employees. Ma Deji noted that a shortage of housing forced over nine hundred workers to live in crude dwellings and shacks around the city. However, plans to construct dormitories for workers and staff were delayed until the second half of 1948, and the building that was eventually completed housed only 200 workers on a temporary basis.[67] The delays are attributed in one source to the factional battles between Ma Deji and the head of the Naval Garrison Command, Gui Yongqing. Gui refused to approve budget allocations for the dormitory, suspecting that Ma was building it to win workers' support.[68] Ma also began a workers' cooperative store that provided discounted consumer goods from the United States. This was part of his effort, according to CCP sources, to limit the powers of the Workers' Welfare Committee to the sphere of handling basic welfare issues, rather than production and wage matters.[69] In any event, expenditures on such items as food, uniforms, medicine, and other employee welfare measures at the Jiangnan Shipyard amounted to 24.1 trillion yuan, or 16.6 percent of the total expenditures in 1947. Subsidies distributed in 1947, at 6.86

[66] SMA, Series Q6-8.1-316.
[67] Shanghai Jiangnan Shipyard Labor Movement History Group, *Jiangnan zaochuanchang gongren*, 54.
[68] SASS Economics Institute, *Jiangnan changshi*, 293.
[69] Shanghai Jiangnan Shipyard Labor Movement History Group, *Jiangnan zaochuanchang gongren*, 204.

trillion yuan, nearly equaled the amount spent on salaries and wages, which totaled 7.31 trillion yuan.[70] These expenditures represented a response to soaring commodity prices, as factory officials substituted nonwage forms of compensation for cash.

Mounting pressures to reduce the size of the workforce led to layoff announcements in the spring of 1947. Management convened a series of Factory Conferences (*gongchang huiyi*) to discuss how to handle the crises of spiraling inflation and declining revenues. At a March 30, 1947 "emergency conference," Director Ma announced that the monthly wage bill was to be reduced by 100 million yuan, meaning layoffs or work cut-backs of another 50 percent from the present level of roughly four thousand employees. The monthly payroll of staff would be cut back so that it did not exceed 20 million yuan, and coal consumption would have to be brought below 500 tons a month. If these labor reductions were in the form of actual layoffs, it meant that 1,600 of the present 3,600 hourly workers would lose their jobs, along with 100 of the 430 staff. To handle these layoffs, management instructed production department engineers and shift leaders to rate each worker on a scale of 100, with 40 points for skill, 30 points for age, 30 points for "attitude and performance." Those who scored lowest would be cut.[71] Despite the use of such quantitative criteria as age and skill, management nonetheless allowed the shipyard's foremen to determine a worker's fate based on "attitude and perfor-mance." In another measure to lower the wage bill, Ma Deji and ship-yard officials permitted several dozen foremen to carry out the functions of staff members, in a procedure called "labor replaces staff" or "artisans replace staff" (*gongdaizhi, yidaizhi*), a move that clearly enhanced the power of foremen relative to professional staff.[72]

Efforts by management to invoke job cutbacks, however, failed when Jiangnan Shipyard workers organized a march in Nanjing, where they presented petitions at the Executive Yuan, the National Defense Min-istry, the Ministry of Social Affairs, and the Naval Garrison Command (NGC). Government officials agreed that the NGC would remit its unpaid bills and that 306 employees who had been dismissed previously would be restored to their jobs.[73] By July 1947, the ambitious plans to cut back labor had resulted in only 294 of the intended 1,600 workers

---

[70] SASS Economics Institute, *Jiangnan changshi*, 281.
[71] Jiangnan Shipyard, Factory History Archives, Series 28.
[72] SASS Economics Institute, *Jiangnan changshi*, 288; Jiangnan Shipyard, Factory History Archives, Series 28.
[73] SASS Economics Institute, *Jiangnan changshi*, 308–9.

being laid off.[74] As late as September 1948, personnel records show that employment at the shipyard had actually expanded, to over 3,700 employees, consisting of 3,318 production workers and 435 staff.[75]

Political controls over the workforce at the Jiangnan Shipyard were also less dramatic than might seem the case from partisan accounts by either Nationalist or Communist historians. A fairly reliable recollection by the vice-director of the shipyard recorded during the early 1960s noted that Nationalist Party supervision during the late 1940s and re-pression of the CCP organizers was simply too strong for there to be a viable CCP underground at the shipyard.[76] Besides this, partisan leaders changed sides with some frequency, if the case of shipyard worker Jin Huashan is indicative. Jin, who would go on to become an all-Shanghai Model Worker in the 1950s and eventually the party secretary of the Jiangnan Shipyard, cultivated clients as an "elder" during the 1940s and became a leading cadre with the Nationalist Party–sponsored municipal Welfare Association and a "Welfare Team" of the BSA. Other workers during the early 1960s identified Jin as a "gangster" (*liumang*) during the early 1940s. When a fellow worker introduced Jin to a handful of Communist organizers attempting to establish a party cell there in 1945, his true political stance was likely the source of some confusion.[77] No viable party cell was established at the shipyard until the second half of 1948.

Like his counterpart at the much smaller Huangpu Shipyard in Guangzhou, Ma Deji faced a difficult choice in the waning days of the Nationalist regime. Under Nationalist government orders to dismantle the shipyard's productive equipment and to destroy whatever machin-ery could not be transported to Taiwan, Ma instead aligned himself with shipyard workers who had organized teams to protect the shipyard and its capital equipment.

Private Enterprises in Shanghai

Nationalist government policy to cope with inflation during the late 1940s also promoted employee welfare provision in private enterprises in Shanghai. The Shanghai BSA issued guidelines in February 1946,

---

[74] Jiangnan Shipyard, Factory History Archives, Series 28.
[75] SMA, Series Q6-6-39.
[76] Jiangnan Shipyard, Factory History Archives, Series 22.
[77] Jiangnan Shipyard, Factory History Archives, Series 19, 20, 21.

based on national laws, for all medium-to-large enterprises to manage employee welfare funds (*zhigong fulijin*). The laws and regulations called for enterprises with 200 employees or more to establish Employee Welfare Committees (*fuli weiyuanhui*) and to operate Welfare Societies (*fulishe*) that were to provide a range of nonwage benefits, such as dormitories, dining halls, and medical care facilities. (Enterprises with fewer than 200 employees were to set up networks for cooperative welfare provision.)[78] As the following discussion of the Shenxin Number Six Mill illustrates, these Welfare Societies became the unofficial channels through which Nationalist Party labor organizers attempted to establish ties with workers and dispense patronage in return for political support.

In early 1947, as inflation skyrocketed and the civil war with the Communists intensified, the Nationalist government's Executive Yuan attempted to strengthen wage and price controls during a declared "economic emergency." The decrees froze standard-of-living indexes, the critical multipliers that converted the basic wages of workers to changes in commodity prices. To administer such wage controls, the Ministry of Economics established a Wage Appraisal Board (*gongzi pingyi hui*), which set wages in "important industries," defined as those that produced daily necessities such as rice, coal, oil, salt, cotton, cloth, and sugar.[79] The wage freeze was lifted, in practice, when managers at numerous enterprises consented to demands from workers to raise wages.

Collectively, by contrast, various associations of private factory owners in Shanghai warned Nationalist officials that neither public nor private enterprises could maintain wage levels so high. The Shanghai branch of the All-China Association of Industry (*Zhongguo quanguo gongye xiehui*) and its individual industrial federations claimed that factory managers had "without exception done their best to shoulder the burden within the scope possible of workers' incessant demands for increased pay and benefits, because they understand the government's difficulties in eradicating labor disputes." The association also noted that factory directors were not to blame for the soaring inflation.[80] Basic wages of workers in some industries, especially cotton spinning and weaving, were increasing much faster than warranted by factory output and productivity. In the cotton-spinning and weaving sector, for example, the pre-1937 basic wage of 11 yuan per month had risen to over 35 yuan per month in the post-1945 period. (The basic wage was multiplied by an index

---

[78] MEA, Series 18-22-90.   [79] SMA, Series S30-1-299.   [80] MEA, Series 24-03-40.

number to determine the actual amount of pay.) On top of this, "treatment" (*daiyu*), a catchall category including benefits and subsidies, had more than doubled, even accounting for inflation. There was no way, at present output, that factories could maintain this level of welfare distribution, the report warned.[81] Notwithstanding these pleas from Shanghai industrialists, Nationalist officials maintained the ultimately futile policy of linking wages to prices and attempting to control both by freezing the latter.

During the late 1940s the Nationalist government in Shanghai also sought to cope with a rising unemployment crisis by controlling factory shutdowns and related closures. Unemployment was mounting as a grave problem in Chinese cities by 1946, and as many as 250,000 were out of work in Shanghai by the end of 1946, largely as a result of business failures. Unemployment and business closures also put large portions of the working population out on the streets in Guangzhou, Tianjin, and other centers of industry and commerce.[82] In the summer of 1946, a Labor-Capital Arbitration Committee (*laozi pingduan weiyuanhui*, LCAC) under the BSA was established to curb the growing number of layoffs and strikes. The BSA stipulated that factory managers had to go through the LCAC first for permission to dismiss workers. The Shanghai branch of the LCAC gradually expanded its claim over labor-management issues by also regulating factory shutdowns. Factory owners had to seek approval from the LCAC before they could suspend or cease production. With the disruption of transportation networks in 1947, raw materials grew more difficult to come by, and many factories had to close for lack of goods to process. The LCAC then required factory owners to support workers left jobless by the closures by having the owner provide food and partial pay to employees when production had halted. Throughout the late 1940s, the Shanghai LCAC also had the authority to inspect enterprises and, if necessary, "make suitable adjustments to stabilize workers' lives and maintain production, preventing disputes."[83] It is certainly unlikely that the LCAC was able to enforce all the powers that it acquired to regulate private industry in Shanghai. Nor was the LCAC very effective in curbing strikes in Shanghai, where disputes reached a high of 2,538 in 1947.[84] Still, the significance of the LCAC lies more in how state intervention during the economic crisis, by establishing

---

[81] Ibid. [82] Pepper, *Civil War in China*, 109. [83] SMA, Series Q193-3-253.
[84] Pepper, *Civil War in China*, 109. Nationwide, almost half of the strikes in seven cities were responses to layoffs and dismissals.

specific rules governing employment and pay, had the effect of channeling the demands of workers and the unemployed directly toward their respective places of work, and toward those who owned or managed the enterprise. In 1949 and the unsteady political transition that followed the Communist takeover, labor protests would continue to be staged at individual enterprises, rather than at city hall.

Labor Politics in Shanghai's Cotton Mills

In many of Shanghai's cotton mills during the late 1940s, labor disputes by workers in privately owned mills centered around the demand that management provide them with welfare measures equivalent to those in the city's state-owned mills. In mills owned by the Rong family's Shenxin Corporation, the provision of subsidies to purchase basic commodities became commonplace and, as hyperinflation raged on, management soon turned to distributing commodities rather than cash for workers to purchase them. Management at the Shenxin Number Six Mill, which employed 4,700 workers by 1947, gave out subsidies for rice and other staples, and rent subsidies to those who did not live in company dorms.[85] Mill employees also received two sets of company uniforms and regular allotments of cloth.[86] A dining hall set up for employees became the center of controversy in early 1946, at the same time as union organization and wages were topics of debate. The poor quality of the food led the union to organize a Dining Hall Supervisory Team, whose members would accompany dining hall managers to produce markets and supervise the procurement of food staples.[87] Many of these measures were the result of the industry-wide labor dispute settlement agreed upon in February 1946, known as the "Eighteen Clause Agreement." Private and public mill managers pledged to index wages to municipal cost-of-living indexes and to provide consumer cooperatives, child care centers, nursing rooms, worker dormitories, schools for children of employees, night schools for workers, hospitals or clinics, showers, and cooking facilities.[88]

Nationalist officials continued to urge that mills provide employees with nonwage benefits in February 1947, during the failed attempt to

[85] Author's interview, Factory Director's Office and Personnel Department, Shanghai Number Thirty-One Mill, January 14, 1995.
[86] SMA, Series C16-2-99.
[87] SMPC, *Shanghai disanshiyi mianfangzhichang*, 98.
[88] SMA, Series Q193-3-253.

freeze the standard-of-living index at January's levels. By 1948, the industrial unions and employers' federations levied several orders for mills to supplement the inflation-eroded incomes of mill workers. Those who had worked for over six months received additional subsidies in the form of cloth. The agreement between federations of labor unions and employers also set specific guidelines on how workers would be compensated if a mill had been shut down in recent months.[89]

The provision of welfare to employees extended to areas such as bonus and incentive pay. The Shenxin General Corporation (SGC), established at this time to standardize management practices at all its mills, developed explicit criteria for wage and bonus determination. Year-end bonuses were to be calculated from the number of days worked during the year, a worker's wage level, "service achievements" (*fuwu chengji*), and standards issued by the Cotton Spinning and Weaving Industrial Federation.[90] At Shenxin Number Six, management also distributed bonuses to those with between one and six years of factory experience, an acknowledgment of the importance placed on seniority.[91] However, in both wage and bonus determination, explicit standards gave way to personalistic criteria such as loyalty. At traditional holidays, especially the lunar New Year, the distribution of bonuses to a loyal worker could amount to the equivalent of four months' wages. Shenxin Number Six managers, despite paying lip service to company standards, were said to distribute even larger bonuses to high staff and labor supervisors.[92] A melee erupted in February 1948 at the Shenxin Number Nine Mill over New Year's bonus payments and led to the shooting deaths of four women workers by Nationalist police forces. The incident sparked city and nationwide protests.[93] In early 1949, managers at Shenxin Number Six and at other mills agreed to provide a year-end bonus equivalent to four to six weeks' wages, tied to the standard-of-living index for the second half of December 1948. The year-end bonus by the late 1940s had evolved from a merit-based incentive payment to an automatic distribution of at least two months' pay, known as "double salary" (*shuang xin*).

---

[89] SMA, Series Q202-1-117.
[90] SASS Economics Institute, *Rongjia qiye*, 2:720.
[91] SMPC, *Shanghai disanshiyi mianfangzhichang*, 28.
[92] SMA, Series C16-2-99.
[93] Shanghai Municipal Labor Union, *Jiefang zhanzheng shiqi Shanghai gongren yundong shi* (History of the Shanghai Labor Movement during the War for Liberation) (Shanghai: Shanghai yundong chubanshe, 1992), 192–205.

The distribution of such bonuses would be an accepted practice well into the early 1950s.

These efforts by state officials, private mill owners, and unions to establish a more uniform pattern of wages and benefits for the city's textile workers were a response to labor disputes that engulfed the textile industry in early 1946. In late February, forty-seven of the city's mills shut down briefly in an organized display of force by several district trade unions.[94] BSA officials quickly forged a compromise. This settlement, imposed by local Nationalist officials and representatives of district unions and industrial associations, standardized minimum and maximum wage levels at all major mills in the city, including those owned by the state, and stipulated rules for leaves, holidays, and medical benefits. In exchange for these terms, labor representatives promised to organize only with official permission from the BSA. They also gave assurances that there would be no strikes and promised to use official arbitration methods if a dispute arose. In the event of a strike, no pay would be given during the shutdown. Management, by agreeing to hire "old workers," or those on the payroll before 1938, in theory gained the explicit power to recruit new workforce entrants.[95] For workers, the wage reform took into account the soaring cost of living and required management to link wages to the municipal government's standard-of-living index (the multiplier reached several million by the late 1940s).

The new wage structure, in theory at least, strengthened management's position vis-à-vis shop floor bosses and their wage-setting powers by linking wage levels with a measure of skill and by offering incentives for increases in individual output. Industry-wide wage agreements in the textile industry had the potential to put wage determination under a new set of state rules, but Number Ones still exerted some control over the wage levels of individual workers. The financial chaos in Shanghai meant that management at the Shenxin mills, like their counterparts at other private enterprises in the city, could rarely distribute wages at the specific levels called for in the soaring official index.[96] According to several

---

[94] Chinese Communist Party, Shanghai Municipal Committee, Party History Research Office, and Shanghai Municipal Labor Union, *Shanghai dishier mianfangzhi chang gongren yundongshi* (The History of the Labor Movement at the Shanghai Number 12 Cotton Spinning and Weaving Mill) (Beijing: Zhonggong dangshi chubanshe, 1994), 142–4.

[95] SMA, Series Q193-3-253.

[96] Author's correspondence with Shanghai Number Thirty-One Mill factory official, April 1995.

sources, labor bosses in mills undermined the skill and incentive criteria that management pushed during the late 1940s with a de facto wage regime based on seniority.[97] Supervisors, who had to comply with wage guidelines issued by the company, could easily classify workers at management's prearranged wage levels by using seniority rather than skill or output as the critical determinant. Number Ones also retained the ability to place those personally loyal to them at work posts that might earn them higher rates of pay through piece rates and incentive bonuses.

Managers at the Shenxin mills also developed a system of written codes, but they had insufficient resources to enforce all fifty-three articles and thirty-one subclauses that governed hiring, work hours, days off, wages, benefits, bonuses, punishments, and dismissals of the workforce. In subsequent recollections by retired workers, many described a more "strict" management system during the late 1940s, but codes, regardless of how much managers wanted them applied, were no protection against the arbitrary actions of supervisors. Number Ones still ruled through personal force, beating and scolding workers for minor infractions.[98] Shift leaders and Number Ones retained extensive powers even though personnel staff handled the hiring process, because supervisors had the ability to allocate new workers to their posts, each of which in theory had a fixed wage rate. Many "traditional" practices continued. As before the war, workers at the Shenxin Number Six Mill were expected to present their labor supervisor with expensive gifts on holidays and for weddings, births, and funerals.[99] In return, the worker could expect better treatment in the form of wages and job security in the event of a downturn in production.

Shenxin Number Six was also a hotbed of partisan activity in the late 1940s. After the Japanese surrender, the rapid expansion of the textile industry demanded that mills quickly take on new workers. With labor in great demand, dozens of Nationalist, Communist, and "independent" labor organizers slipped into the ranks of new hires.[100] Despite efforts by mill management to organize an enterprise union unaffiliated with the Nationalist Party, in early 1946 the Nationalist Party's Welfare Committee sent an official to the mill to direct union work. He quickly

---

[97] SMA, Series C16-2-42; Author's interview, Factory Director's Office and Personnel Department, Shanghai Number Thirty-One Mill, January 14, 1995.

[98] SMPC, *Disanshiyi mianfangzhichang*, 91.

[99] SMA, Series C16-2-99.

[100] SMA, Series Q193-3-363; SASS Economics Institute, *Rongjia qiye*, 2:709–10.

linked up with several employees in the maintenance department, the highest-paying and male-dominated section in charge of repairing the mill's machinery and maintaining its electrical supply. The mechanics received training in union organizing from cadres in the Welfare Committee, who in turn appointed the workers as official Nationalist Party cadres. Subsequently, the mechanics at the mill established intrafactory associations from which they recruited new supporters. They set up several athletic teams under a "Sports Association," (*tiyu xiehui*) whose participants had privileged access to loans and other benefits. Membership in the Sports Association was said to be a guarantee of future employment at the mill. About 100 males participated in the sports teams.[101]

Many of these mechanics gained nomination as candidates in an election for representatives to the mill's Union Supervisory Council, a branch of the industry-wide cotton textiles union.[102] The plan of the GMD union organizers to enlist the support of loyal mechanics on the Union Supervisory Council went awry when a significant number of suspected Communist Party members, most of whom were women from the spinning department, won seats in the election. A few days after the results were announced, fights broke out that triggered a four-day slow-down at the mill. According to Communist sources printed after 1949, a squad of Nationalist mechanics seeking to intimidate the women elected to the union council set upon Council Director Cai Huijun using steel bars and pipes after she ignored earlier threats from mechanics to name two GMD-backed candidates to leadership posts in the union.[103] She and several fellow council members escaped harm by fleeing the factory, but one office employee was hospitalized with injuries. Mill management, in correspondence with local authorities, gave an entirely different account of events. Shenxin Corporation Chairman Rong Hongyuan and Shenxin Number Six Director Rong Esheng told the Shanghai BSA that the real culprits were Cai and her associates, who were seeking to take over the union by force. It was Cai who had ordered a squad of workers to beat up the staff member and then to wreck several spinning frames (photographs of which the Rongs submitted to the BSA). "The principal reason for the strike is that women workers have monopolized the union and men workers have been expelled," the Rongs claimed. Cai and others, whom they suspected of Communist sympathies, had directed

---

[101] SMA, Series Q193-3-363.
[102] SMPC, *Disanshiyi mianfangzhichang*, 95; SMA, Series Q193-3-363.
[103] SMA, Series Q193-3-363.

"good and honest workers to blindly follow them and start this great calamity."[104] The Rongs considered the whole matter a "labor-labor" conflict, not a "labor-capital" (*laozi*) dispute, and requested help from the BSA in punishing the principals.

Despite the initial setback in the union elections at Shenxin Number Six, GMD officials ultimately managed to reassert control over the branch union there. One step was to offer a generous bribe to the father of Cai Huijun, to persuade her to quit her job.[105] (The extent of her devotion to the Communist Party was also short-lived. She later served as a high cadre in the GMD's Welfare Committee and was an alternate to the National Assembly.) It is little wonder that CCP reports in the early 1950s deplored the "complex political situation" that existed at the mill prior to 1949, calling it "one of the enemy's reactionary fortresses in East Shanghai."[106]

The relationship between unions and parties, as seen in the Nationalist regime's efforts to establish a presence in factories, was convoluted. The welfare committees offer parallels to the later model of party branches in factories during the Maoist era, but the Nationalist branches were never as closely linked to the party center, nor were they able to assert the supervision and controls that work teams of party cadres would during the CCP campaigns in the 1950s. Moreover, Nationalist Party cells do not appear to have enjoyed any genuine political constituency in the workforce. Gangs and other unofficial associations were just as common as officially sponsored unions, given the patronage and relative job security the former could offer.

There was an economic logic behind the creation of what might be labeled "workplace welfare." To curb labor turnover, state officials in the wartime economy enacted legislation and policies that compelled enterprises to provide their employees with housing and other basic living needs. The hyperinflationary environment, during and especially after the war, only strengthened this practice. Workers, with the earning power of their wages severely eroded each month, increasingly relied on their enterprises to meet their everyday living needs during the late 1940s. The phenomenon of a vanishing urban consumer goods market is vividly illustrated in A. Doak Barnett's observations of Shanghai in the autumn of 1948:

[104] SMA, Series Q6-8.1-119.   [105] SMA, Series Q193-3-363.
[106] SMA, Series Q193-3-364.

Theoretically, all prices are frozen, at the August 19 level, but actually, despite energetic attempts at control, black markets have reappeared and the prices of commodities are gradually climbing. Furthermore, many goods have disappeared from shop counters and cannot be found by the average purchaser. . . . Existing stocks of commodities have been almost completely cleaned from the counters by panic-stricken buyers. . . .[107]

Because wages were also frozen, workers found it increasingly difficult to buy food and other basic necessities. Contrast this to Barnett's notes of a year prior, in November 1947: "Shops, stores, and markets are filled with all sorts of manufactured consumer goods and foodstuffs."[108]

The pattern of informal autocratic rule by shop floor overseers, discussed in Chapter 2, might have receded during wartime economic emergencies as state officials and private factory managers took unprecedented steps to establish formal controls over hiring, wage determination, and the provision of critical needs such as food, housing, and medical care. Workers once dependent on shop floor supervisors now relied on the enterprise for basic necessities. The evidence from this chapter shows that the personalistic powers of labor supervisors may have been eroding during the 1940s, but they were certainly not eliminated. Highly personalized authority relations could easily coexist alongside personnel departments with their formal rules and codes governing the employment relationship. The "liberation" of cities by the CCP in 1949 and the mobilization of the workforce would level the most serious challenge yet to the ability of shop floor supervisors to rule the factory floor.

[107] A. Doak Barnett, *China on the Eve of Communist Takeover* (New York: Frederick A. Praeger, 1963), 71.
[108] Ibid., 18.

4

Takeover Policies and Labor Politics, 1949–1952

AS units of the PLA advanced into urban areas of north China in early 1949, then into the cities of east, central, and south China during the remainder of that year, Communist Party officials faced a new and in many ways unfamiliar set of challenges. CCP cadres had gained some limited exposure to the complexities of urban government and industrial policy during their takeover of cities in Northeast China in 1948. Stabilizing labor relations and maintaining industrial production had been one of the critical, if not easily grasped, lessons of the 1948 urban takeovers.[1] Yet the stakes were immensely higher in 1949, as Communist forces entered China's major commercial and industrial centers of Beijing, Tianjin, Shanghai, and Guangzhou. Industrial production and commercial activity in many of these cities had all but collapsed, but both had to be restored quickly and carefully, for political as well as national security purposes. The consequences of mismanaging the urban economy through mistaken monetary, fiscal, and industrial policies were ever present. It had only taken a few years between 1945 and 1948 for the Nationalist regime, with its much broader knowledge base of administrators and technocrats, to drive urban areas to financial ruin.

CCP officials therefore relied, however reluctantly, on the existing pool of expertise that remained from Nationalist government personnel. At the factory level, this meant a policy of retaining enterprise managers and technicians, many of whom were Nationalist "officials" simply by virtue of the fact that their enterprises were state-owned. Depending on their degree of loyalty to the Nationalist Party, and their activities prior to the takeover, enterprise directors and their staff accepted the CCP's

---

[1] For a summary of these lessons in CCP labor policy areas, see Pepper, *Civil War in China*, 350–76.

assurances of leniency and autonomy with measured caution. Owners and managers of private-sector enterprises, whom the CCP also urged to participate in the restoration of the economy, had reason to treat carefully the assurances from the government of the "New China." Workers had high expectations from a regime that mouthed promises of a new socialist society in which the working class would become "rulers" (*zhuren*) of the factory. Thousands of private-sector employees left unemployed by the collapse of industrial activity during the civil war returned to their factories to demand their jobs back. They wanted higher wages, improvements in benefits and working conditions, and guarantees of full-time employment. In state factories, Communist military cadres who had been placed in certain critical factories to "supervise" factory directors often seized power from them, with predictable upheavals in basic operations.

A more serious problem within enterprises emerged by the early 1950s with the onset of party-led political campaigns. Political campaigns, by enjoining party "work teams" outside the factory to investigate, report, and sanction the activities and attitudes of all enterprise personnel, left managers and staff politically vulnerable, regardless of their performance by technical standards. To further their investigations of enterprise personnel, CCP cadres relied heavily on workers to provide information and to spearhead attacks on selected factory personnel. Those workers whose factory experience dated from the pre-1949 era could use the CCP's own rhetoric to elevate their status by claiming to have suffered at the hands of exploitative capitalists, foreigners, and Nationalist officials. Enterprise managers were thus caught between the political demands of their superiors in the government and party and their subordinates on production lines who could undermine their authority through political criticism. An analysis of developments in Shanghai and Guangzhou during the early 1950s, and within particular firms in those cities, reveals how these campaigns had important consequences for how existing labor management institutions would evolve.

CITY AND FACTORY TAKEOVERS

Factories were a key testing ground for the political and administrative skills of the CCP. Before 1948, the party had gained a mixed record in this regard. First, in the highly uncertain conditions of military engagement during the civil war, the CCP's urban "policy" in Northeast China in 1946–7 was to mobilize residents to dismantle productive equipment, if not destroy it, in the event Nationalist forces regained control of the city in question.[2] Second, a largely rural-based party of peasant cadres and military personnel applied the lessons and procedures of land reform to the urban workforce: they mobilized workers to struggle against factory owners, to demand higher wages and benefits, and even to redistribute property. Factory equipment not being as neatly divisible as land, the chaos and confusion that resulted was predictable.[3] As it came to the realization that victory might be sooner than once thought, the CCP leadership in 1948 developed a much more coherent policy of urban takeover, one that emphasized above all else the preservation of basic urban services such as electricity and transportation. This emphasis on stability had as a corollary the careful handling of labor relations in both public and private enterprises.

In some ways, the CCP's new imperative to maintain industrial production and to revive it following the takeover of urban areas represented an important shift from labor measures enacted in CCP-held urban areas in 1945–7. In Zhangjiakou (Kalgan), which the CCP had controlled for a year before Nationalist forces recaptured it in October 1946, cadres had aggressively organized factory workers into unions and pushed for immediate changes in wages and other labor policies. Wages were doubled by decree, and raised further to keep pace with inflation. The CCP cadres and their unions also endeavored to establish piece-rate wages and bonuses for output that exceeded quotas. Such decisions on wages and bonuses had to be agreed upon jointly by employers and workers. Zhangjiakou employers were required to pay the medical expenses of their workers, and to seek approval from factory unions and factory management committees (of workers and management) before firing an employee. CCP unions also organized consumer cooperatives to give workers access to basic necessities.[4]

Less than two years later, however, CCP leaders sought to rein in these and other labor management policies whenever factory-level cadres in Harbin and other cities demanded them. Wage increases, once a matter of course in Zhangjiakou, were now labeled as "leftist tendencies" in Harbin. The reorientation of the CCP's labor policy was encapsulated at the Sixth All-China Labor Congress (ACLC) in August 1948 in

---

[2] Kenneth G. Lieberthal, *Revolution and Tradition in Tientsin, 1949–1952* (Stanford, CA: Stanford University Press, 1980), 29–30; Pepper, *Civil War in China*, 386–7.
[3] Pepper, *Civil War in China*, 386.   [4] Ibid., 332–40.

Harbin.[5] The resolutions of the Congress stressed that in wages, work hours, benefits, and the like, "egalitarian" practices had to be curbed. Wage rates in state enterprises of CCP-controlled cities were to be maintained at current levels. Given the inflationary environment, adjustments could be made based on prices of staple goods, but state enterprises were also encouraged to distribute these through the enterprise if possible.[6]

The Sixth ACLC marked an important step in the evolution of CCP labor policy in several respects.[7] It was significant that the previous five labor congresses had been held during the 1920s, when the CCP had considered itself primarily a party of the urban proletariat. Though continuity with earlier congresses was maintained through the person of Li Lisan, who presided at the Sixth ACLC, there was an evident moderation in the party's stance toward factory management, especially in private-sector enterprises. The emphasis on labor-capital cooperation had been stressed in 1948 at a conference on business and industry and was reiterated at the Sixth ACLC.[8] The labor congress also revealed the importance of the Soviet Union and its factory management methods as models that the CCP would seek to emulate, particularly in the area of labor insurance and in production competitions.[9] Relations with capitalists and the viability of the Soviet Union's industrial and labor management as a model would undergo important changes over the course of the 1950s, but the short-term significance of the Sixth ACLC was its articulation of the need for labor restraint in the impending takeover of major urban centers in China. It was a call that would on several occasions go unheeded in 1949.

In private industry, ownership of factory property and output remained an open question in the days following the takeover of Beijing, Tianjin, and Shanghai. Private enterprises, put at over 1.2 million units, accounted for 63.3 percent of production value and 53.7 percent of workers.[10] For a regime whose agrarian policy was to enact swift and

[5] William Brugger, *Democracy and Organisation in the Chinese Industrial Enterprise, 1948–1953* (Cambridge: Cambridge University Press, 1976), 67.

[6] Pepper, *Civil War in China*, 354–64.

[7] Important works from the Sixth Labor Congress are catalogued and described in Ming K. Chan, *Historiography of the Chinese Labor Movement, 1895–1949* (Stanford, CA: Hoover Institution Press, 1981), 152–4.

[8] Pepper, *Civil War in China*, 369–70.

[9] Ibid., 364–6.

[10] Yuan Lunqu, *Zhongguo laodong jingjishi* (History of Chinese Labor Economics) (Beijing: Beijing jingji xueyuan chubanshe, 1990), 76.

violent redistribution of land to those without it, there was certainly reason to believe that the CCP might also expropriate the private assets of factory owners and merchants. Party declarations preached the notion of "democratic management" in which workers would participate in managerial decisions. Indeed, in Northeast China the process of taking over factories had led to "leftist excesses" as inexperienced party cadres struggled with remaining managers.[11] In Tianjin, workers took matters into their own hands by organizing industrial cooperatives in direct con-travention of CCP orders.[12] On the other hand, Mao Zedong declared in the 1949 essay, "On the People's Democratic Dictatorship," that capital-ists and capitalism would be controlled but not eliminated during the transition to a socialist economy.[13]

The substantial portion of industry that already was publicly owned under the Nationalists – about one-third of China's total value of indus-trial output – was immediately transferred to state control under the Communist Party authorities. By the end of 1949, the state had confis-cated from the Nationalist administration a total of 2,858 enterprises with over 750,000 employees, in each case retaining the staff. Factory directors and engineers who remained in such enterprises naturally had cause for concern, because they technically had been officials in the Nationalist regime. The CCP's initial stance was to offer leniency and promises to retain them at their previous salary levels, a policy referred to as "original jobs at original pay" (*yuanzhi yuanxin*). The policy was aimed at retaining the skills and knowledge of technicians, and it set their pay based on the level of real wages averaged for the three months prior to "liberation," along with bonuses and insurance.[14]

Hyperinflation loomed as the most severe problem in urban areas in 1949. Nationalist government policy in the regime's final year had made paper currency virtually worthless, and wages, though linked to monthly cost-of-living indexes, still failed to keep up with runaway daily inflation. To counter inflation, the CCP adopted a number of fiscal and monetary policy measures that would ultimately bring inflation under control but at a substantial short-term cost. In terms of fiscal policy, largely under the leadership of Chen Yun at this time, the government imposed a vast reorganization of revenue collection that emphasized the extraction

[11] Brugger, *Democracy and Organisation*, 71.
[12] Ibid., 73.
[13] Mao Zedong, "On the People's Democratic Dictatorship," in *Selected Works of Mao Tse-tung, Vol. IV* (Beijing: Foreign Languages Press, 1969), 421.
[14] Yuan, *Zhongguo laodong jingjishi*, 122–3.

of urban taxes by central government authorities and a reduction in government expenditures.[15] With respect to monetary policy, CCP officials guaranteed the purchasing power of wages, bank deposits, and bonds by adroitly linking these to the value of a basket of commodities. Rather than emphasize price controls, as the Nationalist regime had done in the late 1940s, the CCP essentially channeled cash out of the economy and into savings. To accomplish this required high interest rates, which reached 70 to 80 percent at the end of 1949.[16] Moreover, savings deposited in the new currency, the *renminbi* (RMB), would be adjusted for commodity prices prevailing at the time a depositor went to withdraw funds.[17] Sales of government bonds would also absorb cash and stifle consumption. The final prong in the attack on inflation was the effort to tie the new currency to commodity prices. Municipal governments stockpiled basic food and fuel commodities, and could release these supplies on markets when prices began to rise. To work effectively, however, it was necessary to use state trading companies rather than private distributors, because merchants were known to manipulate prices. State trading companies set up cooperatives to sell directly to consumers. To further curb speculation, cooperatives were established within enterprises and offices, where only employees could make purchases, not the general public.[18]

The Takeover of Shanghai

As the CCP moved south in the first half of 1949, local underground party members within factories received orders to organize factory protection teams to safeguard facilities and equipment. The effort proved modestly successful, as critical enterprises such as the Shanghai Power Company, the French Water and Power Company, and the twenty-eight facilities belonging to the National Resources Commission remained operable.[19] The story of the CCP's takeover of Shanghai factories, as told through party sources and relayed through scholarly accounts that have relied on these sources, has generally been portrayed as a stable transition in which party stalwarts among the workforce bravely stood guard over factory compounds and prevented retreating Nationalist forces

---

[15] Alexander Eckstein, *China's Economic Development: The Interplay of Scarcity and Ideology* (Ann Arbor, MI: University of Michigan Press, 1975), 198.
[16] Ibid.   [17] Pepper, *Civil War in China*, 396.   [18] Ibid., 397.
[19] Ibid., 391–2; Brugger, *Democracy and Organisation*, 73.

from inflicting damage to production facilities. While many important factories in Shanghai remained intact as the Nationalists hastily retreated, damage to Shanghai's industrial base quickly ensued in two forms. First, Nationalist air raids beginning in June struck critical facilities in the city. Second, CCP economic policies brought rampant bankruptcies, unemployment, and eventually labor unrest. Before turning to these episodes of posttakeover instability, it is worth qualifying the overall picture of tranquility at the time of "liberation" by a look at how the Jiangnan Shipyard experienced the change in regimes.

The candid recollections in 1960 by a group of then-elite party members at the Jiangnan Shipyard reveal a much more complex picture of partisan loyalties and action during a time of extreme crisis. In August 1948, the shipyard had no functioning Communist Party underground organization and only a handful of workers who identified themselves with the CCP. It was that month that Zhang Sidan joined the workforce at the shipyard and promptly set up a branch with himself as the party secretary. Zhang established connections with the Workers' Welfare Committee, heavily dominated by Nationalist Party loyalists, and representatives of both went to the shipyard director, Ma Deji, with a proposal to organize a factory protection team. Ma agreed to the idea, and in late 1948 some seven- to eight-hundred workers were organized for a "Three-Antis" campaign to oppose the dispersal, transport, or destruction of the shipyard's machinery. The effort proved successful, and in early 1949 when Nationalist military officials ordered Ma to break down the shipyard's machinery for transport to Taiwan, he refused. On May 21, Nationalist troops forced the shipyard's employees out of the facility and began detonating bombs to destroy vital equipment rather than let it fall into CCP hands. After securing the shipyard on May 25, PLA troops organized civilian squads to prevent looting. The situation remained tense, and matters were made worse on May 28, when a typhoon struck the region and brought severe damage to the shipyard's dormitories. Military representatives now in control of the shipyard hung a portrait of Mao Zedong in the Number 1 cafeteria. This symbolic gesture was undermined when military personnel then announced that the shipyard's Nationalist staff and managers would be retained. Workers asked with some puzzlement, "This is Liberation?"[20]

---

[20] This account of the Jiangnan Shipyard's takeover is found in the Jiangnan Shipyard Factory History Archives, Series 22. It is not clear what happened to Nationalist official Ma Deji after his refusal of orders to transport facilities and equipment to Taiwan. An

As much as efforts by CCP organizers in other factories may have prevented serious damage to Shanghai's industry and urban infrastructure, mobilization of this kind was incapable of stopping what followed in rapid sequence soon after the city's takeover. Nationalist air raids began in early June, striking the Shanghai Power Company and cutting off electric power to much of the city and its factories.[21] Later that month, the Nationalist naval blockade reduced Shanghai's access to vital shipping routes. In July, yet another major typhoon brought flooding to areas in and around Shanghai.[22] Further air raids in July succeeded in shutting down the Jiangnan Shipyard altogether, after bombs destroyed several factory buildings. The threat of more raids forced PLA officials to disperse production to seven satellite locations around the city, and it was not until May 1950 that concentrated production was resumed. Through a makeshift provision system used by CCP military units, shipyard management provided employees with minimal grain and cloth subsidies along with their wages.[23]

Whereas Tianjin could claim that 90 percent of its enterprises were back in operation within one month of the CCP takeover in January 1949, conditions in Shanghai were grave in the months following "liberation." In July, only 26 percent of the city's industrial facilities were operating, and this portion would reach just under 62 percent by December 1949.[24] Speculation was rife in Shanghai as uncertainties prevailed about the government's ability to back up the new renminbi currency. The RMB fell against the "parity unit," the measure that reflected a group of basic commodities and from which wages were calculated. Beginning in June 1949, the conversion stood at 100 RMB for one parity unit, but by August the rate was 967 RMB for one parity unit. This reflected in part a sixfold increase in the price of rice (one of the commodities included in parity units) between May and June 1949.[25]

The CCP's monetary policy ultimately brought prices under control by March 1950, but not without serious social and political turbulence.

estimated 300 employees and technicians from the Jiangnan Shipyard did find their way to Taiwan, where they worked at one of four shipyards under the Naval Garrison Command.

[21] Pepper, *Civil War in China*, 392.
[22] Ibid., 401.
[23] Jiangnan Shipyard, Factory History Archives, Series 22.
[24] Sun Huairen, *Shanghai shehuizhuyi jingji jianshe fazhan jianshi, 1949–1985* (A Concise History of the Establishment and Development of the Socialist Economy in Shanghai, 1949–1985) (Shanghai: Shanghai renmin chubanshe, 1990), 40.
[25] Pepper, *Civil War in China*, 398.

While economists have noted the national-level consequences of the CCP's early policies, the effects such austerity brought to urban areas and enterprises within them have not previously been explored. The antiinflationary measures resulted in the opposite extreme of deflation, which caused widespread bankruptcies and urban unemployment in 1950.[26] Nationwide, an estimated 1.66 million urban residents were unemployed or semiemployed by June 1950.[27] Between January and May 1950, a total of 1,454 private-sector factories had ceased production, representing about 12 percent of Shanghai's total number of factories.[28]

Many of the social costs of the CCP's early monetary and fiscal policy were felt in the private sector, which accounted for large portions of the economy and employment base in urban areas, nowhere more so than Shanghai. CCP authorities in Shanghai and other cities sought to enforce a Nationalist government law enacted in 1948–9 to limit sharply the ability of private enterprises to dismiss workers. Municipal authorities also issued regulations to force private enterprises to hire more full-time than part-time workers and to seek approval from the local branches of the Ministry of Labor before doing so. Only if there was a compelling reason that a firm or an industry was being shut down could an enterprise fire workers.[29] In a further effort to curb unemployment, new regulations prevented both state and private enterprises from adding shifts or lengthening the work day to over ten hours.

Well before the imposition of monetary and fiscal austerity measures, however, CCP officials in Shanghai described the labor relations issue, citywide and within enterprises, as extremely "complex" (*fuza*). Weeks after the occupation of Shanghai, the director of the East China Military region, Rao Shushi, made a speech in which he told factory owners that labor disputes were their problem, not the government's. He also urged workers not to make excessive demands and warned that they would be dealt with severely if they harmed factory equipment, raw materials, or finished goods.[30] Yet at the same time, Rao and local officials instigated a round of disputes when they issued orders stating that any worker who had left the factory two months before May 25, the date of the city's "liberation," could be restored to his or her job at the original level of pay.

[26] Alexander Eckstein, *China's Economic Revolution* (New York: Cambridge University Press, 1977), 167.

[27] Li, *Zhongguo gongzi zhidu*, 16–17.   [28] Sun, *Shanghai shehuizhuyi*, 55.

[29] Yuan, *Zhongguo laodong jingjishi*, 78.   [30] SMA, Series Q202-1-136.

This policy applied whether or not the factory had reopened for production.[31]

Virtually overnight, Rao and CCP officials had a strike wave on their hands that by some measures could be considered the largest in Shanghai history. According to Shanghai Labor Union records, in the twelve months between June 1949 and May 1950, workers in privately owned factories engaged in 3,939 labor disputes (*zhengyi*).[32] The magnitude of this strike wave surpassed all previous ones in a city known for its contentious working class.[33] Fights over the inability or unwillingness of factory owners to resume production and restore jobs were leading causes of disputes. Disputes over wages, which fell into arrears when employers closed their factories, ranked third among sources of the 1949–50 strike wave. Virtually every industrial and commercial sector in the city was affected. In 1950, disputes in the Shanghai textile industry accounted for 314 of 1,565 cases, or 20 percent. Cotton-spinning and weaving mills saw the largest number of disputes in the manufacturing sector that year (102), second only to newspapers, publishers, and printers (104).[34] The situation was often complicated by workers who returned from the countryside after the CCP takeover to demand reinstatement to their previous jobs. The CCP's order for workers to return to their previous posts triggered a great deal of confusion in hundreds of factories. Factory owners in the Shanghai machine industry's federation urged the city's Industrial Association to repeal the policy, noting that it was leading to incidents of "surrounding" in public, private, and foreign-owned enterprises. Employers in the shipbuilding federation claimed they could not so easily rehire former workers; doing so would only encourage other workers to "surround" bosses and make demands. "If this behavior continues and is accepted, it will spread from plant to plant, and industry to industry," warned the shipyard employers.[35]

There were even scattered reports of clashes between Communist troops and workers in Shanghai. A U.S. consular official reported in August 1949 that "persistent rumors widespread throughout Shanghai" alleged that workers in a large cotton mill (the specific mill varied with different versions of the story) had fought with PLA troops after

[31] Ibid. [32] SMA, Series C1-2-232.
[33] Elizabeth J. Perry, "Shanghai's Strike Wave of 1957," *China Quarterly* 137 (March 1994): 1.
[34] SMA, Series C1-2-232. By some calculations, wages became the leading cause of labor disputes in 1950, with 626 cases recorded affecting 100,784 workers.
[35] SMA, Series Q202-1-134.

employees "exploit[ed] Communists own propaganda [and] declared [that] mill belonged to them." Workers in the mill "soundly booed" pictures of Mao Zedong and PLA commander Zhu De, telling the soldiers to "go back to [their] farms." The resulting melee, according to different rumors, had led to anywhere between two and one hundred deaths of workers and soldiers. Even if the stories were fabricated, the U.S. official noted, the willingness of Shanghai residents to believe them was a sign of the "growing dissatisfaction with industrial policy [of the] Communist regime."[36] It might be easy to dismiss such a report as wishful thinking on the part of the American allies of the Nationalist regime, but the tense labor situation in Shanghai – and the fact that similar worker seizures of factories had taken place in Tianjin – lends it a degree of plausibility.

Uncertainty and tensions only grew worse in early 1950, when yet another wave of Nationalist air raids on February 6 did extensive damage to the Yangshupu area of East Shanghai. The attack forced the closure of the Shanghai Electric Power Plant, the only source of electricity to many of the cotton mills in the area. With production at a standstill and the lunar New Year approaching, mill owners had no way to distribute back wages, let alone the ample year-end bonuses that all employees expected. In many mills, former employees demanding to be rehired were joined by current employees seeking back pay and wage adjustments to counter persistently high rates of inflation. Workers from the Shenxin Number Seven Mill and the Rongfeng Dyeing Mill, both owned by the Rong family, surrounded the offices of corporate headquarters. Shenxin Number Seven workers proceeded to the home of Rong Esheng, the director of the Shenxin Number Six Mill, and helped themselves to the entire spread of special New Year's dishes prepared for his family holiday celebration.[37]

Mechanics and metalworkers who had been dismissed in late 1948 demanded their jobs back by returning to their places of employment and literally surrounding enterprise officials until they consented. At two machine and shipbuilding yards, former workers used this mass encirclement tactic to trap managers for ten hours.[38] Workers at the Dalong

[36] U.S. Department of State, *Internal Affairs of China, 1945–1949*, 893.655/8-1249.
[37] SMA, Series Q193-1-431; Elizabeth J. Perry, "Labor's Battle for Political Space: The Role of Worker Associations in Contemporary China," in *Urban Spaces in Contemporary China: The Potential for Autonomy and Community in Post-Mao China*, Deborah S. Davis, et al., eds. (New York: Cambridge University Press, 1995), 307.
[38] SMA, Series Q202-1-134.

and Taili Machine plants, both owned by the same person, held an "eat-in" at the factory's canteen, gorging themselves on available food stocks to protest the suspension of wage payments, which the owner had invoked because of stagnant sales. Communist officials in Shanghai sided with employers in such cases, accusing the mechanics of having an "extremely leftist attitude."[39]

Communist officials in Shanghai blamed incidents of "overly leftist" behavior on workers and individual counterrevolutionaries seeking to destabilize the new regime. But many of the Communist Party's own cadres were faulted for their "excessive egalitarianism." More often than not, it was they who led strikes against factory owners or expropriated control of enterprises from capitalists during the transition period. In the second half of 1950, a rectification campaign led by the party committee of the Shanghai General Labor Union to curb such excesses among CCP cadres failed to eliminate labor-management disputes. Such union activists, most of whom were known as "mass cadres" and had no CCP or Communist Youth League affiliation, supposedly helped spread a malicious "emancipation feeling" (*fanshen gan*) among workers. Reports stated that some union leaders with "ultra-leftist thought," especially those representing retail shops, encouraged colleagues to surround and compel the owner to raise wages. Meetings between Shanghai workers and party cadres sent to "rectify the masses" turned into a situation in which workers instead "rectified party members and leaders."[40]

The party also faulted union activists for refusing to cooperate with capitalists and foreign managers, thinking that to do so was tantamount to "sacrificing class position." The union members on the Shanghai Cotton Spinning Mills Union Committee admitted that in late 1949 and early 1950, "We did not fully understand how to use the method of labor-capital consultation. We didn't take the initiative in compromising, or in uniting with management to educate workers and overcome difficulties. In our ideology, we only looked after the interests of workers and had overly leftist behavior." Following the February 6 air raids such "leftist tendencies" increased.[41]

It is important to note that the provision of nonwage benefits to enterprise employees, a practice begun in the 1940s and earlier in some cases, continued during this period of tension and uncertainty. A Shanghai General Labor Union survey of 277 factories in 12 sectors ranging from light to heavy industry and employing over 48,600 workers revealed that

[39] SMA, Series C13-2-19.   [40] SMA, Series C16-2-1.   [41] Ibid.

most were providing meals and housing to employees. Table 2 shows that 77 percent of the enterprises provided housing to some or all employees, while 71 percent provided meals to employees. Over 90 percent of the enterprises distributed some form of annual bonus, ranging from the equivalent of one-half to two months' pay. From this "snapshot" of benefits distribution across a number of sectors in late 1950, it is not possible to discern whether such practices represented responses to the CCP's fiscal and monetary austerity program or were actually a continuation of practices from the 1940s. One of the largest industries in Shanghai, cotton spinning, had established a standardized agreement for employee benefits before 1949, and this agreement remained operative in 1950. The thirteen cotton-spinning mills that figured into the Shanghai GLU survey of late 1950 used a Cotton Spinning Industry Association agreement, in which mills that provided three meals per day to employees would deduct 0.2 yuan from workers' base pay. Enterprises that did not provide meals to employees agreed to distribute to each worker sixty liters of rice per month and to deduct 6 yuan per month from base pay. The agreement also stipulated annual bonus payments, which were divided into five grades ranging from the equivalent of twenty-four to thirty-two days' wages.[42] The CCP's enactment of harsh deflationary measures in 1949–50 in effect served to maintain, if not expand, existing practices to distribute in-kind goods and services through the enterprise. Indeed, such practices furthered the CCP's goals of monetary contraction and the reduction of consumption among urban residents. However, the cash distribution of annual bonuses or subsidies, also noted in the survey, directly undermined the regime's antiinflationary strategy. Municipal authorities in Shanghai and elsewhere would act to curb annual bonus payouts in the private sector in subsequent years.

Another source of conflict arose as state enterprises and other large production facilities came under the control of military representatives in 1949–50. The personnel in charge of Shanghai and other cities were almost exclusively military officials from rural backgrounds with little experience in industrial management, to say nothing of urban administration.[43] Many of the local officials sent to Shanghai were rural cadres from the Communist border regions in northern Jiangsu province. The new administrators and their functionaries in factories thus had to contend with a long-held animus of Shanghai residents who viewed them

[42] SMA, Series C1-2-338.
[43] Brugger, *Democracy and Organisation*, 70–1; 74–5.

Table 2. *Shanghai Factories and Welfare Provision, Late 1950*

Industry	Factories In Survey	Total Employees	# Factories Providing Meals	# Factories Providing Housing	# Factories Providing Annual Bonus	# Factories with Incentive Bonuses	# Factories Providing Rice Subsidies	# Factories Providing Other Subsidies
Generators	19	2,739	13	11	19	4	2	2
Ship Building	20	6,966	15	14	20	1	3	0
Machinery	22	3,908	15	19	22	4	0	2
Steel	17	1,925	12	13	11	1	0	0
Dyeing	49	9,821	43	48	46	15	1	3
Silk Weaving	21	1,535	12	7	21	1	4	1
Wool Spinning	14	1,685	13	14	13	6	0	1
Knitting	23	2,327	8	9	21	1	0	2
Paper	14	2,739	8	7	12	3	0	4
Pharmaceuticals	37	2,466	26	28	28	0	2	2
Rubber	37	4,982	27	34	32	1	6	2
Tobacco	10	7,540	5	10	8	0	4	0
TOTAL	277	48,633	197 (71.1%)	214 (77.3%)	253 (91.3%)	37 (13.4%)	22 (7.9%)	19 (6.9%)

Source: Shanghai Municipal Archives, Series C1-2-338.

as "bumpkins" lacking urban sophistication and tastes. For many of the PLA troops in Shanghai, factories were completely alien terrain.

As Shanghai workers came into direct contact with PLA officials and troops sent to patrol factory floors, predictable misunderstandings arose. Jiangnan Shipyard workers resented the presence of troops they nicknamed the "yellow uniforms." Idle workers used their local dialect to warn each other when a soldier was on the way to put an end to their extended breaks. Associating the five-pointed red star on PLA caps with the brand of American gasoline marketed in Shanghai, workers sent out the alert, "Here comes Texaco!" at which point they would make themselves busy. With the call "Texaco's passed" (*deshigu paisi*) workers would resume loafing. In a further sign of the distinctions that Jiangnan Shipyard workers made between themselves as urban sophisticates and the CCP's rural origins, they accused the new management of "lowering" the Chinese character for labor (工) to that for "earth," "soil," and "coarseness" (土). What was all the talk about "Liberation," workers asked, if wages and the organization of work remained as they had been before? Many remarked to the shipyard's military representatives, "You want prior jobs with prior pay under the prior system, then I'll keep my prior attitude!" Workers also made demands to reform the "unreasonable" wage system that they felt no longer connected pay with one's skill level.[44]

The military's style of factory management drew unified condemnation from employees. Strict rules, labor representatives pointed out, meant that many workers came to work ill rather than lose two days' wages. Despite rules, punishments were arbitrarily distributed. Cadres from "red areas" who had extensive military combat experience but virtually no industrial expertise rarely received sanctions for their mistakes, but management meted out serious punishment to production workers whenever they violated a rule.[45] Military control of critical enterprises, and disputes that arose among the civilian workforce, were also evident in Guangzhou following its takeover.

The Takeover of Guangzhou

By the time PLA forces arrived in Guangzhou on October 14, 1949, CCP leaders had gained considerable experience in the difficult tasks of taking

---

[44] SMA, Series C1-2-729.   [45] Ibid.

over and securing urban areas for eventual control under military commissions. As Ezra Vogel observed, the military and party cadres who established CCP rule in the first months following the takeover of Guangzhou "were men experienced in liberating and organizing cities."[46] The most powerful official in the first months and years of Guangzhou's new government was Ye Jianying, who had been the mayor of Beijing following its takeover. Other party and military officials in Guangzhou had served as administrators in the posttakeover periods of Shanghai and Harbin. This group of elite officials, along with much less experienced and younger civilian cadres, was known as the Southbound Work Team. With the exception of Ye, who had extensive local connections dating from his military training in the 1920s, virtually all of the Southbound Work Team consisted of northerners unfamiliar with local customs and certainly the Cantonese dialect. Obvious tensions therefore existed within various parts of the local CCP establishment, consisting as it did of northerners, local CCP guerrilla fighters from rural areas of Guangdong province, and those who had served in the CCP underground in Guangzhou. Given the pressing need for administrators, the leaders of the new regime were compelled to turn, however reluctantly, to the technical expertise of civil servants from the government it had toppled.[47]

As had been the case in other cities, CCP leaders moved quickly to implement a monetary policy that would absorb as much cash as possible out of the inflation-ridden urban economy. Guangzhou's proximity to Hong Kong and the prevalence of Hong Kong dollars complicated matters. In industry, wage earners fought with management over the complex conversion system by which wages were calculated using rice prices, then converted to Hong Kong dollars and distributed to workers. After the local authorities banned the use of Hong Kong dollars for wage payments in early 1950, the action triggered a set of strikes among the tobacco, textiles, rubber, and electrical machinery industries, including two strikes at the Guangzhou Number Two Cotton Mill.[48] Municipal

[46] Ezra F. Vogel, *Canton Under Communism: Programs and Politics in a Provincial Capital, 1949–1968* (Cambridge, MA: Harvard University Press, 1969), 43.

[47] Ibid., 51–5.

[48] Guangzhou Municipal People's Government Labor Bureau, Investigation and Research Office, *Laodong zhengyi huibian* (Reports on Labor Disputes) (Guangzhou: Labor Bureau Investigation and Research Office, 1951); Guangzhou Labor Bureau, "Guangzhoushi laodong zhi," 7.

officials then had to "conduct persuasive work (*shuofu gongzuo*) among certain workers whose demands were overly high."[49] Incompetent factory owners came in for most of the blame in reports on the labor disputes in Guangzhou, but the Municipal Party Committee (MPC) later noted in a 1952 document on the posttakeover period that Communist cadres also contributed to the problem by taking sides in the disputes, or even starting them. "Some of our cadres also were not unified in thought, some purely stressed production and didn't care about labor welfare, and others purely stressed welfare, but did not grasp production."[50]

At large-scale enterprises, outright labor disputes were rare, but the workforce proved unruly for the new officials. Labor discipline at the Guangdong Textile Mill declined precipitously after the CCP takeover. Loafing on the job, even "boldly sleeping" at one's workstation were commonplace. "Just say the word to your supervisor and you can leave," seemed to be the general rule, and there was no wage deduction for unexcused absences. Daily absentee rates rose from 2.8 per 100 workers in January 1950 to 7.4 in March and April. Although Nationalist air raids during the spring partly accounted for the rise in absenteeism, taking the day off to attend local opera seemed to be the more common excuse. Mill employees looked upon production campaigns and anyone who worked too hard during them with great disdain. During an April 1950 production competition, those who participated with excessive enthusiasm drew the wrath of their fellow workers.[51]

CCP investigators found that the military representatives who ran the mill were afflicted with "extreme bureaucratism" and had alienated nearly everyone. The officers held both staff and workers in contempt, calling the former "petty capitalists" and the latter "stinking workers." During meetings the military representatives would hurl "unspeakable" insults at employees. Most of the blame lay with the head military representative, an officer surnamed Yang, who had taken over the mill's operations with his tyrannical style. He was a chronic drinker who rarely came to the factory and lived far from the mill. Everyone suspected the

---

[49] Li Qing, Chen Wenwu, Lin Shecheng, eds., *Zhongguo zibenzhuyi gongshangye de shehuizhuyi gaizao* (The Socialist Transformation of Capitalist Industry and Commerce in China), *Guangdong, Guangzhou*, by Editorial Leading Group on Guangdong and Guangzhou (Beijing: Zhonggong dangshi chubanshe, 1993), 51. (Hereafter cited as Li, Chen, and Lin, eds., *Shehuizhuiyi gaizao, Guangzhou*.)

[50] Li, Chen, and Lin, eds., *Shehuizhuyi gaizao, Guangzhou*, 115.

[51] GMA, Series 92-475.

sources of his income. Employees resented the fact that he prohibited workers from using the factory's supply of firewood, yet he had employees haul it to his house for personal use. He used hot plates and lamps in his office, when workers were not allowed to have them in their dorms. Yang's meetings with union officials frequently erupted into shouting matches. He also could send a wave of fear through an assembled group of employees by announcing, as he once did at a meeting, that he had a blacklist of targeted individuals in his pocket. Despite his military background, Yang disdained military cadres as well, denying them entry into the mill's workshops. Yang believed it was better to cultivate cadres from the retained staff than from military cadres, who knew little if anything about production.[52] As a military representative, Yang was quite likely among the Southbound Work Team and its cohort of northerners.

Labor relations were scarcely better at the Huangpu Shipyard outside Guangzhou. Zhang Yu, the shipyard director, had undergone a well-timed conversion to the CCP while in Hong Kong earlier in 1949. This decision, and no doubt his experience in running the shipyard during the late 1940s, gained him reappointment as shipyard director. Despite this continuity in management, CCP reports from 1950 cited serious problems in production, administration, and overall employee morale. New shipyard employees from the region found the pace of work and managerial competence at the Huangpu facility far below those at other shipyards where they had gained work experience. A party report quoted one of the recent hires from Hong Kong as saying, "When we worked in Hong Kong under the rule of capitalists and imperialists, we could loaf for three to six hours every day and the capitalist would still make money. Now, we work here for eight hours every day and still lose money." Many of these workers demanded that management transfer them to more agreeable workplaces, while others simply abandoned their jobs.[53]

In early 1950, over three months after the takeover of Guangzhou, only 23 percent of the city's factories were at normal operating capacity and 45 percent were completely shut down.[54] Industrial stagnation in 1949–50 caused by austerity policies was in part responsible for the outbreak of labor disputes in Guangzhou. During the fourteen-month period from November 1, 1949 to the end of 1950, a total of 593 disputes

---

[52] Ibid.   [53] GMA, Series 8-8.

[54] Tang Guoliang, ed., *Guangzhou gongye sishinian, 1949–1989* (Forty Years of Industry in Guangzhou) (Guangzhou: Guangdong renmin chubanshe, 1989), 13–14.

(*zhengyi*) took place, with ground and waterway transport workers accounting for 273 of the cases (46 percent).[55] Other sources, calculating labor disputes for 1950, show that the vast majority (243 of the 327 disputes in 1950) arose when employers fell behind in wage payments. A substantial proportion of factories had shut down in the first half of 1950 (609 out of 2,229, according to partial statistics), but Guangzhou workers, unlike their counterparts in Shanghai, appear not to have returned as frequently to their places of employment to demand their jobs back.[56] Both cities had large handicraft sectors and small-scale production that might have absorbed some of the unemployed factory workers, but workers in Guangzhou appear to have pursued employment options elsewhere in the towns of the Pearl River Delta, including Hong Kong.

THE FAILURE OF LABOR-MANAGEMENT COOPERATION

Party leaders attempted to calm the tense labor situation in urban areas by establishing municipal trade union organizations and labor-management consultative bodies. Following the intervention of Liu Shaoqi in the turbulent labor relations of Tianjin in 1949, the CCP's strategy of labor control involved the organization of a citywide Federation of Trade Unions and a Federation of Industry and Commerce.[57] Within factories, the CCP sought to rein in private owners and to give workers a forum to discuss their concerns and reach joint agreements with enterprise management on labor issues. Later known as Labor-Capital Consultative Conferences (LCCCs), these bodies were to mediate labor disputes within individual factories and to come up with solutions for how to increase production. LCCCs spread quickly throughout the private sector. In a departure from the past, when compulsory arbitration and mediation by local Nationalist officials was the norm, the LCCCs allegedly gave privately owned factories the ability to resolve labor issues on their own, within the enterprise. According to guidelines issued by the Shanghai Military Control Committee in April 1950, the boards were to have an equal number of representatives from both sides, labor and management, and to include the factory director, union chair, and head engineer. The LCCCs could make agreements on how to improve

---

[55] Guangzhou Labor Bureau, Investigation and Research Office, *Laodong zhengyi*.
[56] Guangzhou Labor Bureau, "Guangzhoushi laodong zhi," Wages ch. 7–8.
[57] Lieberthal, *Revolution and Tradition*, 47–8.

production and how to handle hiring and layoffs, wages, work hours, and other labor welfare issues. However, the LCCCs were not to get directly involved in factory management and administration.[58] In the second half of 1950, such factory councils rose from a total of 188 in Shanghai factories in June 1950 to 430 by September.[59] Ma Chungu, head of the Shanghai Labor Bureau, attributed the decline in labor disputes and incidents of "surrounding" to the spread of the LCCCs. Still, Ma and other municipal officials noted, the factory councils spent too much time taking up labor issues and resolving labor disputes rather than fulfilling their other purpose, which was to increase production. It turned out that a majority of LCCC members surveyed had not even read the regulations on the councils. Ma wanted LCCCs to establish a system of material incentives, so that output could rise, and to improve the very lax labor discipline reported in some enterprises.[60] LCCCs in other enterprises were faulted for spending too much time haggling over welfare questions rather than production issues.[61]

Along the same lines, CCP authorities set up Factory Management Committees (FMCs) in state-owned enterprises. Like LCCCs in the private sector, these boards gave roughly equal representation to workers and management, with the factory director, the enterprise union chair, and others seated on the panel. In practice, however, the FMCs lacked legitimacy in many enterprises as the factory director or a military representative attempted to dictate rather than consult on labor issues. This was unequivocally the case at the Jiangnan Shipyard. On orders from the central government, an FMC was established to act as a forum for the resolution of labor management issues. In theory, managers and workers had representation on the board, but workers soon viewed it as a "tool" of management. Workers felt, according to a party report, that labor representatives simply "kowtowed" to management, which acted in an entirely too "bureaucratic" manner. The board quickly abolished the pre-1949 practice of making emergency loans available to employees.[62] The attitude of workers toward the FMC was perhaps justified, because its director, Meng Yaren, was the factory's military

---

[58] Li Qing, Chen Wenwu, and Lin Shecheng, eds., *Zhongguo zibenzhuyi gongshangye de shehuizhuyi gaizao* (The Socialist Transformation of Capitalist Industry and Commerce in China), *Shanghai*, by Editorial Committee on Shanghai (Beijing: Zhonggong dangshi chubanshe, 1993), vol. 1:69. (Hereafter cited as Li, Chen, and Lin, eds., *Shehuizhuyi gaizao, Shanghai*.)

[59] Ibid., 1:72, 83.   [60] Ibid., 1:84–5, 88.   [61] SMA, Series Q193-3-566.

[62] SMA, Series C1-2-729.

representative and also the secretary of the shipyard's party committee.[63]

Jiangnan Shipyard workers were also dissatisfied with their new officially sponsored union. As a party report noted, "They feel it's a 'union of the Military Committee' and is incapable of representing their interests." Union cadres, the report said, "cannot even look workers in the face because of the growing discontent toward the union." Workers referred to the Welfare Association under the Nationalist managers before 1949 as the "black union" because of its strength and resolve in pressing workers' demands. The Communist-sponsored union, on the other hand, lacked any authority, and a number of unspecified "heresies" were on the rise.[64]

In addition, union cadres at the Jiangnan Shipyard took problematic political stances. On the one hand, they were unfamiliar with union administrative work, and too often adopted a "union outlook" toward administrative tasks. One CCP member and union committee member, Zhou Xingquan, said that "If we don't increase wages, there's nothing else for our union to do." Zhou and others took the view, party authorities noted with some dismay, that the union should manage only benefits and not mobilize the workforce for production. Zhou and others who were supposed to help shipyard officials solve the problem of "economism" were obviously contributing to it. Another problem was the fact that forty or so union cadres were not involved in production, and the six section heads of the union had manifested "departmentalism" (*benwei zhuyi*) at meetings. Leading union officials from Beijing, including an officer of the All-China Federation of Trade Unions, Liu Ningyi, visited the shipyard in early 1952 and found "severe problems" in management and the overall attitude of workers.[65]

Elsewhere in large state enterprises, the collaborative labor-management boards encountered similar problems. At the Guangdong Textile Mill, those responsible had been slow to set up an FMC, despite direct orders from the new Provincial Industrial Department (*gongye ting*). Eventually thirteen members were elected to the panel: six from management and seven from the union. The problem, according to the investigators, was that the workers on the panel who were elected from their departments thought the FMC was primarily a managerial

---

[63] Jiangnan Shipyard Factory History Research Office, "Factory Chronology," mimeo, n.d., 36.
[64] SMA, Series C1-2-729.   [65] Ibid.

structure. The factory director, the head of the personnel department, and others always made suggestions at meetings, but workers' representatives never said anything except, "It's an administration matter" whenever items such as bonuses were brought up.[66] Worker representatives also never seemed to know the agenda or the resolutions passed at meetings. Elsewhere in Guangzhou, workers were unwilling to meet with work teams sent to factories to organize unions and educate them in political doctrine. Women workers, who accounted for most of the city's knitting and weaving workforce, feared that under Communist Party rule they would be "assigned" to male cadres, and kept a safe distance from them.[67]

The small and selective branch committees of the Communist Party within factories lacked power or prestige in the early 1950s. At the Huangpu Shipyard, the party branch could claim only two production workers as members as late as year-end 1953. The remaining thirty-eight party members all held administrative posts, and most of these had been transferred to the factory as military cadres.[68] In a 1953 survey of steel mills in Northeast China, the percentage of party membership was found to be 1 to 2 percent of the workforce.[69] At the Guangdong Textile Mill, there were only nine party members in 1950, all of whom were office personnel. Those who sought membership in the factory's party committee were told there were no vacancies. A Communist Youth League with forty members had strained relations with the party committee.[70] Prior to the 1951–2 campaigns that would eliminate its leaders, the GMU enjoyed far more popular support within the mill. As a Communist Party member at the mill noted of the GMU, "They take advantage of our shortcomings, especially on issues of direct personal interest of workers."[71] Despite various divisions within the mill's workforce, workers were united in their mistrust of the Communist Party and the work teams sent to the mill. During meetings, only a few "progressive" workers spoke up. Even then, they expressed a misunderstanding of Communist labor

---

[66] GMA, Series 92-475.

[67] Guangzhou Municipal Trade Union Preparatory Committee, *Guangzhou gongyun* (Guangzhou Labor Movement) (Guangzhou: Guangzhoushi gonghui lianhehui, 1950), 85–6.

[68] GMA, Series 8-8.

[69] Chongwook Chung, "Ideology and the Politics of Industrial Management in the People's Republic of China, 1949–1965" (Ph.D. diss., Yale University, 1975), 165.

[70] GMA, Series 92-475.

[71] Ibid. Another source of complaints to the work team was the existence of two "meal groups" (*shantuan*), divided by native place, with the Hunan employees reportedly being served better food than the local Cantonese workers.

policy. One frustrated work team investigator said, "I can't get any material from them. They just won't talk to me."[72]

Local CCP officials responded to these and other failures to control workers, unions, party cadres, and factory owners and managers in a style reminiscent of the party's handling of rural areas in previous decades. Campaigns had evolved as an effective tactic of social control during the party's base area experiences in the 1930s and 1940s, but it was not assured that they would achieve the same results in urban areas. With labor discipline plummeting and gradual reform efforts having failed, the party turned to mass mobilization, investigation, and punishment to remove personnel and overturn practices that hindered efforts to jumpstart industrial expansion.

FACTORY CAMPAIGNS, 1951–1952

Since the takeover of urban areas in 1949, CCP cadres had consistently organized campaigns of various sorts to establish new production goals or to educate workers in party ideology. With China's entrance into the war on the Korean peninsula in the fall of 1950, campaigns were flavored with patriotic appeals and expressed in martial language and style. During the campaign to Resist America and Aid Korea (*kangmei yuanchao*) in 1951, workers and factory owners were persuaded to "contribute," in the form of accumulated wages and capital, particular armaments such as a tank or an aircraft.

The Democratic Reform Campaign (*minzhu gaige*) in spring 1951 took place in factories as an effort to break up ties of affinity and "feudal" relationships that existed between bosses and workers. The campaign had its origins in Northeast China in the late 1940s. At the Wusan Factory in the city of Shenyang, party cadres organized workers in November 1948 for the Democratic Reform Campaign, in which workers were to "speak bitterness" in much the same fashion that peasants had vented their past hardships in front of arrested and accused landlords. Party cadres also registered workers and others who had participated as members of "reactionary organizations" in the past.[73] Notwithstanding these efforts, the party encountered difficulty in breaking up gang and other affective ties between workers and shop floor bosses.[74] In mining and transportation industries, secret society leaders

---

[72] GMA, Series 92-475.   [73] Brugger, *Democracy and Organisation*, 90–1.
[74] Ibid., 91–7.

often took over the grassroots union organizations that the party had established.[75]

In the Suppression of Counterrevolutionaries Campaign, also in 1951, the primary targets were ex-functionaries in the Nationalist military, police, or party organizations accused of industrial sabotage during the transition.[76] The campaign in the spring of that year coincided with the military mobilization following China's entrance into the Korean War in the fall of 1950. The Democratic Reform Campaign and the Suppression of Counterrevolutionaries thus straddled the patriotic campaigns associated with the war and the internal security crackdown aimed at former Nationalist officials. Brugger's analysis of official PRC media at this time noted considerable policy debate within the party over how to deal with gangs and other rival organizations among the ranks of workers. In contrast to those in the party who favored a sudden purge, some CCP leaders favored a gradual approach using administrative reforms, such as output competitions or comprehensive labor insurance. Registration, it was thought, would reveal gang leaders by their suspiciously high incomes.[77]

In early 1952 the party launched in urban areas what Lieberthal aptly termed "the second revolution." Municipal party committees sent work teams (*gongzuo dui*) of party cadres to every major enterprise in urban areas to investigate private and public behavior of owners, staff, and other managers, gathering their information from small groups of workers and colleagues of targeted individuals. Work teams had the authority of the upper reaches of the party and the coercive power of its public security forces. The Three Antis (*sanfan*) exposed and punished incidents of corruption, bureaucratism, and waste among state and CCP cadres in state-owned factories and government offices. Privately owned enterprises were the focus of the Five Antis (*wufan*), directed at tax evasion, graft, embezzlement, theft of state property, and theft of state secrets. Because many private enterprises at this time engaged in wholesale buying and selling with the state, opportunities for corruption were numerous and, for those involved, lucrative. Each enterprise or unit was assessed a monetary figure for how much in "damages" it had afflicted upon the nation. These campaigns were not directed at labor management questions per se, but made relations between enterprise managers

---

[75] Lieberthal, *Revolution and Tradition*, 74–7; Brugger, *Democracy and Organisation*, 94, 105.
[76] Brugger, *Democracy and Organisation*, 105.   [77] Ibid., 106.

and employees extremely tense, as many of the latter provided party investigators with materials to put together cases against a factory owner or manager.[78]

Whatever stability had been achieved in factory labor management by late 1950 was quickly overturned by the outbreak of work stoppages and factory shutdowns during the Five Antis. The turbulence hit small- and medium-scale factories especially hard. LCCC meetings more often than not turned into shouting sessions in which nothing was resolved. Some factory owners suffered physical brutalities from workers. Liu Chang-sheng, the chair of the Shanghai GLU, said: "In the past, employers had a bad attitude toward workers; now workers are reversing roles."[79] In part, as Liu also noted, Shanghai workers had made significant concessions in the prior two years in order to restore industrial production.[80] When workers discovered over the course of the campaigns in 1952 that their bosses had been amassing sizable illicit personal fortunes by taking advantage of state contracts, they reacted with perhaps justifiable wrath. Moreover, because trade union organizations and factory union cadres spearheaded the Five Antis Campaign rather than party committees themselves,[81] there may have been less central control over the conduct of the movement than would be the case in subsequent campaigns.

While they would ultimately submit to the authority of the party in a losing battle, private factory and business owners at the outset undertook measures to thwart the campaign and the party and union cadres who were leading it. In many sectors, such as machines, tobacco, and textiles, capitalists tried to preempt the effects of the campaign by giving out generous bonuses and benefits to workers.[82] This exacerbated an already distorted wage structure between private and state factories. In one privately owned paper-making plant, the very lowest paid workers were earning more in wages and benefits than the staff and technicians at a state-owned paper mill. Elsewhere, some owners cited the decline in business as a reason to invoke large-scale dismissals. Disputes over such firings reached a peak during the Five Antis Campaign.[83]

---

[78] Lieberthal, *Revolution and Tradition*, 174.
[79] Li, Chen, and Lin, eds., *Shehuizhuyi gaizao, Shanghai*, 1:153–4.
[80] Ibid., 1:151–2.
[81] Paul Harper, "The Party and the Unions in Communist China," *China Quarterly* 37 (Jan.–Mar. 1969): 98–9.
[82] Li, Chen, and Lin, eds., *Shehuizhuyi gaizao, Shanghai*, 1:212–13.
[83] Ibid., 1:196.

The Campaigns in Shanghai

After two years of unsteady but gradual economic recovery, textile mills in Shanghai soon became targets of the CCP's nationwide political movements. Authorities in the Shanghai MPC sent work teams to the mills to investigate the political backgrounds of mill managers and employees as early as 1951 during the Suppression of Counterrevolutionaries Campaign. Given the Shenxin Number Six Mill's unsavory reputation as an "enemy fortress" during the 1940s, it was a prominent target for party investigators. Suspicions that the political attitudes of the mill's employees had not changed seemed confirmed during the election of a union chair in late 1949. The individual elected was a staff member from a landlord family. Maintenance department mechanics, active in pro-Nationalist labor associations in the late 1940s, also won election to the Union Preparatory Committee and allegedly plotted sabotage and other "reactionary" activities.[84]

Perhaps for this reason, the Suppression of Counterrevolutionaries movement at Shenxin Number Six was not a public affair to mobilize workers against "enemies" of the regime. Instead, public security officials from the Municipal People's Government simply moved in and arrested thirty-three employees in a one-day sweep on April 27, 1951.[85] Among them was the union chair of landlord class background as well as the mill's former director of the Personnel Department, Rong Bendao. (He had been demoted to a staff position within the department after 1949.) Communist Party sources offer no explanation for why personnel officials came under attack. The rationale behind the decision to round up workers from the Mechanics' Department was obvious: most of these had been active in Nationalist unions in the late 1940s. Of those arrested at Shenxin Number Six during the Suppression of Counterrevolutionaries for whom job descriptions are provided in party reports, 57 percent operated or maintained the mill's machinery.[86]

The Democratic Reform Campaign in the second half of 1951 targeted shop floor supervisors, the "Number Ones" of the pre-1949 era who had enjoyed "feudal" authority over workers. Workers called for an investigation of Number Ones and their past transgressions. Party cadres sent to lead the Democratic Reform Campaign at Shenxin Number Six first surveyed the attitudes of workers at the mill. Women workers in the reeling department wanted to attack the line supervisors who had ruled

---

[84] SMA, Series Q193-3-364.   [85] Ibid.   [86] SMA, Series Q193-3-506.

117

them with despotic force before "liberation." Spinning-room workers wanted to struggle against anyone who had a "bad work style." Mechanics suggested, "First raise our wages, and then we can do everything well." The mill operatives demanded some of the same reforms that had taken place in the city's state-owned textile mills. "State-owned mills have been liberated, but we haven't," they complained. "State-owned mills don't have Number Ones anymore, so they benefit." The mill's staff, already shaken down during the Suppression of Counterrevolutionaries Campaign, dreaded the arrival of another campaign. Some uttered with despair, "There's no hope."[87]

During a series of mass meetings, party cadres encouraged workers to come forward and "speak bitterness" of their past hardships during their employment at the mill. The work team members tallied figures on the degree of emotion displayed among the several hundred workers from each department who vented their feelings. Statistics show, for example, that in the spinning room, 554 workers had "spoken bitterness," among whom 269 had cried. Figures were also kept on the numbers who had "cried greatly" (*daku*) and those who had displayed a "normal" flow of tears.[88] An unspecified number of labor bosses, including one who still demanded gifts from her subordinates and who had remained arrogant during the campaign, were brought out in front of workers to make "self-criticism" speeches confessing to their past abuses.[89] Another Number One, sensing that she would be a target of the campaign, gave prior orders to her subordinates that when the party work team sought opinions from them on how she should be punished, they were to make her sweep the floor so that she could avoid having to do the more strenuous work of tending spindles.[90]

After all the investigation and public venting during the Democratic Reform Campaign, a total of just fifteen arrests were made at the Shenxin Number Six Mill, including five who were later released. There is no information on the background of those detained, but it is likely they were members of spy organizations or bandit gangs rather than Number Ones. Neither classified reports about the campaign nor documents published for propaganda purposes claim that the Number One "system" was eliminated, as some workers had demanded prior to the campaign. Despite the broad and unprecedented mobilization of

[87] SMA, Series Q193-3-364.   [88] SMA, Series Q193-3-366.   [89] Ibid.
[90] SMA, Series Q193-3-364.

workers in this campaign, many pre-1949 labor supervisors managed to survive a campaign in which they were the targets.

The Five Antis Campaign, which took place between February and May 1952, had more far-reaching implications for labor relations than the 1951 campaigns at Shenxin Number Six. Party work teams spent several weeks meeting with employees and collecting reports and "materials" on individual "capitalists" in the various departments at the mill. The campaign also involved political meetings with workers, who were said to have expressed a greater interest in struggling against staff and production supervisors than owners and top management. Party representatives and elected activists encouraged workers to "speak bitterness" about life under the old regime and to provide them with "bullets," or information on various instances of corruption and theft of state property. The work team meticulously catalogued all the allegations, then sent them to district level authorities. Offenders then supplemented the charges with their own confessions to work team investigators.

Among the more revealing observations recorded by a CCP work team at Shenxin Number Six were those surrounding the director of the mill's Personnel Department, Zhang Sizhen. Zhang had joined the mill through family connections in the late 1940s and was a department head. During the CCP takeover, he was credited with struggling against the mill's owners and preventing them from shutting the mill down. Zhang achieved much respect at this time for his ability to argue forcefully and persuasively. This earned him seats on several enterprise committees, including a union preparatory committee and the mill's LCCC, where he sat as a representative of labor. Mill management admired Zhang's talents, and subsequently succeeded in drawing him to their side with an appointment as head of the Personnel Department in August 1951. With a salary increase and growing ties to management, Zhang was said to have turned corrupt in 1951, and ultimately "switched sides" on the LCCC in 1953 by becoming a representative of management.[91] The mill's party committee reported detailed information on the attitudes and activities of several other managers at the mill, even if they were not charged with corruption.

The final report on the Five Antis at Shenxin Number Six reads like an accountant's ledger. The total monetary amount in bribes, tax evasion, graft, theft of state property and state secrets between 1949 and 1952

[91] SMA, Series Q193-3-380.

came to 17 billion yuan (in the old, pre-1952 currency). This sum was considered as "damages to the state" and imposed as a sort of uncollected fine on Shenxin Number Six, as it was on other privately owned mills.[92] Despite the lack of overt labor-management issues in the Five Antis, it became clear that workers could serve as valuable informants to CCP officials interested in the transgressions of capitalist owners.

The Democratic Reform Campaign and others at the Shenxin Number Six Mill demonstrated the ability of the new regime to intervene directly in workplace politics and with force when necessary, but party officials in Shanghai were just as concerned (if not more so) that production was restored and workforce discipline maintained. This is not to deny that the campaigns had major consequences for the individuals who were their targets. They eliminated the CCP's most obvious opponents in enterprises that had been "enemy fortresses" before 1949 and organizing grounds of anti-Communist partisans. The Five Antis Campaign also demonstrated the extractive and investigatory capacities of the CCP to curb long-standing tax evasion and bribery among Shanghai industrialists. But the political campaigns, especially those that called for workers to struggle against those in authority, had to be curbed if production was to be restored and a planned economy established. To discipline the unruly workforce, the experience and authority of line supervisors was indispensable.

Campaigns not only had a range of unintended consequences at mills such as Shenxin Number Six, but they were also not as effective in eliminating the actual problem as party authorities boasted. The Democratic Reform Movement at the Shenxin Number Six Mill involved a great deal of sound and fury directed at Number Ones but only a handful of arrests, and even then it was not clear if those detained were shop floor bosses.[93] The Suppression of Counterrevolutionaries also failed to eradicate its intended targets over the long term. Several unspecified incidents of sabotage took place at the mill after these campaigns. Between 1953 and 1955, public security officials monitoring activities at the mill discovered that among 700 new employees was a man who had murdered several CCP cadres in the countryside and another who was active in a spy ring.[94] Party authorities remained wary of enemies in the workplace.

Elsewhere in Shanghai's major factories, CCP officials from industrial and labor departments of the Shanghai Municipal Committee expressed

---

[92] SMA, Series Q193-1-1310.   [93] SMA, Series Q193-3-378.   [94] Ibid.

concern with the political qualities of the workforce but also limited the scope of the campaigns when production needs had to be met. At the Jiangnan Shipyard in 1951 and 1952, CCP officials carried out political campaigns aimed at expelling "reactionaries" and other politically unsavory elements among the workforce and staff at the shipyard. Among some 3,000 employees, the Suppression of Counterrevolutionaries and the Democratic Reform Campaign turned up about 1 percent of the workforce as having "political problems." These two campaigns resulted in twenty-five arrests, and another nineteen employees were placed under surveillance. After "clean confession," eighteen of the nineteen were excused from punishment. The Three Antis took place in 1952 at the shipyard, but it was less directed at production workers and more at cadres and staff. Given the strategic importance of the facility, it would have been difficult for Communist Party authorities to engage in a large-scale purge of shipyard personnel and production workers. Moreover, 300 of the most obvious potential targets of a political campaign in the Jiangnan Shipyard, the staff and technicians who had been officials in the Nationalist Navy, had already fled to Taiwan. The campaigns in 1951–2 aimed at expelling "reactionaries" and their ilk from the shipyard's workforce therefore had a limited range of targets.

Despite having carried out three major national campaigns in the early 1950s, a few years later CCP investigators at the Jiangnan Shipyard turned up an alarming security situation in which nearly a quarter of the shipyard's then-6,300 employees had some "historical problems."[95] A separate investigation found that numerous shop floor supervisors now holding important positions in various workshops had been active participants in secret societies and in the Nationalist government's Labor Welfare Committee.[96] When these supervisors were included with staff and technicians, a total of 75 percent of those holding administrative posts were found to have some "historical problem" or "complex social connections."

The Campaigns in Guangzhou

The GMU and its leadership were a primary target of Guangzhou's campaigns. During the Suppression of Counterrevolutionaries in the summer of 1951, over thirty-six thousand workers gathered for the kickoff of the campaign at the Sun Yat-sen Memorial to denounce the former head of

---

[95] SMA, Series A38-2-148.   [96] SMA, Series A43-1-112.

the GMU, Li Dexuan. During these opening ceremonies, officials from the People's Court issued the death sentence to Li. The campaign continued throughout the summer, when CCP work teams conducted 106 struggle sessions that involved 216 targets. Like Li Dexuan, most of these appear to have been GMU union officials before 1949. CCP reports noted that following the campaign, union leadership was reshuffled in 193 factories. By late 1951, CCP authorities had set up over 1,600 basic-level unions in the city's approximately 4,000 enterprises.[97] In the largest factories, over 90 percent of the workforce was classified as union members.[98]

These displays of force and organizational ability were impressive on the surface. During the Democratic Reform Campaign in Guangzhou, as in Shanghai, the CCP rooted out competing sources of authority from factory workshops. A total of 618 individuals were targeted for struggle sessions in 50 factories during the campaign in Guangzhou.[99] As much as the Democratic Reform Campaign attacked competing bases of authority among workers, the campaign also opened up unanticipated workplace issues. Workers in Guangzhou's privately owned factories, especially the knitting mills, took advantage of this campaign to make demands for higher wages.[100]

During the Five Antis in Guangzhou the following year, labor issues resurfaced. Available documentation on the campaign suggests that it was newly arrived CCP union organizers in these mills who were responsible for making capitalists raise wages. "It was we who pushed workers to make these demands to their bosses," one union report explained.[101] The strongest force behind the wage increases, however, appears to have been factory owners. Some Guangzhou capitalists demonstrated an ability to thwart the Five Antis Campaign by raising wages of workers in an effort to win their protection or support. In the pharmaceuticals industry, the average pay rose from 137.5 wage points in 1950 to 357 points by October 1952.[102] Average wages in Guangzhou's knitting mills, which were already 50 percent higher than weaving mills in the city, tended to rise in a chain reaction in 1951 as one mill owner would raise wages and workers in other mills would press their bosses to follow suit.[103]

---

[97] GMA, Series 92-121. Number of enterprises from Li, Chen, and Lin, eds., *Shehuizhuyi gaizao, Guangzhou*, Statistical Appendix, Table 2.
[98] GMA, Series 92-121.   [99] Ibid.   [100] GMA, Series 92-476.   [101] Ibid.
[102] GMA, Series 92-129.   [103] GMA, Series 92-476.

A year later, after the Five Antis had turned up substantial "ill-gotten gains" (*baoli*) in the city's approximately 400 knitting mills, owners took revenge by using what party officials called the "three stops." These referred to owners who halted wage payments, suspended the provision of meals to employees, or ceased production by simply shutting down. By the fall of 1952, only 262 knitting mills remained open.[104] Guangzhou factory owners were also later accused of trying to gain support from "revolutionary cadres" in the work teams through illicit means. One owner bribed forty-nine CCP cadres with prostitutes and another gave cash bribes to fifty-one cadres, in exchange for their overlooking tax evasion, fraud, or other crimes against the state.[105]

In public factories such as the Guangdong Textile Mill, campaigns ran their course but in retrospect did not achieve the results the party wanted. The Democratic Reform Campaign and the Suppression of Counterrevolutionaries took place at the mill in the second half of 1951. A party work team investigated the "history" of workers, a task that was supplemented with confessions from 323 workers and 53 staff. The "scope of mobilization" was broad, drawing over 75 percent of women workers and a lower percentage of men. During large struggle sessions in July, the work team led struggles against six "scabs" (*gongzei*) and one "destructive element" (*pohuai fenzi*) and also leveled charges against a section head and a shift leader who had been notorious for sharply reprimanding workers. These individuals had to make public confessions in front of workers. A subsequent report by the CCP stated that during the Democratic Reform Campaign not enough employees had been mobilized and that the work team's investigation was insufficiently thorough. The work team had avoided dealing with the maintenance department workers and staff, nearly all men. Factionalism and other divisions persisted among the workforce.[106]

The Three Antis campaign at the mill in early 1952 exposed a total of thirty-nine "corrupt elements." Summaries of the campaign do not identify the specific jobs of these thirty-nine, but given that many of them had channeled large amounts of public funds toward personal use, most of these targets would have been staff with access to financial flows to and from the mill. Investigators found five "small tigers" who had embezzled over 10 million yuan (in precurrency reform units). Another twenty-eight had taken under 1 million yuan. The work team from the Guangzhou MPC calculated the amount of monetary damages done to

[104] Ibid.   [105] GMA, Series 92-121.   [106] GMA, Series 8-8.

state property and finances by embezzlement, which totaled over 109 million yuan (68 million of which was estimated to be direct damages to state property and finances). The party subsequently scaled back the estimated financial losses of their perhaps overzealous accountants to just 23 million yuan in damages to state property and finances. As a sign of the limits to which the party could carry out its political agenda to "clean the ranks" of employees, only three of these staff were dismissed from their posts, one was fined, and another demoted. The remainder received some form of administrative penalty or a warning.[107]

Following the completion of the Three Antis, CCP work teams carried out a campaign to "Unite to Ban the Reactionary Huidaomen," an unidentified sect apparently popular with employees. As was the case in Shanghai, party officials saw that their efforts to purge the workforce of unofficial associations and other networks were subject to constant backsliding after the campaigns had been completed. The purpose of the new movement was described as "suppression work . . . to better grasp the historical situation of workers." Rather than publicly condemning individuals for past abuses, this movement was more investigatory in nature. MPC officials gathered "materials" on 124 workers and 30 staff. Most of these had some form of past association with the Nationalist Party or its Youth League.[108]

At the Huangpu Shipyard, CCP work teams from the Guangzhou MPC led campaigns that by some indications were perfunctory affairs. There is little specific information on the Democratic Reform Campaign and the Three Antis at the shipyard, but it is likely that their cumulative effect was not as large as elsewhere in China. First, the factory director Zhang Yu, despite having had obvious and direct ties to the upper reaches of the Nationalist regime as a naval official, escaped these movements unscathed (in fact, he would serve as the shipyard's director until his retirement in 1960). Second, because the "reactionary" GMU had no presence in the shipyard's workforce before 1949, it is unlikely that very many employees with politically unsavory backgrounds in this regard would have been found here. Finally, because the workforce was expanding rapidly and taking in recruits from all over the Pearl River Delta, it would have been impossible for party work teams to ascertain the political histories of each worker. Unlike other factories where most employees would have been fairly well acquainted with the activities and associations of certain individuals after several years, at the Huangpu

---

[107] Ibid.   [108] Ibid.

Shipyard all but a handful of workers would have been strangers to supervisors and staff, perhaps to each other as well.

Foremen at the Huangpu Shipyard not only avoided political retribution during campaigns but also remained firmly in control of production. CCP officials reported that the problems at the Huangpu Shipyard were not ideological but more "practical" in nature. Production remained decentralized, scattered among disconnected work sites at the plant. Technicians and engineers were extremely scarce, and production was hampered by the turnover problem that had existed since the late 1940s. The shipyard bosses recruited through networks and drew upon the regional labor market that encompassed the Pearl River Delta. Many of the skilled positions at the yard were filled by workers with extensive experience at shipyards in Hong Kong, Kowloon, and Taigu. As it did for most factories in Guangzhou, the party set as its primary task at the Huangpu Shipyard one of bringing order to a highly decentralized production process. Production team leaders operated virtually independent of the factory director and administration. The shipyard was said to have "severe problems" in labor management. Reports claimed that no one took responsibility (*wuren fuze*), and worker morale was very low. More seriously, the Huangpu Shipyard was "still unable to fulfill the present needs of national defense." In some work sites at the shipyard, there was a great deal of new equipment but not enough labor. Because of the labor shortage, skilled masters had to do jobs usually given to apprentices. Other workshops had too much labor and not enough equipment. "The management system creates chaos, to the point that leaders have no way of gaining control of the production situation," observed the Guangzhou MPC's Industrial Work Department.[109]

Unintended Consequences of the Campaigns

In the most important factories in Shanghai and Guangzhou, the campaigns of 1951–2 displayed the ability of the CCP to penetrate and alter workplace relations at the factory level. Direct opposition to the CCP and flagrant violations of industrial, commercial, or taxation policies were exposed and punished. Yet campaigns also created important unintended consequences.

Campaigns undermined CCP efforts to control the growth in wages, which in turn threatened to revive inflationary impulses in the urban

[109] Ibid.

economy. For example, private factory owners in Guangzhou were under immense political pressure from the campaigns in the early 1950s and complied quickly when workers went to them with demands for higher wages. Party officials in the city complained about the periodic outbreaks of "blind wage increases." At times, enterprise owners preempted campaigns targeted at them by offering wage increases in hopes of receiving lenient treatment from workers. The Wage Department of the Guangzhou GLU reported that factory owners used wage increases to "win over" workers following the Five Antis.[110] CCP cadres were faulted for having a "welfare viewpoint" and often supported the demands of workers for higher wages. Other cadres feared provoking the wrath of workers and simply avoided going into factories known to have "wage problems."[111] In the spring of 1953, when a rash of wage increases spread throughout the city, workers who successfully demanded wage hikes "went about everywhere to tell others of their 'experience'."[112] Wage problems intensified later the same year, when local officials were attempting to set up a comprehensive wage adjustment for 1954. Municipal officials also feared that because Guangzhou was close to Hong Kong and Macao, "counter-revolutionaries will invariably take advantage of the opportunity of wage reform to carry out destructive activities, even to the point that they will instigate the minority of backward elements to carry out strikes and slowdowns."[113]

While campaigns may have undermined the personal authority of "feudalistic" work bosses in many factories, workers quickly discerned that the distribution of power and authority had shifted so that one important weapon had been removed from the labor boss's arsenal: the power to dismiss unruly or otherwise disloyal workers. This created enormous discipline problems in many factories, and posed even greater challenges for the CCP's goal to introduce comprehensive planning in industry. CCP authorities had to restore discipline and some set of incentives that would raise productivity among the workforce. As the economy, including labor markets, came under the increasing control of state planners, shop floor bosses lost their coercive and punitive powers.

The changes in shop floor authority relations brought about by the cumulative effects of the CCP takeover and subsequent campaigns were

---

[110] GMA, Series 92-129.
[111] Li, Chen, and Lin, eds., *Shehuizhuyi gaizao, Guangzhou*, 115.
[112] Ibid., 148.
[113] Ibid., 154.

vividly on display at the Guangdong Textile Mill. Here, the campaigns and the CCP's glorification of workers allowed many to defy orders from their superiors. By 1953, the workshop directors and other supervisory staff complained forcefully to a party work team that changes to labor policies had drastically undermined their powers. For example, with the previous bonus for attendance having been abolished, shop floor supervisors had no material incentives to get employees to show up for work. They resented the fact that whenever they did report flagrant insubordination, they were criticized by party officials. "If this was the old society, I'd fire them right away," said one production team leader. Others noted that "Nowadays, if we criticize a worker for an unexcused absence we get scolded for having a bureaucratic, anti-labor viewpoint." Supervisors had no power to cut the wages of workers who arrived late or refused orders. During disputes, workers would lose their temper at production team leaders and go to workshop directors with the politically loaded complaint that, "His behavior is just like a landlord's!"[114] The mill's retained personnel staff and technicians also complained to CCP investigators that in the past, they had the ability to deduct wages and punish workers for infractions, but demanded to know how they were to manage workers now. The party work team that authored the report on the mill observed that the retained staff were also under immense political pressure. They did not dare speak up during meetings, and lived in fear that if they committed even the smallest error they could be labeled a counterrevolutionary.[115]

Well aware that they could take leaves of absence without consequences, the mill's workers favored attending theater, dancing, and banqueting over laboring for the glory of the nation and socialism. When they showed up for work, they were too exhausted from the previous night's round of drinking. Women workers, much to the dismay of party officials, said the only reason they worked at all was to "make money to buy nice clothes." Women made up about 60 percent of the workforce at the mill and refused to follow disciplinary rules, spending their days in the workshop singing, dancing, telling jokes, and sharing their concerns about "marriage and love." If women in the mill came under criticism for their work habits, they were not the most flagrant offenders. The worst discipline was reported to be in the all-male maintenance department. Instead of repairing machines, these workers "sat around smoking, reading the newspaper, and telling jokes." The mechanics were already

[114] GMA, Series 8-11.   [115] GMA, Series 92-475.

under supervision by party authorities after a sworn brotherhood (*jiebai xiongdi*) had been discovered among their ranks during the Democratic Reform Campaign in 1951. Now, an unruly group of mechanics was purposely delaying repairs to machines because they were unsatisfied with their wages.[116]

As earlier studies have found, the urban campaigns of the early 1950s can be understood as responses of a new regime that understandably lacked the financial, technical, and personnel resources to impose uniform administrative controls over urban areas, including factories.[117] The early 1950s urban campaigns followed from the CCP's past experience of rural campaigns and their success at social control and mobilization. Any number of personal accounts of CCP campaigns demonstrate how the new regime exercised power through the penetration of basic units in society, including factories and other enterprises.[118] When viewed from the factory level using the sorts of newly available materials cited in this chapter, the urban campaigns of the early 1950s portray the unprecedented – by Nationalist regime standards, anyway – success of the state in exerting controls over the enterprise workforce. One clear result of the campaigns of the early 1950s was to drastically erode the authority of production supervisors and administrative staff, who in many instances were campaign targets. It was not the case, as seen from the enterprises discussed in this chapter, that campaigns resulted in the arrest, incarceration, or execution of formerly powerful authority figures within factories. Staff and production supervisors appear to have remained members of the enterprise community, though greatly weakened in their power and vulnerable to political charges from their employees.

The early 1950s campaigns also gave workers the opportunity to use the CCP's own proletarian rhetoric to make demands for enterprise welfare measures that had been disrupted in 1949 with the collapse of the industrial sector. This preservation of enterprise welfare distribution

---

[116] GMA, Series 8-11.

[117] The best analysis of the early 1950s urban campaigns from a local perspective remains Lieberthal's account of Tianjin, in Lieberthal, *Revolution and Tradition*, 125–79; for Guangzhou see, Vogel, *Canton Under Communism*, 63–5; 80; 84–8; for Shanghai, see Lynn T. White, III, *Policies of Chaos: The Organizational Causes of Violence in China's Cultural Revolution* (Princeton, NJ: Princeton University Press, 1988), 67–9.

[118] For enterprises, perhaps the most widely cited personal account of the Five Antis is that of a chemical firm manager in Tianjin and his experience of the psychological trauma of "thought reform" during that campaign. Lieberthal, *Revolution and Tradition*, 126–42.

is best illustrated in the example of Shanghai's Shenxin Number Six Mill. Following the Five Antis campaign, management agreed to spend 1 billion yuan (in precurrency reform yuan) on items such as new dormitories and to make repairs to the current one, along with building a new company cafeteria.[119] There was also newfound respect for the decisions issued by the LCCC at the mill. Still, workers had several "pressing demands" that included a new dorm with separate units for single workers and those with families, and an employee bus for those who did not live in the mill's housing units. Male workers especially insisted that they get a hair salon on the factory premises, and then there was the "umbrella problem." It seemed that in the past the Nationalist-controlled union had distributed free umbrellas to employees, and workers couldn't understand the failure of the new union to do so.[120] Both items were provided to workers in an agreement in December 1952.[121]

CCP officials no doubt were familiar with the "provision system" found in base areas and military units during the 1940s, under which leaders of such units were responsible for distributing food and often shelter to workers, in addition to their wages. While some scholars have traced the *danwei*'s expansive welfare benefits to this "provision system,"[122] the evidence from the previous chapter suggests that workplace welfare as an institution had developed independently in Chinese cities, during the hyperinflation of the 1940s. CCP efforts to stamp out inflation were facilitated by continuing the practice of having factories provide food and other basic necessities to workers. By 1951–2, campaigns and efforts to mobilize and recruit workers into the CCP accorded workers the opportunity to demand more from management in terms of welfare provision. Managers in state and private enterprises had little recourse when confronted with such demands.

Indeed, the Five Antis cleared the way for the ultimate liquidation of the private sector in the mid-1950s. After the campaigns of the early 1950s, factory and commercial business owners remained under close union and party supervision. With little hope of profiting from their businesses, capitalists either closed down or gave up the pursuit of financial management altogether. Generally speaking, smaller enterprises tended to shut down, which led to temporary unemployment difficulties. In larger factories and businesses, managers granted "arbitrary" wage

---

[119] SMA, Series Q193-3-364.   [120] Ibid.   [121] SMA, Series Q193-3-566.
[122] Lu Feng, "The Origins and Formation of the Unit (*Danwei*) System," *Chinese Sociology and Anthropology* vol. 25, no. 3 (Spring 1993): 13–19; Lü, "Minor Public Economy."

increases to anyone asking. This was especially prominent in Shanghai, whose pharmaceutical industry saw its wage bill grow five- to sixfold after the Five Antis.[123] Private owners at other firms so mismanaged enterprise finances that unions demanded supervisory powers over finances to ensure that welfare provisions could be maintained.[124] Private enterprise owners offered little resistance when the drive for collectivization of industry began in 1954.

The growth of the state sector continued apace throughout the takeover period and the campaigns. By 1952 the state sector accounted for 67 percent of China's industrial output, up from an estimated 44 percent in 1949. Moreover, by October 1952 the state owned 80 percent of the enterprises in heavy industry and 60 percent of those in light industry, while state banks controlled 90 percent of total loans and deposits. State trading companies administered half of the economy's total wholesale trade and 30 percent of retail trade.[125] These figures should be placed in the context of state ownership of industry during the 1940s, when Nationalist government–owned enterprises accounted for about 35 percent of industrial output. What is most significant about this change in the enterprise-government relationship is that by 1952 the state sector accounted for a significant portion of government revenue: 32 percent of state revenues came from profits and taxes remitted by state enterprises in 1952. This was up from 14.3 percent in 1950, and in marked contrast to the Nationalist regime's largely agricultural revenue base.[126] The stage was set for the introduction of comprehensive planning and with it, rapid accumulation of capital that could be steered toward heavy industry and other strategic sectors.

However, labor problems remained a major challenge as the CCP adopted a centrally administered, planned economy. If left unchecked, the effects of the early 1950s campaigns would lead to a revival of inflation, as managers fulfilled demands from workers for better wages and conditions, and possibly to a slackening of production, as a politically protected class of workers could defy orders from above. And, as noted in Chapter 3, wage differentials remained highly distorted from the late 1940s hyperinflation – light industry workers earned more than those in heavy industry, and common production workers earned as much as

---

[123] Li, Chen, and Lin, eds., *Shehuizhuyi gaizao, Shanghai*, 1:195.
[124] Ibid., 1:481–2.
[125] Eckstein, *China's Economic Development*, 197.
[126] Ibid., 202.

technicians, for example. Wages would have to be reformed, even lowered in many cases, and the now lax labor discipline in private firms especially would need strengthening in order to achieve the desired productivity increases. We turn now to the fate of workplace institutions during China's transition to central planning.

5

Adjusting to the Command Economy

ONE of the central tenets of China's industrialization strategy during the 1950s (and beyond) was the rapid accumulation of investment capital through state-owned enterprises (SOEs). SOEs were guaranteed low state-set prices on raw materials and other inputs, while profits were assured through higher prices on manufactured goods. Almost all SOE profits were turned over to the state in the form of taxes, which could then be used for additional investment capital.[1] The adoption of this capital accumulation development strategy, with its emphasis on heavy industry, arose both from socialist ideology and the CCP's assessment of the hostile international environment in the 1950s. It is worth summarizing the key elements of the centrally planned economy of the 1950s and how in particular these constraints played out within the microeconomy of the state enterprise and its labor management policies.

During the First Five-Year Plan, employment in industrial enterprises (both state and nonstate) rose from 5.1 million in late 1952 to 7.47 million by late 1957, an average annual increase of 9.3 percent.[2] Consistent with China's emphasis on heavy industry, workers in this sector numbered 4.5 million by year-end 1957 while light industry accounted for 2.97 million employees. In 1952, the distribution of employment between light and heavy industry had been much more evenly balanced, with 2.3 million workers in light industry and 2.8 million in heavy industry.[3] Much of the increase among the industrial workforce in the 1950s came within factories classified as "state enterprises" (*guoying qiye*) and not in the

[1] Audrey Donnithorne, *China's Economic System* (New York: Frederick A. Praeger, 1967), 164–8; Lin, Cai, and Li, *The China Miracle*, 282.

[2] State Statistical Bureau, *Zhongguo laodong gongzi*, 83.

[3] Ibid., 36.

formerly private-sector enterprises that had become "public-private joint enterprises" (*gong-si heying*) during the mid-1950s. Total employment in state sector industrial enterprises rose from 2.7 million workers at year-end 1952 to 4.9 million at year-end 1957. "Jointly owned" enterprises, on the other hand, accounted for about 2.3 million employees, nearly exactly the total employment that had existed in 1952 in both jointly owned and privately owned enterprises (though in 1952 the vast majority of these employees were classified as working in privately owned enterprises).[4] Thus, two discernible patterns emerge in the national employment picture at this time: first, nearly all of the total growth in industrial employment (about 2.4 million new workers) went toward state-sector enterprises, and second, the majority of this expansion was accounted for by heavy industry (about 1.7 million new workers).

Despite extensive statistics on the growth of employment in the state sector, far fewer indicators are available to chart the expansion in the actual number of state-owned enterprises nationally during the 1950s. It is well-established that by 1957 a total of 58,000 state enterprises were in operation, and that 9,300 of these were directly managed under the ministries and departments of the central government. This figure of directly supervised enterprises had risen substantially from 2,800 in 1953.[5] One important trend that reveals itself in local statistics from cities such as Shanghai and Guangzhou is the actual decrease in the total number of enterprises, as the private sector was liquidated and consolidated into jointly owned enterprises. In Guangzhou, for example, a total of 4,549 private industrial enterprises that produced 87 percent of the city's industrial output value in 1953 rapidly dwindled to only 91 enterprises in 1956. The number of jointly owned industrial enterprises rose from a negligible 8 in 1953 to 865 in 1956, producing by the latter year 96 percent of Guangzhou's industrial output value.[6] The number of state-owned industrial enterprises in Guangzhou rose from fifty in 1952 to sixty-four in 1956, accounting for less than 2 percent of the city's industrial output value. In Shanghai, 29,485 private-sector industrial enterprises in 1953 (accounting for 99 percent of the city's industrial output) were transformed into 16,768 jointly owned enterprises producing 66.5

[4] Ibid., 83.
[5] Lu, "The Origins and Formation," 43; David Bachman, *Bureaucracy, Economy, and Leadership in China: The Institutional Origins of the Great Leap Forward* (New York: Cambridge University Press, 1991), 21–2.
[6] Li, Chen, and Lin, eds., *Shehuizhuyi gaizao, Guangzhou*, Statistical Appendix, Table 2.

Table 3. *Socialist Transformation of Industry in Guangzhou and Shanghai*

	Guangzhou		
	State Enterprises	Jointly Owned	Private Enterprises
1950	12	5	3,290
1951	22	9	4,398
1952	50	10	3,978
1953	54	8	4,549
1954	64	28	3,875
1955	64	101	3,084
1956	64	865	91
	Shanghai		
	State Enterprises	Jointly Owned	Private Enterprises
1949	142	15	20,149
1950	156	24	20,707
1951	193	59	24,673
1952	221	65	25,548
1953	246	68	29,485
1954	270	244	27,983
1955	262	375	22,602
1956	279	16,758	6

Units: number of industrial enterprises.

Sources: Li Qin, Chen Wenwu, and Lin Shecheng, eds., *Shehuizhuyi gaizao, Guangzhou*, Statistical Appendix, Table 2; Li Qin, Chen Wenwu, and Lin Shecheng, eds., *Shehuizhuyi gaizao, Shanghai*, Statistical Appendix, Table 2.

percent of Shanghai's industrial output value by 1956. The number of state industrial enterprises in Shanghai rose modestly from 246 in 1953 to 279 in 1956, producing just over 33 percent of Shanghai's industrial output value by the latter year (Table 3).[7]

Finally, to repeat the observation made in Chapter 1, 30 percent of industrial output in the FFYP came from Soviet-aided projects and other new or reconstructed plants. The remainder of industrial output during the FFYP is accounted for by "old" enterprises that existed before 1949.[8]

[7] Li, Chen, and Lin, eds., *Shehuizhuyi gaizao, Shanghai*, Statistical Appendix, Table 2.
[8] Rawski, *China's Transition to Industrialism*, 29.

These enterprises, concentrated in cities such as Shanghai and Guangzhou, received only limited investment funds from the central government yet achieved fairly solid gains in production. Most pronounced in economic performance terms was Shanghai, which accounted for 19 percent of industrial output value in 1957 but received on average only a 2.5 percent share of state investment funds during the FFYP.[9]

While state ownership of industry was not new to China in the 1950s, the administrative relationships that developed between enterprises and the state over this decade represented a significant departure from past practices. State enterprises became the linchpins for capital accumulation in a centrally coordinated command economy. Revenues from state enterprises made up 46 percent of the state budget by 1957, a figure that would rise to over 60 percent in subsequent years.[10] The state set the terms of trade in favor of state enterprises by fixing low prices for agricultural procurement and high prices for consumer and capital goods. This made state enterprises "cash cows," as Naughton notes, in that they generated high volumes of savings and investment that became government revenue once remitted to state taxation authorities.[11] To achieve these artificially high profit streams required careful coordination of supply and marketing linkages among all enterprises, to ensure that producers received precise amounts of inputs to fulfill production (and profit) quotas. Each enterprise in the command economy therefore was connected in a vast bureaucratic network. To simplify the chain of command, each enterprise in theory had a primary relationship with one bureaucratic department (*zhuguan bumen*), the sole entity to which an enterprise was said to "belong." During the FFYP, several thousand state enterprises (an estimated 9,300 by 1957) had direct ties with industrial ministries of the central government. This meant that one ministry in Beijing would coordinate production plans, material allocation, investment strategies, and personnel appointments for many hundreds of enterprises throughout China that were bureaucratically attached to the ministry. For generally smaller state enterprises and those in sectors deemed of less strategic importance, the primary supervisory agency would in most cases be a functional department of the government (province, county, city, etc.) in which the enterprise was located.

In principle, all state enterprises remitted their annual plans for approval by central government ministries, but when enterprises had

---

[9] Ibid., 71.   [10] Donnithorne, *China's Economic System*, 368.
[11] Naughton, *Growing Out of the Plan*, 33–5.

local government departments as their primary supervising agency, local politics could easily intercede in decisions about allocations of finance, material, investment, taxation, and personnel, including labor issues. This process of local government involvement in state enterprise administration would grow more complex and multifaceted over the next decades – to say nothing of the highly interdependent relationship that would develop between local governments and state enterprises in the 1980s and 1990s.[12] During the FFYP, those lines of authority from national and local government departments reaching into the affairs of enterprise management were overlapping and in the process of being sorted out. Because our concern here is with labor management institutions within the enterprise, the question arises as to how these administrative relationships in the command economy may have influenced questions of enterprise welfare, wage and labor allocation, and intrafirm organizations such as enterprise branches of the CCP.

At a macroeconomic level, the goal of the command economy was to curb consumption and maximize savings. As Rawski and others have noted, economic planning ministries in China were well aware of the need to control consumption in a policy environment that emphasized the rapid accumulation of investment capital. This meant that tight controls on wage growth were necessary, because increases in disposable income would put pressure on state planners to expand the output of the consumer goods sector. Additional investment in the production of consumer goods would take away scarce investment capital from the all-important heavy industrial sector.[13] With this macroeconomic constraint on wage growth and consumption, where would basic cost-of-living expenses for the growing number of urban residents and state workers come from? The answer to this otherwise troublesome question was simple, because the mechanisms for distributing basic necessities such as housing, food, and medical care had been in place since the 1940s – workers would obtain these items directly from their enterprise.

While the obvious resolution to consumption constraints in the urban industrial sector lay in continuing the practice of workplace welfare provision, it was unclear how much authority SOE managers should exercise in fulfilling two apparently countervailing imperatives: maximize

---

[12] This relationship and its consequences are vividly and persuasively demonstrated in Steinfeld, *Forging Reform in China.*
[13] Thomas G. Rawski, *Economic Growth and Employment in China* (New York: Oxford University Press, 1979), 67; Lin, Cai, and Li, *The China Miracle*, 19–29.

enterprise profits and provide scarce consumer goods to employees. Factory directors thus found themselves in a delicate balancing act when it came to the allocation of scarce resources. Their supervisors in various government departments who distributed investment funds insisted that SOE managers fulfill production quotas under constrained supplies of capital and labor that were subject to limitations set forth in the plan.[14] Factory directors had to make the most of existing resources and had strong incentives to retain any productive asset, including labor, that could be utilized at a future point if a production shortfall loomed.[15] Initially, and throughout the FFYP, factory directors enjoyed substantial authority within the enterprise to see to it that production goals were met with a fixed wage bill and limited technology. Gao Gang, as chair of the State Planning Commission, strongly supported the Soviet-inspired method of labor management known as "one-man management." (In Chinese, *yizhangzhi* or *changzhangzhi*, literally "one leader system" or "factory director system.") Under one-man management, factory officials were directly accountable to central officials, but they also were given extensive decision-making authority and freedom from having to consult with other enterprise organizations, such as trade unions and enterprise party committees.[16]

The reorganization of production departments reflected the principle of one-man management and the centralization of authority within the enterprise. Chinese enterprises adopted a three-tiered production-territorial system found in Soviet factories. The workshop level (*chejian*) had long been a basic subunit of factory administration, with a workshop director (*chejian zhuren*) responsible for matters of production and supervising workers within each workshop. One-man management added two layers below the workshop: work sections (*gongduan*) concentrated responsibility in the individual leading each section, and below work sections, the same principle applied with production teams or work groups (*shengchan xiaozu*), headed by a group or team leader. This structure and the concentration of authority within a single individual at each

---

[14] Rawski, *Economic Growth and Employment*, 67–9.

[15] Richman, *Industrial Society in Communist China*, 462–8.

[16] Franz Schurmann, *Ideology and Organization in Communist China*, 2nd ed. (Berkeley, CA: University of California Press, 1968), 253–62; Stephen Andors, *China's Industrial Revolution: Politics, Planning, and Management, 1949 to the Present* (New York: Pantheon Books, 1977), 54–5; Brugger, *Democracy and Organisation*, 188–9; Peter N.S. Lee, *Industrial Management and Economic Reform in China, 1949–1984* (New York: Oxford University Press, 1987), 26–7.

level meant that other administrative and coordinating departments within the factory were subsumed to the authority of the workshop, work section, or work group leader.[17] For example, the head of the enterprise union or personnel department exercised far less power than the person responsible for these and all other matters within his or her "territorial" domain – the shop, section, or group.

From both macro- and microperspectives, therefore, command economics imposed hierarchical structures on an industrial sector that remained in the 1950s highly differentiated in terms of the organization of production, technology, and labor. The transformation of the nonstate sector, where production and labor management institutions exhibited the greatest degree of variation, would bring serious disruptions as thousands of enterprises were shut down, merged, and otherwise consolidated into the command economy. Within the state sector, an important distinction arose between those beneficiaries of relatively high levels of state investment and those which, like the enterprise cases from Shanghai and Guangzhou, suffered from relative underinvestment. Here too in the older factories that would produce a disproportionately greater share of industrial output during the FFYP, we can observe changes and continuities in labor institutions as enterprise managers, workers, and state officials responded to new constraints and inducements in the command economy. This process of institutional design and modification can be seen in four critical areas: enterprise welfare, wages and bonuses, labor allocation, and the role of enterprise party committees.

ENTERPRISE WELFARE

It is difficult to quantify the expansion of enterprise welfare during the 1950s from the perspective of enterprises, but national investment data reveal something of the magnitude of this expansion. Capital construction investment (CCI) (*jiben jianshe touzi*), a measure of state investment in industry that includes funds for the construction, renovation, or expansion of various enterprises, rose from 2.9 billion yuan in 1952 to 10.5 billion yuan in 1957. (Virtually all capital construction funds at this time came through state appropriations and not bank loans or funds raised by enterprises.) Official statistics also classify the share of capital construction expended on nonproductive investment (*fei shengchanxing touzi*), which in the 1950s meant funds that went toward projects such as

[17] Andors, *China's Industrial Revolution*, 54–5.

Table 4. *Capital Construction Investment in Shanghai, 1950–1957*

Year	Total CCI	Nonproductive CCI	Nonproductive CCI for Residential Housing	Nonproductive CCI as % of Total CCI	Residential Housing as % of Total CCI
1950	16	5	1	31.3%	6.3%
1951	52	27	4	51.9%	7.7%
1952	141	84	28	59.6%	19.9%
1953	259	162	71	62.5%	27.4%
1954	231	124	39	53.7%	16.9%
1955	243	56	9	23.0%	3.7%
1956	267	77	19	28.8%	7.1%
1957	371	116	46	31.3%	12.4%

Units: million yuan (current yuan).
Source: Sun Huairen, *Shanghai shehuizhuyi*, 881.

the construction of residential units, hospitals, and other facilities that did not directly contribute to economic output. A large portion of CCI during the FFYP went toward such nonproductive uses, constituting over one-third of CCI and even reaching 48 percent in 1953 (12.5 percent of all capital construction investment that year went toward residential housing). By 1957, the distribution of productive and nonproductive investment in CCI was about 73 percent and 27 percent, respectively.[18] Table 4 shows data from Shanghai on CCI from 1950 to 1957, along with various components, including nonproduction investment and housing (a category of nonproduction investment). Between 1951 and 1954, nonproduction investment actually exceeded production investment, amounting to 50 to 60 percent of total capital construction investment. Shanghai's average nonproductive CCI for the FFYP was 39.9 percent, compared to the national average of 33 percent during the same period.[19] In some years, much of Shanghai's nonproductive CCI went toward residential housing, construction for which exceeded 27 percent of total CCI in 1953.

In addition to such nonproductive investments for urban residents and state employees, the latter especially benefited from the implementation

[18] State Statistical Bureau, Fixed Asset Investment Statistics Division, ed., *Zhongguo guding zichan touzi tongji nianjian, 1950–1995* (China Statistical Yearbook on Investment in Fixed Assets, 1950–1995) (Beijing: Zhongguo tongji chubanshe, 1997), 96.
[19] Ibid., 98.

of a national labor insurance program. Labor insurance provisions, first announced in February 1951, allowed for partial or full wage payments to employees temporarily or permanently placed out of work because of illness or injury; covered employees' medical expenses as well as those associated with childbirth and funerals of family members; and distributed pensions to retirees based roughly on earnings and years of service at the enterprise. The program expanded gradually, from 1951 regulations that covered only enterprises with greater than one hundred employees, then to a larger section of state enterprises in 1953, with the inclusion of service-sector enterprises as well as urban collective enterprises and handicrafts in 1956. The number of workers covered by labor insurance rose from 3.3 million in December 1952 to 11.5 million in 1957. In the latter year, an estimated 6.5 million workers received some form of medical expenses. National expenditures on labor insurance rose more than threefold between 1952 to 1957.[20]

Urban workers, especially those in state-sector enterprises, were said to have greeted labor insurance with great fanfare, likening the benefits from medical and pension coverage to the distribution of land to peasants during land reform. Under both cases, livelihoods were now putatively "guaranteed" against unforeseen circumstances.[21] One Jiangnan Shipyard welder who had managed to obtain 12 mu of land in 1950 (probably through land reform) as a backup source of income donated this plot to the state after he learned that the labor insurance provisions would see to his needs in retirement.[22] Elsewhere workers now assured of a means of support in their retirements were said to have turned over their accumulated savings to the state for arms purchases in the Resist America, Aid Korea Campaign during China's involvement in the Korean War.[23]

The structure through which national labor insurance was administered is revealing. According to Labor Insurance Regulations of the early 1950s, labor insurance programs were to be handled by enterprise-based unions, which would serve the health and pension needs of their fellow employees. Rather than vest welfare administration within local or regional governments, or even hospitals and clinics, PRC officials in the

---

[20] Yuan, *Zhongguo laodong jingjishi*, 196–9.   [21] Ibid., 197.

[22] SMA, Series C1-2-2257. Known as *yanglao di*, such plots were returned to village governments by workers who had owned them as sources of retirement income. See Yuan, *Zhongguo laodong jingjishi*, 197.

[23] Yuan, *Zhongguo laodong jingjishi*, 197.

early 1950s chose to operate the insurance program for state employees through the enterprise itself. It is perhaps instructive to recall the half-hearted attempt by the Nationalist regime to establish Welfare Associations and Committees within its state enterprises during the late 1940s. By the 1950s, economic and fiscal stability, as well as the various controls that the government attained to coordinate the expanding state sector, meant that enterprise-based welfare programs could more readily be administered. Funds for employee medical expenses, disability payments, and retirement pensions were collected from the enterprise budget or deducted from the wage bill and managed by enterprise unions as part of a collective welfare fund.[24]

Despite the reported enthusiasm over the labor insurance and pension measures developed in the 1950s, the distribution of welfare provisions was anything but uniform. The most obvious distinction in the 1950s was that between public and private enterprises. State enterprises that were directly accountable to Beijing ministries received relatively generous amounts of budgetary funds for welfare provision, whereas the private-sector factories had to raise their own welfare funds from profits or payroll deductions. Employees at the periphery of industrial employment, in the vast urban handicraft sector, received the lowest pay and only meager welfare benefits, if any. After the campaigns of the early 1950s had swept through the private sector, many smaller factories – where the number of employees would have been too small to bring labor insurance coverage – abandoned basic provisions of nonwage benefits that many had established in the inflation of the 1940s. A 1955 Shanghai GLU report argued that enterprise unions in the private sector needed to gain greater supervisory powers over enterprise finances, because financial mismanagement was leading to wage cuts, the closure of medical clinics, and the cessation of food provision. In small factories, desperate workers sought out factory owners in their homes and invited themselves to partake in family meals.[25]

The livelihoods of private-sector workers did not necessarily improve, however, after the collectivization of industry in 1955–7. Known also as the "socialist transformation of industry," this process in labor management terms replaced generally higher wages in the private sector with

[24] Joyce K. Kallgren, "Social Welfare and China's Industrial Workers," in A. Doak Barnett, ed., *Chinese Communist Politics in Action* (Seattle, WA: University of Washington Press, 1969), 548–9; Donnithorne, *China's Economic System*, 190–1.
[25] Li, Chen, and Lin, eds., *Shehuizhuyi gaizao, Shanghai*, 481–2.

greater collective benefits. Still, managers of the new "jointly owned" enterprises had smaller budgets for welfare expenditures than did SOE managers. With the establishment of administrative controls over wages, employees in private enterprises saw their incomes stagnate relative to their counterparts in state-owned factories. Employees in many jointly owned enterprises suffered serious declines in income and benefits following the closure, consolidation, and merger of scattered plants and workshops. State officials quickly abolished numerous schemes that private managers had used to supplement incomes of workers. The most common of these were bonuses paid for attendance, "hidden" wages justified as subsidies for any number of consumer staples, and generous annual bonuses.[26] Workers in newly nationalized textile mills in Shanghai saw their real incomes drop by 50 to 60 percent, as state industrial officials slashed bonuses and hidden wages. To compensate, state officials helped mill management set up child care, recreational, and educational facilities, but these collective benefits were no substitute for individual income, especially to younger workers who might not have had a direct need for some of these services.[27]

The socialist transformation of industry thus created important divisions among workers, primarily between relatively prosperous full-time workers in state-owned enterprises and disaffected temporary and contract workers in underfunded collective enterprises. Asymmetries in welfare provision across enterprises also extended to workers within the same enterprise, divided as they were into full-time, contract, and temporary employees. The largest state enterprises employed virtually all full-time workers, while the collective sector contained the largest portions of contract and temporary workers. Tensions within the workforce over the distribution of workplace welfare festered during China's transition to a socialist planned economy. Open conflict would erupt in many jointly owned enterprises in 1957.

These limitations and skewed distributions of welfare provision notwithstanding, China's leaders in the early 1950s took pride in their achievements in labor policy. For many who had developed national labor policy laws and regulations, as Elizabeth Perry has observed, the formation of an enterprise community that provided exclusive benefits and social security to its members may have represented a throwback to

---

[26] SMA, Series C16-2-178.   [27] Ibid.

the days of urban guilds.[28] Minister of Labor Li Lisan, a central figure in China's labor movement and the Communist Party since the 1920s until his political demise in the 1950s, drew up important labor policies such as labor insurance. If the makers of early PRC labor policy had once been workers in Shanghai and elsewhere, they were familiar with the tradeoff that came with job security and collective benefits of urban guilds – low wages for apprentices and other entrants to the workforce. As apprentices and private-sector workers in Shanghai and Guangzhou would learn after collectivization, enterprise welfare provision and wage growth were inversely related. Growth in the former meant constraints on the latter. Workplace welfare should therefore be understood in the context of wage policy. Factories first became welfare institutions in the eyes of most employees and managers during the inflationary episodes of the 1940s, a period when wage and price spirals made wage levels and differences in pay meaningless. Repairing the distorted wage structure absorbed much attention, and aroused much controversy among managers, workers, and party officials during the first half of the 1950s.

WAGES

Among the most pressing issues in urban areas in the early 1950s was wage policy and its potential to reignite inflation. The CCP authorities in 1949 initially protected workers from hyperinflation by establishing in 1949 a "wage points" system (*gongzi fen*) that tied wages to food prices. This was part of the antiinflationary monetary policy, discussed in Chapter 4, that aimed to absorb cash while instilling confidence in the new currency and banking system. In addition, all enterprise employees, regardless of skill or position, were eligible for in-kind subsidies and other forms of noncash payments that furthered antiinflationary objectives.

The wage structure was another major problem. Pay varied widely across industries and within individual factories. In the highly differentiated manufacturing sectors found in cities such as Shanghai and Guangzhou, the small-scale private sector paid higher wages than those found in large-scale state factories. This "inverted" relationship between skill and pay had several precedents in the late 1940s. Party officials

---

[28] Perry, "Labor's Battle for Political Space," 305–6; Perry, "From Native Place to Workplace," 44–7.

found that in many textile mills, machine maintenance workers received lower earnings than the less technically knowledgeable spinning and weaving operatives, who were paid by the piece.[29] Wage inversion was especially acute in Shanghai and in the South Central region. "Wage reform" in the 1950s would entail a lowering of wages in some industries.[30]

The wage problem remained serious in Shanghai's textile industry, in both private and state-owned mills. In 1952, some textile workers were reportedly refusing to pay their union fees unless something was done about wages. Mocking the CCP slogans that implored citizens to look to the party for leadership, workers at the state-owned Number Nineteen Cotton Mill said, "We've been looking to the Communist Party 'til our vision's gone blurry. From Liberation down to now and still no wage increase?" Union officials tried in vain to alleviate concerns over the wage issue, and workers often bypassed their enterprise union representatives and went to the Shanghai municipal government to press their demands.[31]

Moreover, there was little distinction in pay between skilled and unskilled workers. The Shanghai Municipal Labor Union's Wage Department noted, "A wage system like this will neither stimulate production nor raise skill levels, while at the same time it will foster an egalitarian viewpoint among workers."[32] The authors blamed the poorly managed mills under the Nationalists for placing skill as the last criterion in wage adjustments, and placing seniority first. In 1952, with both state and private mills still maintaining a wage system set up in 1946, Municipal Textile Union officials reported that different pay for the same job was also a common problem in mills, because wages were not set "according to the importance, skill, or physical exertion of a job, but are created mainly according to seniority." The union urged the abolition of this practice of seniority-based wages: "This is one of the most unreasonable forms of the long-term exploitation of workers during the reactionary rule of the Guomindang."[33]

As seen in Chapter 3, the Nationalist bureaucracy's efforts to plan industrial output and control the distribution of resources on a nation-wide scale began in the early 1930s, if not before. Following the Japanese invasion in 1937, the Nationalist government vastly extended its control of both wages and labor allocation under wartime economic

---

[29] SMA, Series C1-2-31.   [30] Howe, *Wage Patterns*, 86–7.   [31] SMA, Series C16-2-42.
[32] SMA, Series C1-2-338.   [33] SMA, Series C16-2-42.

administration.[34] Thus, the critical step that the Chinese state took during the 1950s was not in determining wages for state workers but in the dramatic expansion of the scale involved in this task. PRC officials gained control of the wage bill for over 7 million industrial workers nationwide. The administrative burdens were immense, and perhaps for this reason industrial ministries determined pay rates for relevant occupations within their industries rather than having the labor ministry do so. The eight-grade wage system, deceivingly simple on paper because every occupation was classified into pay grades of eight or fewer categories, could never work in the complex and highly diverse landscape of industries and occupations in China, even after the consolidation of various trades and enterprises in the 1950s.[35]

Under the wage system that China copied from the Soviet Union, industrial ministries established rates for occupations specific to the work tasks and products involved in the industrial sector in question. The central planners also allowed for adjustments based on regional variations in the cost of living. Most state enterprises went through the complex and potentially divisive process of wage reform in 1952, and were followed by jointly owned enterprises in the national wage reform of 1955–6. The announced objective of the wage system, in line with socialist principles, was to reward "each according to his work." This was accomplished by linking each step in a wage ladder – usually of eight grades – with a particular job and its associated set of skills. (Each ministry devised its own skill standards.) In theory, a welder in a Dalian shipyard would earn the same monthly income (after adjustment for interregional price differences) as a welder in Shanghai or Guangzhou. CCP wage policy had the positive effect of keeping the growth of wages well below the growth of labor productivity, and helped spur China's 18 percent annual growth rate in industrial output during the FFYP.[36] Because retail prices rose less than 2 percent annually at this time, real wages grew an estimated 17 percent between 1950 and 1952, followed by a modest 4 percent growth between 1952 and 1957.[37] Wage growth was not stunning during the FFYP, but when combined with the nonwage benefits that state enterprises were distributing to their employees, the change in living standards of Chinese workers was dramatic.

[34] Editorial Committee, *Zhongguo jindai bingqi gongye*, 3: 813–29, 960–80.
[35] Howe, *Wage Patterns*, 108–9.   [36] Yuan, *Zhongguo laodong jingjishi*, 147.
[37] Howe, *Wage Patterns*, 33–4.

Beneath these accomplishments in wage policy, however, lay the demise of wage planning and controls that would characterize Chinese industry in the 1960s and beyond. One of the most serious problems with the wage grade system was that its uniform standards unrealistically assumed that the work tasks and level of technology were roughly similar across all factories of the same industry. Yet production processes varied widely within industrial sectors. Some jobs and skills for which industry-wide wage standards were established simply did not exist in some factories, even if a group of factories could logically be classified in the same industrial sector.

The adoption of national wage standards within a highly differentiated industrial sector meant that enterprise managers and workshop supervisors in charge of wage distribution had very nebulous criteria to set wage grades for particular workers.[38] Discretionary authority over job descriptions and evaluations of the individuals who held such jobs remained at the level of the factory.[39] Misunderstandings inevitably arose and led to frequent disputes over the fairness of an assigned wage grade. An unfair or biased evaluation of a worker's skill level triggered spats between staff and one or more disgruntled employees. It was also common for inexperienced officials, especially after the completion of the socialist transformation of industry and commerce in 1956, to apply the graded wage scales haphazardly to jobs that were not suited for a wage ladder intended to promote skill enhancement in industry. As the authors of a Shanghai General Labor Union report in the late 1950s noted, managers at a Shanghai department store went too far when they applied the skill-based wage scale to their clerical employees. Store clerks had their "skill levels" and pay determined through a "blind taste test" that required them to assess the quality of cigarette brands by puffing on different samples. This wage determination procedure was decidedly unpopular among the store's nonsmoking clerks.[40]

In other respects, local CCP officials and enterprise directors undermined wage reform in the mid-1950s by invoking "retained" wages (*baoliu gongzi*). This practice was especially common in former privately owned enterprises such as the Shenxin Number Six Mill, where pay in the early 1950s was generally higher than in factories that had been under state ownership since 1949. After the complex process of wage reform, a worker whose new pay level on the eight-grade scale was lower than before received income supplements that made up the

[38] Ibid., 108–9.   [39] Ibid., 77.   [40] SMA, Series C1-2-2723.

difference. In short, retained wages simply abrogated the results of wage reform.[41] While office staff were most often the recipients of retained wages, such a practice also clearly benefited pre-1949 workers by protecting their income levels when their wages might have been lowered through wage reform.

Disagreements over wage policy also took place as some factories received investment in new machinery that raised productivity. Following the socialist transformation of industry, the jointly owned Guangzhou Number Two Cotton Mill benefited from generous levels of technology investment from the state. Workers at the mill learned how to operate the new equipment and felt entitled to higher wages. Concerned about keeping caps on labor costs, managers refused to go to the Municipal Labor Bureau to request wage adjustments. Instead, they accused any worker who complained about pay of "economism". (This was a politically loaded term, one that had been applied to Li Lisan in his removal from union work in 1951. Economism essentially implied the pursuit of better wages and benefits, considered self-interested behavior by the CCP and therefore subject to political sanction.) Politically active employees with membership in the enterprise party committee or the Communist Youth League especially feared being labeled as "economistic" and reportedly declined to even use the word "wages."[42]

While wage reform gave state officials central controls over the wage bill, such controls remained at a macroeconomic level. State ministries worked with enterprise officials to set an annual target for the enterprise wage bill, and enterprises had to arrange a fixed number of employees with the relevant officials from the Ministry of Labor. But within these confines, enterprise managers had the power to allocate workers to different jobs and their corresponding level of pay.[43] The initial wage setting, it turned out, was vitally important, because it fixed a worker's income for the short and medium term. As disgruntled textile workers in Shanghai said in the mid-1950s of this first wage assessment, "once it's set, it's yours for life."[44] Subsequent promotions up the wage ladder to higher rates of pay could be made only during infrequent nationwide

---

[41] This practice can be found in most enterprise reports on wage reform in the 1950s. Shanghai Number Thirty-One Mill, Factory Archives, Labor and Wage Department, Series 56; GMA, Series 8-14.

[42] GMA, Series 92-478.

[43] Howe, *Wage Patterns*, 109–10; Richman, *Industrial Society*, 796; Eckstein, *China's Economic Revolution*, 101.

[44] SMA, Series C16-2-99.

wage adjustments – which occurred in 1956, 1959, 1963, 1971, and more often in the late 1970s and 1980s.

WAGE ADJUSTMENTS

In each of the national wage adjustments, relevant ministries (including labor) issued guidelines as to which categories of workers should receive promotions up the wage ladder. A typical wage adjustment might single out for wage promotions all those workers who had entered the state workforce at or before a given year. The actual process of determining individual wage adjustments took place at the factory level, during meetings of production teams, where workers openly discussed and debated among themselves who was deserving of wage promotions and who was not. Party officials conceived of wage adjustments as a "campaign," though as several cadres admitted, it was an entirely different affair from mobilizing workers to attack selected individuals or class targets. Because local CCP cadres viewed and implemented these national wage adjustments as another political campaign, party cadres insisted that workers be organized into small groups to discuss, out in the open, the myriad details of wage reform and wage adjustments. Convening a group of fellow employees to determine who among them were deserving of wage increases, and all the nebulous criteria that might involve, undermined the notion of "state-set wages" in a command economy. CCP officials issued instructions on how to run such meetings to the enterprise party committee, which in turn relayed the guidelines down to party leaders within workshops, work sections, and production teams. Party members inside and outside the factory tried to persuade workers to put the needs of the country and modernization ahead of their personal interests in higher income.[45] During these wage discussions in small group settings, individual workers pursued a number of different strategies to gain status, higher wages, or both. Young party members achieved political standing in these groups as loyal ascetics when they refused to accept wage increases. An astute workshop supervisor or production team leader could dispense wage adjustments to supporters as a form of patronage.[46] These wage adjustment meetings, what we might call

---

[45] Shanghai Number Thirty-One Mill, Factory Archives, Labor and Wage Department, Series 56.

[46] These observations were offered during interviews and informal conversations with factory administrators and labor officials in Shanghai and Guangzhou in 1994–95.

"money talks," also tended to steer wage hikes toward relatively older workers with larger families to support.

The introduction of the national wage scale and comprehensive wage adjustments created a significant and largely artificial generational divide between so-called "old workers" – anyone who worked prior to 1949 – and their younger counterparts (both full-time and otherwise). This temporal division, and the competing views of work and money that spawned it, strengthened an informal seniority wage system in China's new socialist, skill-based wage structure. The distribution of money to factory workers was less a function of state-defined skill levels and more of time, as measured by the politically constructed temporal landmark of "liberation." Those who had entered the ranks of the working class prior to 1949 were venerated as "old workers" (*lao gongren*), regardless of their actual age. Such "old workers" managed over the course of the 1950s to establish a political agenda that subsumed technical skill in wage determination and criticized the pursuit of money for money's sake. Material incentives and overquota bonuses favored by the younger generation of post-1949 workforce entrants were repudiated by the late 1950s and not revived on a similar scale until the 1980s. Wage adjustments, few and far between after national wage reform in the mid-1950s, were carried out within factories by convening such small-group sessions or "money talks," during which the opinion of older workers held sway.[47]

Following wage reform in the mid-1950s and nationwide wage adjustments thereafter, the eight-grade wage ladder gradually came to reflect length of employment rather than skill. Several studies have shown that over time, China's skill-based wage system developed into one based almost exclusively on seniority, as those who had been in the workforce longer – and who had gone without a wage increase – took priority over more recent entrants into the workforce.[48] Wage seniority evolved gradually as enterprises placed new workforce entrants, often apprentices or recent school graduates, on the lowest rungs of the wage ladder. State policy contributed to this de facto seniority system during the 1950s. Employee benefits, such as pension eligibility, were tied to years of

---

[47] The informal processes of wage determination and adjustment are discussed in greater detail in the enterprise case studies in Chapter 6.

[48] Peng Yusheng, "Wage Determination in Rural and Urban China: A Comparison of Public and Private Industrial Sectors," *American Sociological Review* 57 (April 1992): 208–9; David Granick, *Chinese State Enterprises: A Regional Property Rights Analysis* (Chicago: University of Chicago Press, 1990), 54–5; Walder, *Communist Neo-Traditionalism*, 79.

service at one's enterprise, so that a worker who moved to a new work-place would forfeit the accumulated years of service at that enterprise.[49] Moreover, because the enterprise was responsible for the distribution of health care and labor insurance, the incentives to remain at one's enterprise were all the greater. Yet state policy to tie wage adjustments to length of service became explicit *after* this practice was institutionalized within firms in the 1950s. During the 1959 national wage adjustment, for example, wage raises were given only to those who had been employed before 1957, with special consideration to those who had "pre-liberation" work experience. In the 1963 wage adjustment, official directives instructed enterprise managers to promote older skilled workers whose wages had not yet been adjusted since the first wage reform of the mid-1950s. By 1971, state wage adjustment policy was even more explicit: enterprises should adjust wages for workers at grade 3 who had been employed before 1957; for grade 2 workers employed before 1960; and for grade 1 workers employed before 1966.[50]

For the personnel who staffed government offices, military units, and other administrative departments, the concept of seniority also applied in determining wages. As Lu Feng has shown in his account of the *danwei*'s origins, it was government policy throughout the 1950s and 1960s to calculate years of service based on the time that an individual first "participated in the work of the revolution" or entered "revolutionary ranks."[51] This meant that time served in military or administrative units in the party's base areas was included in calculating years of service. For workers in cities that were under Nationalist control until 1948–9, it was clearly more difficult to demonstrate the credentials of having conducted "revolutionary work." Participation in the CCP underground in urban areas before 1949 may have established one's *bona fides* as having entered the revolutionary ranks, but only a handful of workers could make this claim. Despite lacking an explicit legal basis to demonstrate extended years of service prior to 1949, urban workers in state enterprises convinced party and enterprise officials that their participation in work before "liberation" should be considered the equivalent of participation in "revolutionary ranks" in determining wage settings and

---

[49] Lu, "Origins and Formation," 34–5.
[50] For the various criteria involved in each national wage adjustment, see the Guangzhou Municipal Labor Bureau, "Guangzhoushi laodong shi," ch. 5.
[51] Lu, "Origins and Formation," 17.

subsequent wage adjustments. China's seniority wage system was thus rooted in national and shop floor politics rather than mandated by explicit state policy.

As studies of comparative socialist economies during the 1960s and 1970s have shown, the difference in earnings between the highest-paid factory officials and lowest-paid workers in China was a multiple of only between two and three, far narrower than the five to one spread found in factories of the former Soviet Union, not to mention capitalist economies.[52] While such an outcome no doubt reflects the prevailing Maoist egalitarianism of the time, it is also easy to point to the prime beneficiaries of the seniority-based wage system – "old workers" – who used political and institutional forces to maintain low wages for factory managers above them and younger workers below them. It would be an exaggeration to view pre-1949 "old workers" in Chinese factories as a kind of interest group whose preferences changed national level policy over the course of the 1950s. They did, however, constitute a vital knowledge base in terms of technical skills, as well as an important political constituency whose support of the Communist regime was instrumental as the party sought to control urban areas. When strikes erupted in Shanghai, Guangzhou, and elsewhere in the spring of 1957 (see Chapter 7), "old workers" offered pivotal support for the new socialist status quo.

INCENTIVE BONUSES

Burawoy and others who have conducted shop floor ethnographies of workers in a command economy have noted a number of generic points for socialist factories that are useful in understanding work in Chinese factories in the 1950s. First, because supply rather than demand acts as the primary constraint in socialism, central planners and managers compete for scarce inputs, including labor. The constant uncertainty about supplies produces frequent adjustments to the labor process, making the de-skilling of the workforce found in mass production less likely in socialist enterprises. Because managers and workers must make almost constant adjustments to the production process based on shortages and bottlenecks in supplies, skilled and experienced workers benefit from the plant-specific knowledge they have of machines and other

---

[52] Richman, *Industrial Society in Communist China*, 804–5.

equipment in the factory.[53] One corollary to this proposition is that the continual adjustment and adaptation to production contingencies permits workers and their supervisors to enjoy greater shop floor autonomy from management than would be the case in a capitalist economy.[54] Burawoy also asks why, in socialist planned economies dedicated to full employment, have observers noted a remarkably intense pace of work relative to the shop floors of firms in capitalist economies (even of monopolistic firms such as the one in which Burawoy was employed). The key distinction, according to Burawoy, is that monopoly capitalist firms, with their union contracts covering much of the workforce, offer guaranteed wages but not guaranteed employment. In socialist factories, on the other hand, employment is guaranteed while wages are not.[55] Workers in factories of socialist command economies must therefore eke out marginal wage increases by exceeding production quotas. The uncertainty of supply, or not knowing when adequate materials will be available, leads to frantic efforts by workers to get all they can from machines and existing materials on hand.[56]

Under a wage system in which overquota production makes up significant portions of workers' earnings, informal bargaining is common. Workers seek job assignments or work stations where they can easily attain and surpass production quotas, and supervisors who decide which workers will be placed on which machines exercise a degree of personal authority well beyond their formal job descriptions. And the battle over rate setting, or determining what the production quota will be, is highly contentious – at times foremen retain this power to set rates and at other times a technical expert from factory administration will exercise control of rate setting. Socialist factory administrators will frequently utilize "socialist competitions," in which extraordinarily high output "norms" will be set as the standards for which workers must exceed in order to qualify for bonuses. The fact that enterprises enjoy flexible budgets and state-set prices means that they suffer no consequences financially for overproduction. The chief constraints on overquota wage systems are in the supply of adequate raw materials and technology.

---

[53] Burawoy, *Politics of Production*, 162–3; Michael Burawoy and Janos Lukacs, "Mythologies of Work: A Comparison of Firms in State Socialism and Advanced Capitalism," *American Sociological Review* vol. 50, no. 6 (December 1985): 726; Miklos Haraszti, *A Worker in a Workers' State*, trans. Michael Wright (New York: Pelican Books, 1977).
[54] Burawoy and Lukacs, "Mythologies of Work," 726.   [55] Ibid., 727.
[56] Burawoy, *Politics and Production*, 168.

During the FFYP, state-owned enterprises implemented a number of different production incentive wage systems that covered large parts of the industrial workforce. Approximately 200,000 of Shanghai's 974,000 workers were on piece-rate systems of pay in 1957, with another 130,000 workers eligible for extra pay if they produced beyond a set amount.[57] In the mid-1950s, as many as 70 to 80 percent of Shanghai's machine industry workers earned bonuses of some kind, compared to 50 to 60 percent of textile mill workers. Bonuses made up about 5 to 6 percent of the average wage in fourteen large enterprises in Shanghai (including the Jiangnan Shipyard).[58]

In theory, incentive or output bonuses were a logical way to induce greater productivity. In practice, the schemes proved extremely difficult to administer. Central planning created inevitable bottlenecks in the flow of goods and tools. Shortages or delays in the delivery of critical raw materials meant that workers who earned part of the pay through overquota bonuses lost opportunities for additional income not because they lacked skills or initiative but because management failed to provide them with the necessary inputs. As a result, workers paid through such incentive systems grew increasingly frustrated. Such workers also grasped the point of diminishing returns, or when further effort to produce was no longer worth the additional pay. Forgers in the Jiangnan Shipyard slowed down the pace of work once their output had reached a level that provided sufficient spending money for their off-work pastimes. "With cash for two bottles of booze already in hand, work can ease up now," they were fond of saying.[59]

Incentive bonuses proved far too complex to administer, but this did not prevent enterprise managers from devising elaborate ruses to distribute extra pay to their workers in the form of bonuses. Party reports suggest that the portion of the wage bill spent on bonuses was far higher than the officially reported 5 to 6 percent. Even if bonuses as a share of an individual worker's total pay may not have amounted to a substantial portion, state officials condemned enterprise managers for their tendency to distribute bonuses in an overly generous fashion ("extreme egalitarianism" as party officials called it).[60] The large bonuses once

---

[57] SMA, Series A36-1-248.   [58] SMA, Series C1-2-2723.

[59] Ibid. This phenomenon of beating piece-rate systems, known as "making out" in the parlance of the Chicago machinery plant where Burawoy worked, is not necessarily unique to workplaces under monopoly capitalism. See Burawoy, *Manufacturing Consent*.

[60] SMA, Series C1-2-2723.

passed out at holidays were now a thing of the past. But factory directors in the 1950s found a way to direct surplus enterprise funds toward their employees. At the Number Thirteen Cotton Mill in Shanghai, a total of forty-three different bonuses were in place during the FFYP, many of which amounted to outright subsidies. Among the more unusual of these was a "salting and tasting bonus" of 5 to 6 yuan per month paid to cooks in the mill's cafeteria for their steadfast attention to spicing their dishes properly.[61] In Shanghai's machinery and electronics plants, state officials faulted factory directors for paying out bonuses to nonproductive employees such as gate guards, repairmen, cooks, fire prevention guards, day care staff, and night school teachers as a reward for the factory (and its production workers, presumably) having met output and quality standards. The authorities considered this to be a waste of bonus funds squandered on employees who had nothing to do with actual production. At the Jiangnan Shipyard, workshop directors put in place a safety bonus designed to reward accident-free work sites. Yet because the bonus accumulated over time if a work site continued to have a clean safety record, workers were earning substantial bonuses of 20 yuan per month.[62] All of these bonuses represented a far greater portion of basic pay than the amount that managers reported to authorities.

In many Guangzhou factories, piece rates and overquota bonuses also had the effect of lowering production. The so-called "progressive producers" who won accolades for setting or surpassing output records were greeted with suspicion and animosity by their fellow workers, who accused them of selfishly pursuing extra cash.[63] Piece rates also caused workers to avoid learning how to use new production technology, because the time spent in training on a new machine would cause a drop in their output-based income over the short term. When the Li Yuxing knitting mill in Guangzhou acquired a cloth-cutting machine in the mid-1950s, managers ultimately had to put it away in storage after workers insisted on cutting cloth by hand.[64]

By the late 1950s, all output incentive systems in China were suddenly abandoned – an exceptional policy in the history of socialist planned economies (see Chapter 7). This dramatic change in policy toward production bonuses reflected the ideological preferences of many in the CCP elite in the late 1950s (who opposed material incentives of any kind). Yet as suggested here and in the enterprise cases that follow in Chapter 6, the rejection of overquota bonuses and other incentive pay

---

[61] Ibid.   [62] Ibid.   [63] GMA, Series 92-216.   [64] Ibid.

systems in Chinese industry was rooted in the shop floor conflicts during China's transition to a centrally planned economy.

LABOR ALLOCATION

As the Chinese state in the 1950s undertook to nationalize private industry and commerce and to bring all enterprises directly or indirectly under state plans, the average number of employees on the payroll and the enterprise's annual wage bill also were fixed and subject to administrative constraints. Over the course of the FFYP, the process of state labor allocation gradually shifted from "unified introduction" (*tongyi jieshao zhidu*), in which local labor bureaus acted as clearinghouses for unemployed workers and understaffed enterprises, to one of "unified deployment" (*tongyi diaopei zhidu*), in which local branches of central planning ministries assigned workers to particular enterprises.[65] SOE managers had to negotiate each year with the relevant ministries over the number of official workers they would be allowed to employ under the plan as well as the size of the enterprise wage bill in a given year.[66] By the late 1950s, when the registration of urban residents checked the flow of rural migrants to cities, the system of job assignments by central planning ministries became critical in lowering the mobility of workers across areas and to and from enterprises. In the Soviet Union, by contrast, job turnover and labor shortages remained a chronic problem.[67]

During the FFYP, the CCP succeeded in stopping labor turnover, at times an acute problem in the 1930s and 1940s. Pension eligibility was linked to years of service at one's enterprise, and the enterprise retained the authority to release a worker's dossier – the all-important personnel file without which employment at another enterprise was not possible. Moreover, state policy prohibited jointly owned enterprises from dismissing staff and workers who had been employed prior to their enterprise's transfer from private to majority public ownership. By 1956, managers at state and jointly owned enterprises had to seek permission

---

[65] Yuan, *Zhongguo laodong jingjishi*, 93–100.
[66] Author's interview, Jiangnan Shipyard History Research Office, December 26, 1994; Author's interview, Huangpu Shipyard officials, May 3, 1995; Eckstein, *China's Economic Revolution*, 101.
[67] Rudra Sil, "The Russian 'Village in the City' and the Stalinist System of Enterprise Management: The Origins of Worker Alienation in Soviet State Socialism," in *Danwei*, Lü and Perry, eds., 131; Hiroaki Kuromiya, *Stalin's Industrial Revolution: Politics and Workers, 1928–1932* (New York: Cambridge University Press, 1988), 200–26.

from the Ministry of Labor before they could expand or reduce the size of their enterprise workforce. Under a command economy in which enterprise managers had to fulfill annual plans, there was a strong incentive to hoard labor, not reduce it. Factory managers under pressure to fulfill output quotas turned anywhere for surplus labor. State and party officials subsequently criticized them for failing to keep controls on the labor plan and wage bill in their rush to meet production goals.[68] Efforts to control hires by the factory director led to back and forth bargaining among workshop directors. As the Guangzhou MPC's Industrial Work Department noted, "Labor and wage planning, without question, tends to be regarded as just fulfilling the production plan." When labor and wage department personnel complied with state plans and refused to increase a factory's labor force, their superiors in the factory director's office accused them of "conservative thought." Under pressure to maintain enterprise labor plans, cadres in the personnel department at the Tongyong Machine factory in Guangzhou were labeled as "black cadres."[69]

Initially, state controls on hiring placed few restrictions on recruitment from "society," meaning from surplus labor in urban and especially rural areas. When the state eased restrictions on hiring in 1956 and then again in late 1957, enterprises absorbed massive amounts of new labor. The first "loss of control over labor recruitment" (*zhaogong shikong*) took place in 1956, when the Ministry of Labor decentralized recruitment powers by allowing enterprises to go through local labor bureaus rather than industrial ministries for new hires. As a result of this easing of controls, the number of workers hired nearly doubled that called for in national plans – instead of 840,000 workers recruited in 1956 as stipulated in the plan, enterprises hired a total of 1,460,000 new employees.[70] The State Council quickly interceded in early 1957 with orders that strictly prohibited enterprises from "hiring from society" and renewed the requirement that new hires had to be approved by central industrial ministries. (Subsequent directives from the State Council in the first half of 1957 restricting the promotion of apprentices and temporary workers to full-time status led directly to labor protests by these groups in several cities. See Chapter 7.)

The practice of occupational "replacement" (*dingti*) by children of state enterprise employees became common in the PRC by the 1970s,

---

[68] GMA, Series 8-28.   [69] Ibid.   [70] Yuan, *Zhongguo laodong jingjishi*, 98.

but it appears to have developed earlier in larger, older factories, as the cases in the following chapter illustrate. The labor allocation procedures issued by the Ministry of Labor in the 1950s make no mention that sons and daughters of factory workers had to be assigned to jobs in the unit of their parents. Clearly, however, state labor officials listened to requests of factory managers, shop floor supervisors, and workers that new entrants to the workforce be assigned to the same work unit of their parents and relatives. Through its national controls over labor allocation, the Chinese government inadvertently promoted an intensely localistic practice of work-unit occupational inheritance. Family members of current or retiring employees had first priority, if not exclusive access, to jobs in the most desirable work units.[71]

The hiring of family members was not simply the result of some fondness among factory workers for having relatives work alongside them in the same enterprise. Without astute bargaining with relevant officials, an urban family could find its members scattered across distant provinces by the demands of state labor allocation. This appears to have been the case especially in coastal cities such as Shanghai and Guangzhou, with relatively larger pools of skilled labor than cities in the interior (where a massive industrial buildup was underway by the 1960s). Having relatives dispatched to China's far-flung industrial centers created financial and emotional hardships for families, as a Shanghai General Labor Union report from 1955 noted. One unfortunate production team leader at the Jiangnan Shipyard had three members of his immediate family working in three different cities: his mother was in Guangzhou, his father in Hankou, and his younger brother in Lanzhou.[72] The State Council came up with a rather token solution in 1957 when it issued new guidelines on home leave to permit relatives more time to visit one another.

State-controlled labor allocation and the reorganization of production units during the FFYP represented a substantial erosion in power for production supervisors relative to the days when workers could be hired and fired at the whim of the shop floor boss. Workshop directors, as well as enterprise personnel managers, had to accept the allotment of laborers periodically assigned to their plants. Given the scarcity of both technology and labor, enterprise managers had an incentive to retain

---

[71] Michael Korzec, *Labour and the Failure of Reform in China* (New York: St. Martin's Press, 1992), 17–25.
[72] SMA, Series C1-2-2257.

personnel, so they welcomed any additional inputs of labor and were reluctant to dismiss all but the most disruptive of employees. In practice, however, shop floor bosses under state socialism enjoyed certain powers, which they used in their continuing battles with personnel departments within the enterprise. This conflict over the ability to control frontline industrial workers extended back to the 1920s and 1930s, but under the command economy it took different forms. Personnel departments in state and jointly owned enterprises during the 1950s still lacked the necessary technical and administrative skills to decisively subordinate the entrenched shop floor supervisor. Factory directors, especially under one-man management, enjoyed ultimate formal authority to assign new workers to specific posts in the factory, but in large enterprises, directors had to rely on the knowledge of workshop directors, work section heads, and production team leaders in distributing work posts to new workers. Moreover, a new entrant to the ranks of the factory's workforce would find it wise to establish good relations with these supervisors. Because China lacked a system of technical training of any consequence, recent school graduates came into factory employment lacking many necessary industrial skills. Factories therefore had to develop apprentice programs in which new recruits would undergo a period of on-the-job training. These apprentices relied on their skilled elders to develop the techniques to operate complex machinery. Following the apprenticeship, workshop and production team leaders could designate the novice to a less demanding task or to a work post that offered opportunities to earn overquota bonuses.

Shop floor supervisors could no longer fire and hire workers under the command economy, but because many such supervisors in the 1950s had been recruited from the ranks of skilled labor, they retained valuable, plant-specific technical knowledge in the operation of factory machinery. Because virtually all new workers had to be trained on the job, supervisors held a valuable resource. To the extent that a factory's machinery was fairly old, as much of it would have been in cities such as Shanghai and Guangzhou that did not receive the dominant share of capital investment during the 1950s, technical skills were very narrowly restricted to the enterprise, or even workshops within large enterprises. With the new wage and incentive bonus system that in theory rewarded skill with higher pay, machine-specific knowledge was all the more valuable. Personnel officials, white collar staff who more than likely would have been transferred to the enterprise from a bureaucratic agency or educational institution, were no match for the front line supervisors in terms of operational knowledge. While supervisors might have to go to the factory director and staff in order to request additional labor, the latter group was constrained by orders from their bureaucratic superiors in the industrial ministries.

New workforce entrants, as might be expected, suffered the most under the transition to the command economy. Apprentices complained about the extended length of their training period as well as the quality of the instruction they were getting. At the Guangdong Textile Mill, managers manipulated the length of the apprenticeship well beyond the time it took to acquire skills. More than ten apprentices at the mill had trained for over two years, well beyond the official period of four to six months, without being promoted as official workers.[73] In Shanghai, apprentices also objected that they were earning only 2 or 3 yuan during their training period, whatever the length. Some "teachers" were themselves only slightly advanced apprentices from a senior cohort of trainees. Moreover, skilled workers were often pressed to fulfill output quotas and had limited time to show apprentices how to operate machinery.[74]

Formally, the workshop director and the production team leader followed orders issued by state officials and factory staff administrators. In practice, Chinese labor policy left a certain amount of discretion for supervisors to exert informal and personalistic authority over subordinate workers. As enterprise branches of the CCP entered into this shop-floor authority relationship by recruiting supervisors as designated party leaders of workshops, work sections, and production teams, this informal personalized authority based on skill and technical training took on a politicized and ideological dimension by the 1960s.

PARTY-GOVERNMENT RIVALRY

The adoption of the FFYP gave powers to industrial bureaucrats and factory directors that essentially rendered the party secretary and the party branch powerless to set plans and influence the organization and activities of workers within the factory. The adoption of top-down state planning also neutralized what little power Labor-Capital Consultative Conferences and Factory Management Committees had enjoyed. Enterprise unions, never strong in the early 1950s, were also politically

---

[73] GMA, Series 92-478.   [74] SMA, Series C1-2-2257.

powerless under the plan-dominated system of labor management. Party committees continued to function, but their missions were highly ambiguous. The "High Stalinist" principles of party domination that China's industrial officials had copied from the Soviet Union of the late 1940s withered as the alternative Soviet model of one-man management placed decision-making power and authority in the hands of factory directors.

Factory directors and state representatives, with full authority to take whatever steps were necessary to fulfill the plan, cast aside objections from factory party committees that proposed strengthening political work and holding meetings to discuss policy. In Guangzhou, factory directors reportedly canceled study sessions led by party committee members on the grounds that such meetings took time away from production. At the city's electric plant, the factory director prohibited the enterprise party secretary from having access to production records and related information. In several other large-scale Guangzhou factories, the enterprise party cadres were not allowed to go down to the factory floor without prior permission from the factory director.[75] Factory directors often wore two hats, serving concurrently as enterprise party secretaries, in which case there was not even a token party secretary to supervise the actions of the factory director. Despite the fact that more administrative officials had attained party membership, the respective backgrounds of the typical factory director and the typical party secretary were quite distinct. The factory director was usually older, with years of experience and training in a technical field, while the party committee secretary was younger, frequently emerging from the ranks of workers. Guangdong party officials noted that because factory directors often had the status of county-level cadres in the party's administrative hierarchy, they felt little need to listen to enterprise party secretaries, who ranked as subordinate district-level cadres.[76] Administrative relationships and the competition among government and party units for control over labor issues within state enterprises would persist throughout the 1950s and reach a dramatic resolution by 1957, whose consequences will be addressed in Chapter 7.

[75] GMA, Series 8-150.

[76] Guangdong Province Economic Planning Commission, Editorial Office for the "Economic Planning Gazetteer," *Guangdongsheng jingji jihua wenjian xuanbian* (Selected Documents on Economic Planning in Guangdong Province) (Guangzhou: 1990), 1:291.

LABOR COMPETITIONS

Socialist labor competitions, in which party cadres single out model workers and "progressive producers" and propagate them as paragons to the rest of the workforce, is another common feature of state socialist labor organization. Both China and the Soviet Union utilized competitions during the early stages of planning in order to establish production "norms" (*ding'e* in Chinese), or the standards by which overquota bonuses would be set. In Chinese factories in 1950–1, and even earlier in Northeast China, the "Movement to Create New Records" established output standards in factories.[77] This production competition, later known as the "Movement to Increase Production and Practice Economy," also urged factory workers to offer up "rationalization proposals" (*helihua jianyi*) that would help the enterprise to lower production costs and to raise productivity.[78] In 1953, during labor competitions in China, factory cadres organized meetings in which workers studied industrial management systems in the Soviet Union and read accounts of dramatic feats by individual workers from around China. Given the initial constraints on new technology and capital equipment that many enterprises suffered from during this time, the party's use of emulation and education to encourage workers to get more from the existing production capacity of their enterprises was a predictable strategy.

By 1956, however, the focus of labor competitions in China had changed. This was a year in which Shanghai saw a rapid increase in the number of intrafactory competitions, whose number rose from 688 factories in the first quarter to 2,641 in the third quarter.[79] While the idea remained to "popularize progressive experiences" of exceptional workers, the party placed emphasis on propagating the achievements of individuals within the enterprise, as opposed to recounting the achievements of some distant and unknown model worker. The criteria for selecting model workers and progressive producers also had changed by this time. While such honors were once bestowed upon those who demonstrated exceptional dexterity in the operation of existing machinery, by 1956 model workers were selected from among those who had mastered advanced technical skills on newer types of machinery and technology.[80] Model workers in the FFYP were thus more likely to have gained their status through technical achievements rather than physical

---

[77] Brugger, *Democracy and Organisation*, 126–7.   [78] Ibid., 146; 186–7.
[79] Sun, *Shanghai shehuizhuyi jingji jianshe*, 189.   [80] Ibid.

intensity and endurance displayed in "storming," or maximizing the capacity of existing machinery.[81]

This change in criteria for model workers toward an emphasis on skill acquisition is illustrated well in the case of a work-section leader at the Jiangnan Shipyard in 1955. Having been promoted to leader of his work section for his diligence and hard work, he subsequently found himself torn between the competing demands of technical improvements and party imperatives to mobilize workers for education and increased production. After putting in a work day that began at 6 A.M., he would then study designs and blueprints up until 10 P.M. or midnight. He lacked confidence in his ability to learn new skills, and also found it impossible to fulfill the demands of the party committee: "I know I should mobilize the masses, but I'm so busy, and others are busy too – we have no time to hold meetings to mobilize the masses." He also felt that because he had been promoted from the ranks of workers, he lacked the authority to give orders to his former co-workers.[82] This account illustrates the need for caution in overemphasizing the authority of shop floor supervisors during China's transition to the command economy, and it also suggests something of a relationship between technical knowledge and authority within the shop floor. Whenever enterprises acquired new equipment, the powers shop floor supervisors had once enjoyed as a result of technical mastery of older machines were suddenly neutralized. Put another way, the acquisition of new capital undermined the authority of those whose powers lay in mobilizing labor for work on existing machinery. The Great Leap Forward, whose very essence was one of labor-intensive growth, would radically reverse the years of erosion in the authority of shop floor supervisors.

Neither the "High Stalinist" model of Communist Party–led workforce mobilization nor one-man management with its highly concentrated administrative authority at various levels of the factory took hold during the FFYP. Technical and material scarcities alone suggest that Soviet patterns of labor management could never have been immutably grafted on to the Chinese factory. Beyond this perhaps expected failure to adopt Soviet labor management institutions *en bloc* lies a more significant institutional problem that predated the FFYP and even the 1949 revolution. The problem lay in the gap between new institutions, whether those called for by capitalist scientific management of the 1930s or by the imperatives of the command economy in the 1950s, and older institutions

---

[81] Howe, *Wage Patterns*, 130–1.   [82] SMA, Series A43-1-103.

of labor management that workers, supervisors, and staff had relied on to organize work within the factory. Labor management institutions such as those discussed in the preceding chapters (namely, the foreman's fiefdom, workplace welfare, and to some extent, seniority wages with narrow, inflation-compressed differentials) arose in response to technical and material scarcities, and in response to external crises such as war and hyperinflation in the 1940s. In subsequent years, these makeshift solutions became entrenched norms that workers, supervisors, managers, and even state officials readily accepted and in some cases actively sought to preserve. This is not to say that the institutions of the command economy failed to modify existing labor management institutions. Yet these older institutions also decisively channeled subsequent shop floor politics and conflict as various actors defined their interests in relation to the preservation, modification, or transformation of existing labor management institutions. The discussion of enterprise cases in the following chapter illuminates in greater detail how labor management institutions within the Chinese factory generated conflict with the rules and constraints imposed by command economics and the Soviet model that China's planners had so assiduously copied in the early 1950s.

6

Enterprise Perspectives on the Command Economy

MUCH of the scholarship on industrial and labor management in China during the FFYP has focused on the areas of heavy industry in Northeast China, which also received prominent coverage in the state media during the 1950s. This earlier generation of scholarship, based largely on such official press accounts, revealed tensions within China's industrial enterprises over the organization of work and the role of intraenterprise organizations such as unions, party committees, and mass organizations.[1] The opening of PRC archives in recent years has permitted scholars to take a closer look at shop floor politics and labor organization. While the perspective remains an official one, internal reports from city-level unions, Communist Party committees, and government departments offer revealing insights into the politics of the factory and the institutions that managers, workers, and intrafactory organizations pursued or resisted during China's transition to a planned economy. Each of the four enterprises discussed in preceding chapters experienced dramatic challenges to preexisting labor management institutions, as external political and economic controls generated new constraints as well as conflicts.

The purpose of this chapter is twofold: 1) to illuminate patterns of conflict that arose over wages, welfare provision, and labor organization as workers and managers resisted new state-imposed formal constraints and 2) to discuss variations in how these patterns of conflict unfolded across the textile and shipbuilding sectors in the cities of Shanghai and Guangzhou. Central to this second point is the role of the MPC and its Industrial Work Department (*gongye gongzuo bu*) in each city. This little-known functional division of the local Communist Party played a critical

---

[1] Schurmann, *Ideology and Organization*; Andors, *China's Industrial Revolution*; Brugger, *Democracy and Organisation*; Chung, "Ideology and the Politics of Industrial Management."

mediating role in the translation of central political and administrative directives into actual practice within industrial plants.[2] The Industrial Work Departments spurred factory party branches to mobilize workers for factory campaigns, implemented highly complex wage adjustment procedures, and would eventually take over most supervisory functions of certain factories within their cities. The assumption of local controls by the Industrial Work Departments of MPCs had significant consequences for labor management institutions within local factories.

China's transition to a command economy took place concurrently with an equally significant but less visible transition that might be described as the "localization" of enterprise management. As the discussion of command economies in the preceding chapter showed, factory directors in these economies act as middle management in a hierarchy that places executive decisions over finance, investment, production, distribution, wages, etc., in the hands of central government planners. In theory, enterprise managers only implement directives made at central levels. The enterprise cases from this chapter reveal another process at work during the centralization of industrial production in China during the 1950s – the encroachment of MPCs into enterprise labor issues at large local factories. Shop floor politics, the recurring debate among individuals and groups within an enterprise over the distribution of power and pay, had long been influenced by political entities outside the factory, as witnessed in the same enterprise cases during the 1930s and 1940s. During the 1950s, shop floor politics became more directly linked with the state, though in two not necessarily compatible arrangements. On the one hand, central government ministries overlaid a national set of rules for how enterprises would go about hiring and paying workers. On the other hand, local party committees sought to control shop floor politics by engaging in extensive monitoring of how such rules were implemented.

JIANGNAN SHIPYARD

Having been a subordinate unit of the East China Military Region's Naval Headquarters in the three years following the CCP's takeover of

---

[2] While municipal archives in both Shanghai and Guangzhou carry extensive reports authored by CCP Industrial Work Departments, we still know little about the actual personnel staffing these departments, their budgets, missions, etc. Further opening of internal Municipal Party Committee files from the 1950s is likely to bring valuable insights on these and other local CCP departments.

Shanghai, the Jiangnan Shipyard was placed under the control of the Shipbuilding Industry Bureau of Beijing's First Machinery Ministry in December 1952.[3] Under this arrangement, the shipyard was grouped with most other large shipyards in China, among them the Dalian Shipyard, which was known formally as the Sino-Soviet Shipbuilding Corporation. As this title indicates, the Dalian Shipyard was a keypoint enterprise in receiving Soviet technical assistance and in emulating Soviet industrial management systems. The Jiangnan Shipyard, a recipient of little in the way of direct assistance save for forty Soviet advisers housed there in the 1950s, nonetheless sent several delegations to Dalian for managerial training. Following one of these visits, Jiangnan officials abolished the existing Personnel Office and divided its functions into a two sections (*ke*): a Personnel Section and a Labor and Wage Section, staffed by a total of twenty employees. Each section set out to establish output standards and norms to calculate pay, in emulation of Soviet methods.[4] Officials from the First Machinery Ministry also sent work teams to the Jiangnan Shipyard during the early 1950s to advise management on how to reform production and management processes, including the introduction of production incentive bonuses.[5]

Concurrent with these changes in the bureaucratic relationships of the Jiangnan Shipyard were transfers in the chain of command for the shipyard's party committee. In July 1952, the party committee was released from the supervision of the East China Military Region's Naval Headquarters Party Committee to the Shanghai MPC's Heavy Industry Work Department. Formal orders for this transfer came from the Shanghai MPC's Organization Department.[6] This change in party supervision was significant: while the Jiangnan Shipyard's administrative responsibilities lay with a ministry in Beijing (e.g., First Machinery), its party branch reported to local authorities. Moreover, the fact that the Shanghai MPC had a functional department charged with handling enterprises in heavy industry suggests that party officials in the city were not content to monitor only party affairs and appointments within the Jiangnan Shipyard and other heavy industrial enterprises but would also act as an

---

[3] Jiangnan Shipyard Factory History Research Office, "Jiangnanchang de renshi laodong guanli" (Jiangnan Shipyard Personnel and Labor Management), mimeo, n.d., 168.

[4] Ibid., 169.

[5] Jiangnan Shipyard Factory History Research Office, "Renshi laodong guanli," 153.

[6] Jiangnan Shipyard Factory History Research Office, "Factory Chronology," mimeo, n.d., 40.

alternative line of authority over matters of industrial and labor policy. This is precisely what took place over the course of the FFYP.

Wages

The blueprints for intraenterprise wage policy found in the Soviet managerial manuals of the time failed to account for one important problem. This was the fact that production technology in Chinese industry was not only less advanced but also highly variable across enterprises in the same industry. Particular job descriptions laid out by Beijing ministries hardly matched the reality inside factories. Perhaps as a result, and also because of the pressing need to reorganize wages among a demoralized workforce at the Jiangnan Shipyard, managers had rather hastily implemented the eight-grade wage system in 1951. Factory officials did the actual work of setting grades (*pingji*) for each worker, based on national standards issued by the First Machinery Ministry.[7] In practice, ambiguities in the central government standards allowed workshop directors in charge of setting wage grades much discretion.

The issue of pay dominated the meetings of the Employee Representative Congress (*zhigong daibiao dahui*) during 1951–2. This was a new organization established along with a Factory Management Committee in many state factories in 1950 to give workers more voice in the operations of their enterprise. Jiangnan Shipyard management, especially military officials, tried to explain to skeptical labor representatives that difficulties in national finances, as well as the local unemployment situation in Shanghai, meant that wage increases, including some kind of systematic wage reform, would have to be delayed until "further research" could be done. Meanwhile, the lowest paid production workers suffered from what amounted to an 18 percent cut in pay, as a result of steps taken during the final year of Nationalist administration. These production workers received 1.8 "parity units" in daily wages when, they argued, they had been receiving the equivalent of 2.2 parity units during the late 1940s.[8] (Parity units were a monetary measure used in the early 1950s to keep wages in line with prices.)

During the spring and summer of 1952, the Shanghai MPC made perhaps its first intervention into a purely administrative issue when it became involved in the question of wages at the Jiangnan Shipyard. Work teams from the Shanghai MPC convened meetings of over 350

[7] SMA, Series A36-2-072.   [8] SMA, Series C1-2-729.

Jiangnan Shipyard production supervisors. The supervisors argued that wages were the central issue in production. "If the wage problem is not resolved, we won't be able to return to our production teams and account for it," they warned. These leaders complained of several problems associated with the legacy of the Nationalist administration. For example, some workers had been hired through personal connections, and had been given high wage levels despite their relatively low skills. Many shift leaders and highly skilled workers who had been labor contractors in the past had seen to it that production workers personally loyal to them received higher wages. Young apprentices and temporary workers, on the other hand, suffered under this system, because apprentices who had gone through three years or more of training still got their previous low level of wages, as did temporary workers who had obtained full-time status. All of these problems caused what Communist Party authors called "contradictions" (*maodun*) among the workforce: different rates of pay for the same job had to be remedied with the socialist principle of "to each according to his work" (*tonggong tongchou*). Yet, as officials also noted, the shipyard workers based their understanding of wages on the old system, which led to the "egalitarian phenomenon" in which wages were not linked to production.[9] A 1953 report by the Heavy Industry Work Department of the Shanghai MPC on how to carry out wage adjustments in the city's machine and shipbuilding industries remarked that "low labor productivity and other phenomena severely influence production, so this wage adjustment has developed into a task which demands immediate attention."[10]

The party authorities set up a Wage Reform Committee at the Jiangnan Shipyard in mid-1953, and the panel began the tedious process of adjusting wages for production workers. In a mobilizational style typical of the CCP, wage adjustment at the shipyard and other heavy industry enterprises in Shanghai combined the technical leadership of various ministry and local labor officials with mass meetings among workers led by "backbone element" party members. As Shanghai MPC officials put it, "Wage reform work is a political campaign which requires that deep and broad mass education be carried out." The report later noted that "political work and mass education" were "the crux of the success or failure of the entire wage reform." Mass meetings led by such activists revealed several manifestations of "unhealthy thought," however. Many

[9] Ibid. [10] SMA, Series A36-2-072.

workers suspected (rightly, it turned out) that bonuses and subsidies would be abolished after wage reform, or that this wage adjustment would be the last for the indefinite future. Low-skilled workers who were receiving relatively high pay naturally expressed opposition to a more strict application of skill standards that would lower their wage grade (and income). Some party officials called demands for grade promotions by the high-skilled, relatively underpaid workers "100 percent reasonable."[11]

The effect of the 1953–4 wage adjustment at the Jiangnan Shipyard was to reduce the number of workers at the two extremes of the wage scale. The number of grade 7 and 8 workers, who were essentially work section leaders or workshop directors, fell from 441 to 317, out of a total of 4,074 production workers. The number of low-skilled grade 1 workers declined from fifty-five to fourteen, meaning those with wages between grade 2 and grade 6 now made up 91 percent of production workers. The 1953–4 wage adjustment at the Jiangnan Shipyard had thus revived the "egalitarian" tendencies that central ministry officials wanted to avoid in setting up the wage ladder. Enterprise officials apparently preferred a more equitable wage distribution to that pushed by the central government. Jiangnan Shipyard administrators gave wage increases to 88 percent of production workers, but this generous distribution under a fixed wage bill only raised their average annual incomes from 260.9 yuan per year to 264.7 yuan (an increase of about 1.5 percent). At the same time, the adjustment abolished or reduced to under 10 yuan the sources of extra-wage income such as bonuses and subsidies.[12]

In the extremely detailed reports that exist on wage reform at the Jiangnan Shipyard and other Shanghai enterprises, one of the most significant patterns that emerges is the close involvement of the Shanghai MPC, through its Heavy Industry Work Department as well as a separate State Enterprise Management Department, in administrative issues within enterprises. Of course other organizations outside the enterprise had political stakes in wage policy, and foremost among these was the Shanghai GLU, which had a Wage Department that also issued frequent reports on the courses and complications of wage reform in various state and nonstate enterprises. GLU reports proved to be more critical in tone and more prepared to note shortcomings in the eight-grade wage system as well as the implementation of overquota production bonuses.[13] But it

---

[11] Ibid.   [12] Ibid.
[13] Representative GLU reports are those found in SMA, Series C1-2-2408. Municipal Party Committee reports can be found in SMA, Series A42-1-10.

was the MPC's Heavy Industry Work Department that exercised a high degree of informal authority over wage policy. This pattern of MPC dominance is evident in other labor issues, and in other large enterprises in Shanghai and Guangzhou.

Production Bonuses

As factory management at the Jiangnan Shipyard soon discovered, for the overquota bonuses scheme to work, employees had to be provided with the necessary materials in the first place. However, management's insistence in issuing "work slips" (*pai gongdan*) for every conceivable job led to interminable delays as workshops awaited a superior department's approval and orders. To obtain even a single screw required such a work order. Over the course of a year, an estimated one million of these slips had to be written up and processed. Workers, discouraged by such delays, declined to pursue overquota bonuses. Workshop employees also complained that the factory's planning department gave them no power to revise designs and blueprints. This brought further production delays, as workshops had to go to top management to apply for revisions. The inspection department staff in charge of ensuring that goods produced met quality standards set by the First Machinery Ministry were faulted for lacking sufficient skills and technical knowledge.[14]

Incentive systems also generated several unwelcome tendencies in the workforce. The most troublesome to party and union officials was the rivalry between older and younger workers.[15] After recent entrants to the workforce learned the necessary skills, they could earn just as much as a worker with far more seniority who might be several rungs higher on the wage ladder. This younger cohort of skilled workers drew the animosity of their seniors and those in less skilled positions, who accused them of the selfish pursuit of cash: of "serving the *renminbi*" instead of "serving the people (*renmin*)."[16] An older worker, who despite having the status and income associated with a high-wage setting, watched the apprentices whom he had trained take advantage of the overquota bonus system and earn three to four times his own fixed monthly pay. The elder skilled workers recited a refrain to their juniors: "The one who started first was me, the one with better luck is thee; I taught you how to work

---

[14] SMA, Series A36-1-136.   [15] SMA, Series C1-2-2724; SMA, Series A36-1-136.
[16] SMA, Series A36-1-136.

a day, but you're the one with better pay." The production department staff charged with setting the critical quotas beyond which bonuses could be earned were under such pressure that one staff member even requested three times, unsuccessfully, that management send him to the countryside during the Great Leap Forward.[17]

Older workers at the Jiangnan Shipyard looked upon new entrants to the ranks of workers as spoiled beneficiaries of the new policies. They resented that young workers enjoyed the good life of socialism while they had undergone the bitterness and hardships of being a shipyard apprentice during the 1920s and 1930s. One fitter at the Jiangnan Shipyard recalled how at age 14 when he became an apprentice, his master withheld all of his earnings for years. Now, he remarked, "post-liberation" apprentices spend six months in training and then promptly earn at least 50 yuan a month. "So," the old fitter observed, "they brainstorm over how to spend their money. They study dancing, look for girlfriends, and don't put in any time learning technical skills. But skill is something that is acquired from a life of bitter experience. There's a huge difference between the grade 3 worker of today and the grade 3 worker of the past."[18]

Enterprise Welfare

Limited housing and health care had been available to full-time employees at the shipyard in the late 1940s, and socialist management expanded such benefits over the course of the FFYP. Shipyard employees were entitled to labor insurance provisions soon after the first set of regulations came out in early 1951. By 1956, construction of an employee hospital with eighty beds was completed, to go with a smaller clinic that had begun in 1953.[19] The provision of employee housing, begun in June 1953, expanded rapidly so that within a year over one thousand employees and their families had living quarters near the factory. In December 1954, a dormitory for unmarried workers opened, with a capacity for over thirteen hundred employees.[20] Such benefits, as well as improvements to the facilities that had existed before 1949, came with the assistance of state investment in the shipyard and with substantial portions going to "non-production investment." In 1956, for example, 16 percent of state

---

[17] SMA, Series C1-2-2724.   [18] SMA, Series C1-2-2257.
[19] Jiangnan Shipyard Factory History Research Office, "Factory Chronology," 40, 44.
[20] Ibid., 42.

investment funds went to nonproduction items such as dormitories, hospitals, dining halls, and other collective welfare measures.[21]

Labor Allocation

Shanghai's largest and arguably most important industrial enterprise, despite its placement within a central government ministry, suffered from the same treatment in terms of national investment that other enterprises in the city did during the 1950s. This can be seen in the respective growth rates of the labor force and investment. The workforce at the Jiangnan Shipyard during the FFYP expanded from 3,385 in 1952 to 6,347 in 1957, an increase of 87.5 percent.[22] This growth exceeded the increase in capital construction investment, which rose 27.9 percent between 1952 and 1957.[23] In short, planning authorities in Beijing pursued a policy of increasing labor rather than capital at the Jiangnan Shipyard.

Included in this expansion of the workforce were squadrons of state-trained engineers and specialists to keep the extensive accounting records necessary for such a highly coordinated economy. In 1952, there had been 323 engineer-technicians (*gongcheng jishu renyuan*) and 385 managers (*guanli renyuan*) at the Jiangnan Shipyard, a ratio of roughly one technician and one manager for every ten production workers. By 1957 there were 1,492 engineer-technicians and 1,201 managers, an increase in the "supervision ratio" to one technician for every four production workers and one manager for every five.[24]

Many of the new entrants into the ranks of the shipyard's workforce were relatives of current employees, usually the sons and daughters of workers who had worked at the factory prior to 1949. A new apprentice program begun in December 1951 enrolled 162 children of Jiangnan Shipyard employees to study various technical shipbuilding skills.[25] In oral histories conducted in the early 1960s, veteran workers proudly noted how their children had followed in their footsteps and were now Jiangnan Shipyard employees. Bo Tingfu, a riveter, belonged to a family

---

[21] Jiangnan Shipyard Factory History Research Office, "Tongji ziliao" (Statistical Materials), mimeo, n.d., 208.

[22] Jiangnan Shipyard Factory History Research Office, "Renshi laodong guanli," 175.

[23] Ibid., 208. [24] Ibid., 175.

[25] Jiangnan Shipyard Factory History Research Office, "Factory Chronology," 39.

that had sent three generations of sons to work at the Jiangnan Shipyard.[26]

The Shanghai MPC and its Heavy Industry Work Department appears not to have encroached on labor allocation issues directly, though it did exercise authority over appointments of key personnel, such as the designation of a head engineer in the shipyard in 1954.[27] However, the conduct of political campaigns during this time clearly touched upon labor allocation issues within the enterprise. The political qualities of the Jiangnan Shipyard's workforce drew a great deal of attention from municipal CCP authorities.

Campaigns

The FFYP at the Jiangnan Shipyard took place in the context of heightened military tensions over Taiwan and other flash points in the Cold War. As orders for military vessels expanded, so too did the vigilance of CCP authorities concerned about sabotage and spying. (In fact, for over one year beginning in fall 1955 the shipyard took on the code name of "Factory 436" in official communications.)[28] In 1954 the party branch at the shipyard implemented the Shanghai MPC's call for a "cleaning of the ranks" of employees. Branch party committees in workshops educated workers about the need for secrecy, the importance of the enterprise for national defense, and their responsibility in maintaining national secrets. Unlike the Democratic Reform Campaign, which had open struggle sessions and confessions by those guilty, the Cleaning of the Ranks Campaign would have no such public confessions, the reason being the need "to guarantee a smooth transition to military production." The party first investigated what it called the "critical departments," then technicians, and finally the common departments and ordinary workers. An anonymous work section had thirty workers confess to political crimes, among them five who were classified as "principal counterrevolutionaries." Two of these were ordered to be arrested immediately. The party report also said that those who had a history of connections and who still maintained them with "spy organizations" and "imperialists" should be taken through legal channels or arrested, or sent for long-term reeducation through labor.[29]

[26] "Recollections of Jiangnan Shipyard Workers," Bo Tingfu.
[27] Jiangnan Shipyard Factory History Research Office, "Factory Chronology," 41.
[28] Ibid.   [29] SMA, Series A38-2-148.

This Cleaning of the Ranks Campaign was necessary according to party officials because some sixteen thousand workers had entered the shipyard in 1953, bypassing previous campaigns. Party officials found "materials" on 320 employees, about 52 percent of whom were production workers, 13 percent technicians, and 35 percent staff. Among the 320 employees, the party discovered 10 technicians who were "politically unreliable," and 147 from families belonging to or associated with "the enemy." Of these, thirty-one fell into the "five types" of counterrevolutionaries; forty-four had been Nationalist military officials. In addition to the 320 from whom the campaign had produced "materials," there were another 1,152 employees who confessed to "reactionary histories." Those with questionable pasts in the eyes of the CCP then totaled 1,472, or 23.4 percent of the workforce, which at that time numbered 6,300.[30]

Not long after the Cleaning of the Ranks came the New Products Campaign in late 1954 and 1955. This campaign gathered materials on a group of over one thousand technicians and skilled workers who were chosen to undergo training in new techniques of production under some forty Soviet advisers, most likely on machinery imported from the Soviet Union.[31] On the surface this was a simple matter of technical instruction, but the Jiangnan Shipyard's party committee remained concerned about the "purity" of those who would undergo training for these new production methods. "To protect the safety of the new products, the purity of the personnel must be ensured," a report said.[32] Again the party opted for a behind-closed-doors approach to political campaigns rather than open struggle sessions with confessions. An in-house investigation team under the leadership of the party committee researched the background of about one thousand employees for almost a year. Their results found that of 159 individuals at the post of work team leader or above, 120 had "historical problems" associated with membership in the Nationalist Party or its unions before 1949. Of seventy-three production workers listed in dossiers, only seven had been Communist Party members before 1949. How these individuals fared following these investigations is not elaborated in unclassified party reports, but because there was already a critical shortage of technicians and skilled personnel at the Jiangnan Shipyard, all but two were approved for participation in the New Products Campaign. Still, the party recommended that several hundred engi-

---

[30] Ibid.
[31] Jiangnan Shipyard Factory History Research Office, "Renshi laodong guanli," 168.
[32] SMA, Series A43-1-112.

neers, technicians, and administrative cadres who did have the requisite political backgrounds be transferred from outside factories and "mixed" with Jiangnan Shipyard cadres for the training program.[33]

The Cleaning of the Ranks and the New Products Campaigns combined production with political goals and targeted new members of the workforce who entered under labor allocation plans. These later "campaigns" also involved more secret investigation by specially appointed teams and less open confession and mass criticism than had been the case with the campaigns of the early 1950s. Perhaps it was not without coincidence that Zhu De, vice-chair of the Central Committee and veteran PLA general, visited the shipyard in January 1955 to "inspect party discipline work."[34] While enterprise party committees languished at other factories, the Jiangnan Shipyard's party committee enjoyed close ties with the Shanghai MPC and was carving out an important role for itself in supervising the workforce.

SHENXIN NUMBER SIX MILL

Like many other large privately owned enterprises during the early 1950s, the Shenxin Number Six Mill established an LCCC in 1950 to discuss labor-management issues. The mill's LCCC was not, however, free to make labor regulations as it wished. In late 1950, the Shenxin Number Six LCCC agreed to follow the minimum wage guidelines of the Shanghai Municipal Textile Industrial Federation (which had its own LCCC).[35] Later the mill's LCCC also set a standard workday of ten hours, with provisions for a 50 percent increase in wages during overtime hours.[36] The LCCC was charged with implementing the PRC Union Law and Labor Insurance Law in 1951.[37] Under orders from the Shanghai Municipal People's Government in 1954, the LCCC abolished the mill's practice of distributing a year-end bonus that amounted to two months' wages, known as "double salary." This "irrational" bonus practice was so labeled because all workers received it regardless of their performance or rank.[38] Yet despite this exercise of power over labor issues within the enterprise, the LCCC's powers quickly receded once the Shenxin Number Six Mill underwent state acquisition in the mid-1950s.

---

[33] Ibid.
[34] Jiangnan Shipyard Factory History Research Office, "Factory Chronology," 43.
[35] SMA, Series Q193-3-1032; SMA, Series Q193-3-566.
[36] SMA, Series Q193-3-506.   [37] SMA, Series Q193-3-566.   [38] Ibid.

Private industry nationwide had been placed under different forms of state control early in the 1950s, when unified sales and purchasing agreements drew enterprises into state commercial and distribution networks. But in the mid-1950s, the state rapidly nationalized industry by forcing owners to sell the vast majority of shares in their firms to the state. Following the socialist transformation of industry, textile bureau officials directed the mostly medium- and small-scale enterprises to establish wage scales of the kind already found in state-owned enterprises and to quickly increase productivity. Larger privately owned enterprises like the Shenxin Number Six Mill in Shanghai were placed under "joint" state-private ownership in 1954–5. The government's rationale in exerting control over the enterprises owned by the Rong family was that production costs at these and other privately owned mills remained far too high.

The Rongs were hardly in a position to oppose nationalization of their mills, and their remarks supporting it must be treated with skepticism, but Shenxin mill managers and the Rongs anticipated certain benefits from a transfer to joint ownership. The factory director of the Shenxin Number Six Mill, Qin Defang, was said to have welcomed joint ownership, out of sheer frustration with trying to manage an unruly, undisciplined workforce. "They won't obey us, but now there's someone to manage them," Qin remarked in reference to the new "boss" of the state. He, like others in the Shenxin group, argued that production costs were high and productivity low because workers couldn't be controlled.[39] Rong Yiren, head of the Shenxin General Corporation (who would become China's state vice president in the early 1990s), praised the upcoming socialist transformation of industry during meetings in the spring of 1954, saying it would help raise quality standards to those set by the state, increase output, and introduce the "democratization of management" in the mills.[40]

But not everyone appeared convinced of the benefits of joint ownership, particularly stockholders in the SGC and workers in the mills. During the same meeting, the labor union chair of the Shenxin Number Six Mill, Ni Zhirong, compared the socialist transformation of industry to "a streetlight illuminating the path that the nation should take," but he pointed out that from the expressions of several stockholders at the meeting, some had not yet been "enlightened."[41] Stockholders in the

---

[39] SMA, Series Q193-3-378.   [40] SMA, Series C1-2-1327.   [41] Ibid.

SGC were not the only ones suspicious of what would happen after the mills were nationalized. Workers, despite hours of meetings with supervisors and CCP cadres, harbored doubts about what life would be like under "joint" ownership with the state. Some felt that nationalization would bring an easier pace of work. "After joint ownership, we'll be able to work seven and a half hours [per day] and live comfortably like workers in state factories."[42] Other workers were more skeptical, and sensed that following the move to joint ownership, work would become more intense, with stricter labor discipline. Party reports do not make clear how these attitudes divided along department or gender lines, but older workers were said to fear being brought under joint ownership, because they doubted they could increase their productivity enough to maintain their income levels. Still others, the report said, suspected that state supervision would bring with it lower overall wages and an end to subsidies.[43]

In terms of its relations with the bureaucracy and party, the experience of the Shenxin Number Six Mill differed from that of the Jiangnan Shipyard in several respects. First, the mill's administrative responsibilities fell to the Textile Bureau of the Shanghai Municipal People's Government, not to a Beijing ministry as was the case with the Jiangnan Shipyard. Second, while the Shanghai MPC appears not to have become as directly involved in wage and other labor issues as it did at the Jiangnan Shipyard, the branch party committee within the Shenxin Number Six Mill quickly asserted powers over administration and the politically vulnerable set of managers retained from the Shenxin Corporation. Thus Qin Defang, who remained the mill's director after its conversion to state property, came under harsh criticism from the Textile Bureau one month following the handover because he had failed to fulfill production quotas. "They're just ruthless, they don't save any face," Qin said of bureau officials following the meeting.[44] More serious was the assertion of controls over administrative issues by the mill's party committee.

Campaigns

The transformation to public ownership and the new presence of party operatives placed unprecedented political pressure on managers. The mill's party committee supervised day-to-day operations and its treatment of managers and staff foreshadowed what would follow elsewhere

[42] SMA, Series Q193-3-378. [43] Ibid. [44] Ibid.

in Chinese factories after party committees took over factory management in the late 1950s. Well before the orders came from the upper
reaches of the party hierarchy to "send down" technicians, staff, and
directors to the factory floors in 1957–8, the branch party committee at
the Shenxin Number Six Mill was directing a "send down" campaign of
its own.

The movement of office staff down to production lines, where they
could observe operations and also interact with workers, proved a
popular measure among workers. For party authorities, this was part of
the "thought transformation" (*sixiang gaizao*) of capitalists, but it also
was felt to be useful for production. Workers welcomed seeing their
office-bound superiors engaging in production. Such occasions, the
factory party committee noted, helped improve management's understanding of production issues, but it also achieved the political effect of
having them "worship workers as masters."[45] Guo Fengxian, a vice-
director of the mill, learned on one such visit that several women who
worked on production lines had to walk over three miles to get to the
mill each day. On several occasions, factory director Qin Defang and
others received large character posters that workers had penned. The
most welcome sight on the factory floor was the arrival of Long Weiyang,
a vice-director and dyeing specialist who had been at the mill for thirty
years and had acquired a reputation for his arrogance. Long, known as
the "Old Fox," had a network of skilled recruits among the employees,
and most workers were said to have been gripped with fear whenever
they encountered him. But after the transition to joint ownership, party
cadres frequently brought Long down to the shop floor to participate in
production. "I haven't engaged in production for over ten years. I feel
backward and I should participate," Long conceded. In addition to top
management from the "capitalist side," state and party cadres who had
in the past remained in their offices all day were reported to be working
closely with the "masses" on the shop floor.[46]

Wages

The long-awaited wage reform at Shenxin Number Six took place in
July 1955.[47] The average wage for workers at the mill was 74 yuan a

---

[45] Ibid.   [46] Ibid.

[47] Shanghai Number Thirty-One Mill, Factory Archives, Labor and Wage Department,
Series 56.

month following wage reform.[48] This was, on paper, an increase of 4 percent in the average wage of production workers. But apparently this wage reform left many wage issues unresolved, and it was not until November 1956 that the mill had brought its wage system under state guidelines. During the process of wage reform in 1956 – actually a wage adjustment based on the initial wage reform in 1955 – the issue of income inequality emerged as the most contentious of all. While all workers wanted the higher pay that they knew their counterparts in neighboring state-owned cotton mills enjoyed, Shenxin Number Six production workers felt that the mill's staff were vastly overpaid for doing very little. Party committee members and the Labor and Wage Department cadres at the mill spent hours in meetings trying to persuade representatives from workshops and production departments that staff and technicians needed higher pay. The party's argument was that lowering staff incomes too drastically would also lower their initiative and motivation, in turn affecting production and the fulfillment of national plans. These party and personnel department cadres (who may in fact have suffered a decline in income if the production workers had their way) turned to the example of state-owned mills to point out how sharp reductions in high-income earners caused them to lose their motivation. Despite these arguments, Shenxin Number Six production workers responded with a proposal to further reduce the wages of staff and to redistribute the surplus among themselves. The mill's party committee labeled this as "egalitarian thought," though several party cadres sided with these demands to lower staff pay.[49]

Party reports from the 1950s at the Shenxin Number Six Mill complained that these group meetings allowed workers to introduce to the wage adjustment process nonskill criteria such as a worker's tenure, family conditions, attitude, and "work style." Such meetings also led to bickering and what party cadres felt were highly arbitrary criteria in setting wages. Too often Shenxin Number Six workers employed the "five irrelevants" (*wu buguan*): experience (years worked), tenure (years at the mill), labor attitude, "backward thought," and family circumstances. It was also common for workers in these sessions to attempt to

---

[48] *Rongjia xitong qiye shiliao* (Rong Family Group Enterprise Historical Materials) vol. 7, no. 2 (June 1957): 215, in CBHRC, Series R-03-4.

[49] Shanghai Number Thirty-One Mill, Factory Archives, Labor and Wage Department, Series 57.

deny wage increases to a colleague they considered to be too arrogant or "conservative."[50]

To all involved, holding meetings of work groups to determine the wages of colleagues was a novel practice. Party officials at the mill were aware that unlike the political campaigns that had taken place there before, in which face-to-face meetings were convened over sensitive and personal issues, the wage reform "campaign" involved issues of money as well as status or class. As one cadre put it,

> Wage reform concerns everyone's personal interests. The communication of principles and policy is not like the communication in other political campaigns in the past. It not only has to be reasonably stated, but also must be connected with reality, so that the masses understand that the party's guiding principles and policies are set by considering the comprehensive and long-term as well as the individual and present interests of the working class.[51]

Workers felt that the method of group meetings to set wages was an improvement over the past, when the single word of the boss decided one's wages. But others also felt that engaging in such a drawn-out mutual consultation over issues of pay was too time consuming and complicated.[52]

Over time, this insistence by the party that group meetings be used to determine wages, subject to constraints of state policy and the approval of workshop directors, evolved into a situation in which wage raises were distributed almost exclusively on the basis of seniority. Personnel officials at the Shenxin Number Six Mill's successor, the Shanghai Number Thirty-One Mill, noted in interviews in 1995 that work experience and job tenure (*gongling*) served as the primary criterion when wages were adjusted in these small group settings. As one official explained, "This was done because it was felt that someone with more seniority, who had worked in the mill before liberation, for example, had contributed more to the nation." This practice of placing seniority *and* politics as the foremost standard for wage adjustments eventually led to a situation in which younger employees who might have attained an equal level of technical

---

[50] Shanghai Number Thirty-One Mill, Factory Archives, Labor and Wage Department, Series 56.

[51] Shanghai Number Thirty-One Mill, Factory Archives, Labor and Wage Department, Series 57.

[52] Ibid.

skills would earn far less than a worker who had entered the factory workforce in earlier years.[53] While seniority wages were found in some factories in China during the pre-1949 period, it was during the transition to socialist planning, with its centrally administered wage system based on skill, that seniority wages became an institutional feature of the Chinese industrial workplace. The importance of seniority as a factor in receiving wage adjustments had its roots in factories such as the Shenxin Number Six Mill, where workshop leaders and factory officials rewarded workers who had "contributed to the nation" by enduring the sufferings of pre-1949 factory work.

Labor Allocation

As was the case with national wage controls, state control of labor allocation in the 1950s contributed to substantial productivity gains. At the Shenxin Number Six Mill, Shanghai party officials in 1951 blamed management for "chaotically" hiring too many temporaries, who worked for well over the six months allowed under regulations.[54] The labor department of the Shanghai Municipal People's Government exercised control over the mill's labor recruitment by 1953, when officials began dispatching college graduates to work at the Shenxin Number Six Mill's personnel department. Partial employment records show that all hires from mid-1953 to early 1955 were from regional and local labor departments.[55] Between 1950 and 1955, the number of workers at the mill rose from 2,877 to 3,610.[56] Labor productivity also rose dramatically, doubling between 1950 and 1954 at the Shenxin Number Six Mill and at the Shenxin Number Nine Mill. The other three Shenxin mills in Shanghai saw 60 to 70 percent increases in productivity during the same time.[57]

Enterprise Welfare

Privately owned textile mills did not keep pace with the impressive expansion of welfare provision in state enterprises. Managers at the

---

[53] Author's interview, Factory Director's Office and Personnel Department, Shanghai Number Thirty-One Mill, Jan. 14, 1995.

[54] SMA, Series Q193-3-566.

[55] SMA, Series Q193-3-506. Only ten of the 103 workers assigned to work at the mill were women.

[56] *Rongjia xitong qiye shiliao* 7, no. 2 (June 1957): 191–4, in CBHRC, Series R-03-4.

[57] Ibid., 190.

Shenxin Number Six Mill established a school for employees and expanded a child care center and a cafeteria, but major improvements to employee welfare provision were delayed until after the mill was converted to formal state ownership.[58] In 1958 the mill was combined with two adjoining mills to become the Yangshupu Cotton Spinning and Weaving Mill. (Still later, in 1966, it would be renamed the Shanghai Number Thirty-One Cotton Spinning and Weaving Mill.) Following this merger, factory officials built two new dining halls with a full-time staff of forty cooks and seating capacities of five hundred in each hall. Management also expanded the existing living quarters for employees.[59] Spending on medical costs associated with labor insurance, as a percentage of the wage bill, rose from 7 percent in 1951 to over 26 percent by 1958.[60]

The FFYP imposed new institutional arrangements for the hiring, pay, and organization of the workforce, institutions that spread quickly to large enterprises in Shanghai such as the Jiangnan Shipyard and the Shenxin Number Six Mill. More striking from the observation of these two cases is the influence, on labor issues at least, of the local party committee or the enterprise party committee in an era usually associated with overcentralization and overconcentration of authority in industrial ministries. The Shanghai MPC developed specialized departments to become involved in the minutiae of wage reform at the Jiangnan Shipyard, and local party officials closely monitored the workforce through campaigns and other measures. At the Shenxin Number Six Mill, the enterprise party committee appears to have gained considerable power over management following state takeover of the mill, a development not found in most state enterprises at this time. In both enterprises, with workforces made up largely of older employees with pre-1949 experience, workers neither enthusiastically endorsed nor passively accepted the new regime of production that came with command economics. Unintended consequences arose in the Jiangnan Shipyard as older and younger workers divided over the issue of incentive pay. In the Shenxin Number Six Mill, seniority wages prevailed as a way of resolving disputes over skill-based pay. In both enterprises, more senior workers benefited from political status even though they did not necessarily have the skills

---

[58] SMA, Series Q193-3-364.
[59] Shanghai Number Thirty-One Mill Factory Director's Office, "Number Thirty-One Mill History," mimeo, n.d.
[60] Ibid.

to match their younger counterparts who adapted more flexibly to the new rules and in some cases to newer machinery. Farther south in the less industrially developed city of Guangzhou, a similar process of "localization" of enterprise management was under way, but the content of the local party committee's intervention took a clearly different pattern.

HUANGPU NAVAL SHIPYARD

During the 1950s the Huangpu Naval Shipyard conducted repairs on naval vessels, making it the primary base for warship repair in the strategically important South China region.[61] The sensitivity of the work involved at the shipyard did not seem to prevent Zhang Yu, who had been the shipyard's director under the Nationalist government, from retaining his post throughout the 1950s. Zhang had fortuitously converted to the Communist Party in Hong Kong in 1949. Officials in the South China Military Region returned him to his post in 1950. Unlike the Jiangnan Shipyard in Shanghai, which was turned over to the First Machinery Ministry in late 1952, the Huangpu Shipyard remained under the naval department of the South China Military Region until 1960. This administrative relationship, plus the fact that the shipyard engaged primarily in repair work, gave shipyard officials more flexibility than if they had been placed under the plans and budgets of a central government industrial ministry. Zhang Yu ran the shipyard through seven sections directly under his office, including a Labor and Personnel Section that was in charge of labor insurance, wages, and welfare measures.[62] The number of employees had risen to a total of 722 by 1953 (up from 163 in 1950). Of this 1953 total, 113 were classified as managers, resulting in a ratio of 5.4 production workers for each manager. This figure is comparable to the worker-manager ratio that the Jiangnan Shipyard would achieve by the end of the FFYP. Employment at the Huangpu Shipyard rose during the 1950s to a total of 1,110 in 1956 (though precise figures breaking down workers and managers are not available for that year), and 1,678 by 1959, the only year for which precise employment data are available. The latter year is not exactly a representative one because it was at the peak of the high-employment years of the Great Leap Forward. Still, it is safe to surmise that by 1957 employment remained above 1,000, or at least 39 percent above 1953 levels. As the workforce expanded, pressure to reform wage and welfare measures intensified.

[61] Tang, *Guangzhou gongye sishinian*, 151–2.   [62] GMA, Series 8-8.

Wages

Wages were a central source of dissatisfaction among Huangpu Shipyard workers in the 1950s. The Guangzhou MPC criticized the "unreasonable" wage system that prevailed during the 1940s for its "serious egalitarianism."[63] In the days following the CCP takeover, employees supposedly requested lower wages "to take care of the state's financial difficulties after liberation." Director Zhang "responded to the call of upper levels" to lower the wage bill. But wages remained at this discounted level for two years. They were based on the skill standards from before 1949, in which employees were ranked by only four or five grades, with each corresponding to a basic salary linked to the price of rice.

As had been the case at the Jiangnan Shipyard, factory officials at the Huangpu Shipyard reformed the pre-1949 wage system with adverse consequences. The "egalitarianism" that followed during the 1949 to 1952 transition period was manifested in numerous wage levels with very little difference between them. There were now nineteen wage grades, but the difference in earnings between one level and the next was equal to the price of a pack of cigarettes – hardly enough to spur a worker into investing in the time to learn the skills that would bring promotion to the next wage level.[64] The average wage during this time had risen considerably over the 1940s, when the range between skilled and unskilled workers had been equivalent to a ratio of eleven to five *jin* of rice per day. By the early 1950s, before the shipyard underwent national wage reform in late 1952, the average wage span had doubled for the skilled, from 11 to 22.4 *jin* of rice per day, and more than tripled for the unskilled, from five to eighteen *jin* per day. Thus, the average wage differential between unskilled and skilled under these "egalitarian" conditions had fallen from the pre-1949 ratio of 2.2 to 1 down to the early 1950s range of 1.24 to 1.[65] Despite generally higher wages when compared to the pre-1949 period, without wage reform, factory officials reported, "not only would there be no way to raise production, but the dissatisfaction among workers would have the opposite effect of lowering production and causing them to leave the factory (*tiaochang*)."[66]

---

[63] GMA, Series 8-14. [64] Ibid.

[65] Calculations for the 1940s based on author's interview, Huangpu Shipyard officials, May 3, 1995; author's correspondence with Huangpu Shipyard official, May 16, 1995. For the pre-1952 period, calculations based on figures in GMA, Series 8-14.

[66] GMA, Series 8-14.

Wage reform at the shipyard began in September 1952, after all other state enterprises in Guangzhou had already completed revisions to the wage structure. While wage reform at the Huangpu Shipyard stalled, workers who had learned of the generally higher rates of pay being distributed through wage reform began demanding a hasty wage reform from factory administrators. Because the Huangpu Shipyard remained under military administration, shipyard officials were confused about which civilian ministry's skill standards to deploy in implementing the eight-grade wage system. First, officials copied the skill standards of the Jiangnan Shipyard, but because the Huangpu Shipyard had a far lower level of capital and technology, officials had to revise the skill standards to better reflect actual conditions. The Huangpu Shipyard ultimately adopted the standards of the Electric Power Bureau rather than those of the First Machinery Ministry, because the latter had more stringent standards that would make it difficult for workers to attain higher levels of income. Eventually 154 of 187 (83 percent) employees received wage increases, amounting to a 15 percent increase in the overall wage bill. The thirty-one employees whose wages were lowered received "retained wages," supplemental payments to make up for the difference between their old rates and the new, lower levels of income.[67] For those receiving such subsidies, wage reform amounted to no change in earnings at all, except that their official wage rate had been lowered.

When management made the grade settings public, many workers pointed out that some of their colleagues who had been assigned relatively high wage grades fell far short of the skill standards required for their grade number. Younger workers were especially dissatisfied with their relatively lower grade settings. One of them expressed surprise that his membership in the Communist Youth League was of no help when it came to his wage grade setting. "It didn't matter how beautifully someone had spoken out during study sessions," a party report noted, "Once the rankings were posted, everyone immediately went to see what their own grade was. Some were happy, others issued complaints."[68]

According to central plans, overall wage levels were supposed to be about 15 to 20 percent higher in Shanghai than in Guangzhou, but the wage spread in heavy industry was to be slightly greater in Guangzhou. For Shanghai heavy industry, for example, the official wage gap between grade 8 and grade 1 workers was set at 2.75 to 1, and for South China it was 2.82 to 1.[69] As noted previously, wage reform at the Jiangnan

[67] Ibid.   [68] Ibid.   [69] SMA, Series A36-2-072.

Shipyard in 1953–4 resulted in some 90 percent of workers receiving wage grades between levels 2 and 6, where there was a narrower differential of 1.77 to 1. Detailed wage distributions from the Huangpu Shipyard are not available, but given its slight wage differential of 1.24 to 1 in the early 1950s, it is unlikely that wage reform would have brought its wage system up to the standards of industrial ministries. Reports on wage reform at the shipyard even stated that the skilled workers were unwilling to receive grade 7 or grade 8 wages because they "feared the responsibility" that would have placed them in charge of a workshop, work section, or production team. Younger workers, who received grades 3 and 4, expressed dissatisfaction and demanded higher wage settings.[70] Local party officials in Guangzhou in the early 1950s had a different explanation for why wage reform went so poorly at the Huangpu Shipyard in 1952. They blamed the party committee at the shipyard for doing poor "ideological work" among employees, because so many workers expressed dissatisfaction with the result of their wage grade setting.

With wage reform at the Huangpu Shipyard, the party had clearly come up against something that could not be framed as a "campaign." As the shipyard's party committee noted, "This campaign was not like others. There was no mobilization of the masses beforehand . . . this was a test of whether individual interest and the interest of the party could be unified. For example, if contradictions arose, could principles be preserved, could the interests of the party be put first?"[71] CCP officials throughout China were learning that whether they mobilized the masses or not, wage planning was a highly contentious issue.

Enterprise Welfare

The Huangpu Shipyard in Guangzhou had extended only marginal benefits to workers and staff prior to 1949. Most workers at the Huangpu Shipyard viewed their employment as a temporary endeavor, and they simply looked elsewhere for work when economic conditions prevented the shipyard from meeting its payroll. The goal for shipyard managers in the 1950s was to curb turnover by introducing for the first time in the factory's history the level of welfare provisions that had come to be the norm in many of China's largest enterprises by the mid-1950s. Huangpu

---

[70] GMA, Series 8-14.   [71] Ibid.

Shipyard workers in the early 1950s still expressed dissatisfaction with living conditions there, because the remote location, an hour's ferry ride from Guangzhou, limited their off-work activities. They referred to the island where they lived and worked as "Siberia." (In reference to nineteenth-century Tsarist prison camps, a CCP report hastily clarified.) Military installations covered most of the island, and only two small villages lay near the shipyard. Young workers voiced numerous complaints about the isolation during meetings.[72] Shipyard Director Zhang oversaw the construction of a new workers' dormitory that housed over six hundred, plus a cadres' dorm that held twenty-four families. Separate family quarters were established with a living capacity of 300, along with a dining hall that could seat 500. Management also built a hospital, swimming pool, elementary school, and a credit cooperative at this time.[73]

Campaigns

Campaigns during the 1950s at the Huangpu Shipyard centered on increasing productivity and efficiency rather than investigating unsavory individuals in the ranks of the workforce, as was the case in the Jiangnan Shipyard in Shanghai. The apparently misnamed Anti-Bureaucratism Campaign (*fan guanliao zhuyi yundong*) at the Huangpu Shipyard in 1953 illustrates this emphasis on productivity over politics during the FFYP. The campaign's goal, despite its title, was to establish more rules and procedures to improve the notably slack labor discipline at the Huangpu Shipyard. The shipyard's Personnel Section in fact was set up in late 1952 in conjunction with the Anti-Bureaucratism Campaign. The Personnel Section established a set of inducements and punishments to increase productivity and reduce absenteeism. The campaign also introduced reforms in production, such as an unspecified "work card" system, as well as bonuses based on output. These measures reportedly improved the problem of workers arriving late and quitting early, refusing to obey orders, and taking leaves of absence without permission. The work site with the worst discipline, the carpentry workshop, allegedly had the best discipline after the campaign.[74]

---

[72] GMA, Series 8-8.
[73] Author's correspondence with Huangpu Shipyard official, May 16, 1995; GMA, Series 8-8.
[74] GMA, Series 8-11.

If Huangpu Shipyard officials had relatively less stringent supervision and controls than their counterparts elsewhere who managed under central government ministries, who was responsible for conducting the Anti-Bureaucratism Campaign and others like it during the 1950s? Here it turns out that the Guangzhou MPC played an important role. The MPC's Industrial Work Department placed much emphasis on improving productivity during the FFYP. During the Anti-Bureaucratism Campaign at the Huangpu Shipyard, the Industrial Work Department showered criticism on managers. Why hadn't shipyard officials taken greater initiative to remedy disciplinary and associated problems caused by the wage reform of 1952? asked the Industrial Work Department. Why had managers simply relied on a work team from the Industrial Work Department to make the rules and develop wage standards? Huangpu Shipyard officials responded to such criticism frankly and tellingly: "We lack experience, educational materials, and we very much need the top levels of the party to regularly give us advice."[75]

As in Shanghai, it appeared that wages were too sensitive of a problem, or perhaps too irresistible as a political issue, for local party officials not to intervene. Elsewhere in Guangzhou, the MPC's Industrial Work Department led several other mobilization efforts to standardize work procedures and motivate the labor force to sacrifice high wages for the good of the nation. This pattern varied distinctly from that of Shanghai, where the local Industrial Work Department engaged in a more politicized and mobilizational effort to investigate and control the workforce. In Guangzhou, the MPC's Industrial Work Department played a more administrative, apolitical role in simply bringing small enterprises like the Huangpu Naval Shipyard up to minimal compliance with the bureaucratic mandates of the command economy. Far from mobilizing workers to engage in wage reform, the local Industrial Work Department was called in to assist insecure managers at the shipyard. The Guangzhou MPC also enjoyed close ties with a handful of large factories in Guangzhou. By the mid-1950s the MPC's Industrial Work Department was directly administering ten of the city's largest factories, among them the Guangdong Textile Mill.[76]

---

[75] Ibid.

[76] The Guangzhou archival sources fail to reveal precisely where profits from these enterprises went, though it would not be astonishing if their relationship with the

GUANGDONG TEXTILE MILL

Unlike the Huangpu Shipyard and many other factories in China during the early 1950s, employment at the Guangdong Textile Mill actually declined from a high of 970 employees in 1950 to 895 in 1953. While this decrease resulted in a worker-management ratio of about seven workers per manager, only 76 percent of the workforce was involved in direct production, with a large portion of the remainder occupying positions such as guards, medical staff, and other service occupations at various welfare facilities at the mill.[77] In 1950 the mill had adopted seven sections, including a Labor and Wage Section and a Personnel Section with six staff. One of the problems noted in a 1953 report was that these and other sections had little conception of how to carry out their functions because the mill's director stressed fulfillment of annual finance and production quotas, without putting much thought into maintaining labor and wage ceilings.[78]

Administratively, the Guangdong Textile Mill had a rather complicated set of relationships with the bureaucracy and the local party committee. While the MPC's Industrial Work Department retained control over this and nine other key enterprises in the city, the Textile Bureau of the Municipal People's Government of Guangzhou had obvious claims to the city's largest and oldest textile mill. It was the MPC's Industrial Work Department that remained the dominant influence over labor and production issues at the mill, especially after 1956 when the Guangdong Textile Mill absorbed the Guangzhou Number Two Mill as part of the socialist transformation of industry. The latter enterprise had in fact been owned by the Rong family of Shanghai, who had opened the mill in Guangzhou in the late 1940s. The merger of the two mills resulted in an employment level of roughly two thousand six hundred by 1957.[79] While the city's Textile Bureau kept close records on production and employment at the postmerger mill, it was the Guangzhou MPC's Industrial Work Department that supervised many of the administrative functions at the mill. The local party's assertion of administrative controls over the mill meant that officials would address both production and political concerns.

Municipal Party Committee resulted in at least some financial flows directly to that organization.
[77] GMA, Series 8-8.   [78] GMA, Series 8-8, Series 8-28.   [79] GMA, Series 227-24.

Wages

The Guangdong Textile Mill underwent its first wage reform in April 1951. The new wage structure was supposedly developed by a study group of representatives from the mill's party committee, the Communist Youth League, the enterprise union, and administrative cadres, all of whom came to a collective decision about how pay rates would be set and for whom. Employees in each department received wage increases of 8.5 to 18 percent.[80] The wage reform took place following the Three Antis Campaign at the mill, after relations between workers and the party were supposedly "more intimate." A party report quoted one worker saying, "I had often heard before that the Communist Party was for the interests of the workers, but I had some doubt in my mind and I never believed it. Now, seeing this wage reform . . . I genuinely believe that the party is the political party of the working class." The popularity of the "reform," it turns out, was also because of a generous "grandfather" policy that allowed those whose wages were cut to receive "retained wages" or subsidies that supplemented the difference between their new wage level and the higher amount they had earned before.[81] Most employees remained on piece rates, which had been reformed by establishing new standards.

The overall result of wage reform at the Guangdong Textile Mill, in terms of productivity, was a success. Between 1950 and 1953 different departments raised productivity between 100 and 360 percent, whereas average wages at the mill rose at a far more modest rate of 32 percent between 1949 and 1953.[82] Yet the draconian wage measures soon created problems. Average wages at the mill, having risen since 1950, leveled off by 1953–4, and because of cotton shortages and production cutbacks in 1955, started to fall. After a 21 percent climb in wages between 1950 and 1952, the cancellation of the bonus for consistent attendance in 1954 led to further declines, so that wages in 1955 stood at just 10 percent above 1950 levels.[83]

By late 1955, MPC officials faulted managers at the Guangdong Textile Mill for keeping far too tight a rein on the wage bill, so much so that they declined to give raises to employees who had fulfilled the skill standards necessary for promotion to the next wage level. Probably to

---

[80] GMA, Series 8-14.   [81] Ibid.

[82] GMA, Series 8-8. If average wages in 1949 are set at 100, then the rise in the average wage level in subsequent years was as follows: 1950 = 109; 1951 = 118; 1952 = 129; 1953 = 132.

[83] GMA, Series 92-478.

prevent complaints and "stirring up the wage problem" (*nao gongzi wenti*), management did not even make public what the skill standards were. Workers who had mastered a particular skill thus never knew what wage grade they were entitled to. The wage squeeze also applied to the majority of the workforce who earned some form of piece-rate wages. Factory officials set high wage quotas and did not make adjustments in rates when, for example, spinning department employees had to produce finer grades of yarn that required more time. Income for workers in one department fell from 63 to 52 yuan a month for this reason in late 1954, and when workers took their complaints to management, cadres chided them for being "economistic." The spinning department employees then reportedly returned to their dormitories in tears, and production declined rapidly thereafter.[84] Furthermore, the unsteady provision of raw materials meant that production often had to cease, which punished workers on piece rates through no fault of their own. Workers told union officials, "We don't fear a hike in the quotas. We most fear that the mill won't be open."[85] The Guangzhou Municipal Labor Union, which authored the report, argued that the mill's wage stance was "in violation of the wage policy of the state."[86]

Factory officials at the mill also lowered the pay of the more costly skilled workers and caused what the union described as "divisions among the work force." These "egalitarian errors" had been committed in the past, and in some cases there was still "severe egalitarianism" across jobs. This compression of wages was another attempt by management at the mill to deal with the problem of surpassing the enterprise wage bill. Employees who had obtained a skill were often stuck with a wage level far below what they were entitled to under the state wage determination guidelines. Skilled electricians and machine maintenance workers labored at apprentice wages, despite having long ago passed through the apprentice program. An electrician at the Guangzhou Electric Power Plant who was transferred to the Guangdong Textile Mill was relegated to a minor post so that management would not have to pay him at the maximum grade 8 level.[87]

Labor Allocation

The Guangdong Textile Mill's ties with the MPC's Industrial Work Department appear to have served it well in a 1954 dispute that arose

[84] Ibid.   [85] GMA, Series 92-482.   [86] GMA, Series 92-478.   [87] Ibid.

when the mill's managers refused to take on thirty apprentices sent by the Municipal Labor Bureau, on grounds that their education was insufficient for employment at the mill. The mill's management took the case to the Industrial Work Department, requesting not only to turn down the apprentices but also to hire family members of current mill employees. The views of the Labor Bureau prevailed, however, and its officials noted that allowing the mill to pick and choose among the workers allocated to the enterprise would set a bad precedent and undermine state efforts to control the distribution of new employees to private and jointly owned enterprises in the city.[88] Nonetheless, mill managers succeeded in obtaining jobs for family members of employees, as the Guangzhou Labor Bureau would point out in 1954. Bureau officials said that mill management was hiring relatives of not just any employee but apparently exclusively of party members. One mill worker had complained to the bureau, "This textile mill takes special care of party members' families."[89]

Enterprise Welfare

Being placed under the supervision of the Guangzhou MPC's Industrial Work Department also had positive results in terms of welfare provision, which expanded rapidly during the 1950s. The ten enterprises under Industrial Work Department auspices had all established comprehensive labor insurance, medical clinics, and nurseries by the mid-1950s. Eight factories offered "wellness cafeterias" (*baojian shitang*) and four provided living quarters for workers and their families. All of these factories had Workers' Recreation Clubs, which oversaw factory athletic teams and bands, along with dance, drama, and choral groups, including a Guangdong opera troupe. Labor insurance outlays were estimated at about 20 percent of the average wage of an employee. Among this elite group of enterprises, the Guangdong Textile Mill ranked at the top by several measures. The Guangdong Textile Mill offered employees generous housing by Guangzhou standards.[90] The Industrial Work Department noted that other welfare provisions at the mill were unsurpassed by any other enterprise in the city. More than nine hundred employees enjoyed the city's largest child-care center, as well as the best medical facilities, with both Chinese and Western clinics available. Union officials reported that the existence of clinics and greater attention to women's

---

[88] GMA, Series 8-28.   [89] Ibid.   [90] GMA, Series 92-192.

health issues had "gradually abolished the feudalistic thought of women workers who wouldn't notify anyone if they had gynecological illnesses (*fuke bing*)." Over 72 percent of women workers in the mill were said to "suffer from various degrees of gynecological illnesses," which union officials had sought to remedy with education and the establishment of a "menstrual cycle registration card system."[91] A Guangzhou's Textile Bureau report noted that in 1957, expenditures for measures related to workers' livelihood and collective welfare had exceeded planned allocations by over 100 percent.[92]

Campaigns and Labor Competitions

At the behest of Industrial Work Department officials, the mill's party branch and factory managers launched a Campaign to Increase Production and Economize in late 1953. The party committee engaged in "persuasive work" in workshops and during union meetings to improve the tepid morale of the workforce. As part of a mobilization and propaganda effort, party officials deployed radio broadcasts, large character posters, blackboard reports, "achievement charts," "honor rolls," "ground slogans" (chalk characters written on the surface of shop floors), and Cantonese songs, all to inspire workers to produce beyond quotas and to show them how the fulfillment of the factory's plan was critical to the national plan, which in turn affected their own well-being.[93]

The party branch at the mill proudly reported a positive change in the attitude and morale of employees, but the broader evidence suggested otherwise. One maintenance worker, who unfailingly took his extended cigarette break after making each repair to a piece of machinery and whose workday lasted only four hours, reportedly had given up smoking and was "playing a leading role in his production team as a result of the campaign." But the mill's workers were well aware that the campaign was an effort to intensify work without extra pay. Part of the campaign involved giving out "Red Flags," a nonmonetary reward for the hardest-working individuals and production teams. Workers responded to this form of incentive with predictable apathy and suspicion. "A Red Flag is nothing special," one production worker remarked. "With money you can at least buy something," she reasoned, "A Red Flag isn't as good as having pretty clothes for myself." Both old and young workers were reported to manifest similar forms of "economistic thought." Some

[91] GMA, Series 92-478.   [92] GMA, Series 227-36.   [93] GMA, Series 8-10.

wanted Red Flags so that they could be used to justify wage increases in the future. Others told their production teams that they should earn them to prevent "losing face." Some cadres were also worried about winning Red Flags because they feared that others would accuse them of "trophyism" (*jinbiao zhuyi*), or striving for personal achievement. Others complained about the poor provision of materials and of equipment problems. They noted that no amount of labor competition could solve technical problems.[94]

The failure of the campaign to accomplish either its production or ideological goals is reflected in moderate productivity increases in 1953 and 1954. In 1954, wages grew faster than the value of output.[95] A bonus for consistent attendance, despite making up only 6 percent of wages, was still a critical supplement to workers' incomes, and some came to work sick rather than pass up the bonus. The year-end "double salary" bonus was abolished at the Guangdong Textile Mill and other state factories at the end of 1953, but workers still received a bonus of one-month's wages at the end of the year. They also continued to express dissatisfaction with the state of wages at the mill.[96]

COMMAND ECONOMICS, LOCAL CONTROLS

In all four enterprise cases discussed in this chapter, the imposition of new labor management institutions such as state job assignments and state wage determination generated patterns of conflict within enterprises. In Shanghai, older and younger workers divided over the issue of incentive pay, whereas in Guangzhou the resistance to the new wage regime appeared to have been more uniformly directed against managers and administrators. While municipal party committees in both cities asserted control over aspects of enterprise administration, specialized industrial work departments became directly involved in wage reform and campaigns. In Guangzhou as well as Shanghai, state enterprises acquired two sets of supervisors: those from the central government ministries and those from the MPC's Industrial Work Department. The historically wide variation in industrial development and labor movement strength in the two cities probably best explains the variation in how the local party's Industrial Work Department operated in the two cities. In Guangzhou, with its relatively underdeveloped industrial base

[94] Ibid.   [95] GMA, Series 8-28.   [96] Ibid.

and smaller concentration of industrial workers, the role of the local party committee was to push managers and workers to adopt the formal labor management institutions of the command economy. Predictably, party-led campaigns turned out to be drives to establish rules and incentives to increase production. In Shanghai, by contrast, the local party committee and its branches within enterprises took on far more ideological and politicized roles in investigating the actions of employees and staff, especially in recently nationalized enterprises and in sensitive sectors such as shipbuilding.

Party committees, at the factory level or the municipal level, had always exerted a greater degree of control over administrative matters in the regions of East and South China than in Northeast China, where the Soviet model of one-man management had a stronger influence.[97] The enterprise cases in this chapter confirm that observation, but they also allow us to understand more clearly the consensus among workers and managers to resist the mandates of the Soviet model. By 1956 the CCP leadership explicitly rejected the Soviet model of shop floor organization in favor of a less technical, more mobilizational approach to labor management. This policy shift would dramatically enhance the power of enterprise party committees at the expense of administrative personnel, with lasting consequences for labor management institutions.

[97] You, *China's Enterprise Reform*, 35.

7

The Rise of
"Party Committee Factories"

> *Why is it that many industrial enterprises have not been able*
> *to break away from old bonds in the systems and methods of*
> *management?*[1]
>
> editorial, Renmin Ribao (People's Daily), 1965.

China's transition to a command economy in the 1950s created administrative relationships that in effect pulled state industrial enterprises in two directions. Centralized, "vertical" relations emerged as enterprise managers received investment and inputs from, and submitted profits to, central government ministries and commissions in the State Council. At the same time, localized or horizontal relations also developed as municipal and provincial committees of the CCP claimed administrative authority over enterprises within their territorial "jurisdictions." While local party committees had no legal claim to do so, they frequently usurped managerial prerogatives over wages, bonuses, and other labor management issues. These competing central and local claims on enterprise labor management generated growing tensions over the distribution of jobs, wages, and enterprise welfare benefits. Complicating matters, for central government agencies at least, was the fact that its personnel and departments oversaw by 1957 a total of 58,000 state-owned enterprises and 112,000 jointly owned enterprises, representing an increase of 200 percent from 1955.[2] As the number of industrial enterprises and the administrative burdens to manage them increased, pressure mounted for local authorities to assert greater control over local industry.

---

[1] Quoted from *Survey of China Mainland Press*, no. 3555. The original appeared in *Renmin Ribao* (People's Daily), September 24, 1965.

[2] Bachman, *Bureaucracy, Economy, and Leadership*, 21–2.

The ambiguous lines of authority between the central government departments and local party committees shifted rather suddenly, and decisively, in favor of the latter by late 1957. The Central Committee of the CCP issued a sweeping directive that turned administrative authority over to local governments, which in effect gave new powers to local party committees. With national controls over capital investment and labor supply essentially suspended in 1958 at the onset of the Great Leap Forward (GLF), the size of China's industrial labor force doubled almost overnight after having expanded gradually in the early 1950s.

A few years later with the onset of the industrial recession and a famine of epic proportions in the countryside, industrial enterprises saw their investment budgets cut substantially. In the early 1960s, the central government undertook drastic measures to control the growth of the urban population through urban registration and rationing of consumer staples. The effect was to freeze labor mobility and wage growth for two decades. Despite the apparent recentralization of industrial policy to higher administrative levels at this time, local party committees maintained even stronger administrative controls over state enterprises and their labor management. The employment practices and authority patterns within work units became firmly entrenched by the mid-1960s and remained in place until the mid-1980s. This chapter traces how these changes in the external political environment during the late 1950s and early 1960s altered the existing framework of enterprise labor management institutions. The dominance of enterprise party committees over factory managers might lead one to expect substantial changes in job allocation, wages, and benefits following the ascendance of enterprise party committees in late 1957. Yet in certain respects, factory party committees revived and even strengthened the very labor management institutions that had existed prior to, and in conflict with, the constraints of the command economy.

STRIKE WAVES, RECTIFICATION, AND DECENTRALIZATION

Mao Zedong's call for a frank public assessment of the party and government in the Hundred Flowers Movement of 1956–7 unleashed strident criticisms among China's intellectual and artistic communities. In the industrial sector, criticism of the government and party became most visible in the numerous labor disputes in large cities in China during the spring of 1957. In May and June of 1957, a series of strikes broke

197

out in Shanghai that in quantitative terms surpassed the historic episodes of strike activity in 1919, 1925, and 1946.[3] These labor "disturbances" (*naoshi*, so labeled by the authorities at the time) were first and foremost disputes over the perceived unfairness in the distribution of wages and benefits. Workers in the small and medium enterprises that had been converted to state ownership in the mid-1950s protested against cuts in benefits and bonuses. Apprentices reacted violently to the State Council's decision in early 1957 to extend apprentice training periods, delaying the time before they could attain status as full-time state employees. More broadly, the strikes appear to have been a reaction against the conversion to state planning. According to Shanghai GLU reports, in strikes involving 548 factories and 27,000 workers, 88 percent of the cases centered around wages and benefits. Investigators also discovered that 82 percent of the strikes were in formerly private enterprises which, in the course of transformation to joint public-private ownership in the mid-1950s, had dramatically cut back on numerous bonuses and benefits.[4]

In Guangzhou, labor disputes broke out a year earlier, in 1956. Guangdong Provincial Party officials reported that construction workers in Guangzhou and other cities in the Pearl River Delta engaged in slowdowns in the summer of 1956. Workers in several factories used the "Hungarian incident," as the popular protest against the Communist government in Budapest in 1956 was called, to demand higher wages. One worker in a tobacco plant told the factory director, "You don't care about workers' livelihood. Remember the Hungarian incident? We can show you what it's like!"[5] As would be the case in Shanghai in 1957, Guangzhou workers protested against wage reform discrepancies in the new jointly owned enterprises. According to subsequent investigations, party authorities found that workers in these factories also engaged in deliberate slowdowns, turning around the phrase "to each according to his labor" (*anlao fuchou*) into "labor according to one's pay" (*anchou fulao*).[6]

In both Shanghai and Guangzhou, factory officials were the targets of several violent incidents and more numerous "surroundings" in which

---

[3] For a full treatment of Shanghai's strike wave of 1957, see Perry, "Shanghai's Strike Wave of 1957." As she notes, the period following the CCP takeover of Shanghai in 1949 brought by far the largest number of strikes: 3,324 compared to 587 in 1957 (p. 1, fn. 3).

[4] SMA, Series C16-2-178.   [5] GPA, Series 219-1-21.

[6] *Guangzhou Ribao*, May 15, 1957, 2.

hundreds of angry workers immobilized managers by encircling them and refusing to move for hours on end. Workers demanded the restoration of nonwage income and assorted benefits that they had enjoyed under private ownership. The managers who bore the brunt of workers' frustration were frequently central government officials responsible for streamlining production, reducing waste, and bringing operations in the formerly private sector enterprises in line with and subservient to the mandates of the command economy.[7]

While labor disputes swept through the newly nationalized factories in 1957, one group within these enterprises stood out for their service in preventing the labor unrest from growing more acute. Communist Party reports cited "old workers" for their leadership in mediating disputes between angry apprentices and factory office administrators. It is unclear if these "old workers" held positions of rank within production teams and work sections, but given their experience and seniority, many old workers would have been promoted to these posts by the late 1950s. CCP reports urged that because they had placated intrafactory disputes, older workers should continue to gain promotion to supervisory posts within factories. "Old workers are not just the backbone of production; they're also the backbone of politics," claimed one report from the Shanghai party branch of the China Textile Union in September of 1957. In promoting cadres during the 1950s, enterprise officials in the textile sector had paid insufficient attention to the contributions of old workers and their skills. The report's authors admitted, "We have insufficiently utilized the rich life experiences of old workers to educate new and younger workers."[8] If older workers in the industrial sector benefited from their role in the strike waves of 1957, the same could not be said of technicians and other specialists.

Rectification

The reaction to the Hundred Flowers Campaign brought grave consequences to those in white collar or administrative roles in factories, and especially to those who had at Mao's request offered up criticisms of the Communist Party. During the Anti-Rightist Campaign that ensued in the summer of 1957, party authorities arrested factory staff who had spoken out against the party. Within enterprises, technicians and staff who were not sent to rural areas to engage in agricultural labor or to prison camps

---

[7] SMA, Series C16-2-178.   [8] Ibid.

for "thought reform" were invariably transferred to production jobs in their places of employment. National-level union officials who had taken "economist" or "syndicalist" stances by advocating wage increases for workers and some level of union autonomy from party control also came under attack.[9]

However, limited evidence on the Anti-Rightist Campaign in Shanghai factories suggests that the Shanghai MPC's Industrial Work Department may have curbed attacks on supervisors and staff in critical sectors and enterprises. At the Jiangnan Shipyard, the Anti-Rightist Campaign began late and ended rather quickly. The campaign was not launched until October 1958 and was concluded by April 1959. During this time, a total of forty-nine employees, mostly administrators and technicians, were accused of being "rightists" (out of several thousand staff). In September 1959, the party committee had already begun to "discard labels" or vindicate some of those accused. By early 1962, there were only eighteen employees (nine cadres and nine technicians) whose labels as "rightists" had not been removed.[10] The forty-nine "rightists" all were party members who held administrative posts. When they were sent to the countryside, they served as officials in communes.[11] In the machine industry in Shanghai as a whole, the Anti-Rightist Campaign saw a total of 810 personnel sent to the countryside (again, the vast majority were cadres and technicians). The critical capabilities and skills possessed by technical staff in industrial enterprises more than likely constrained party officials from purging the already thin ranks of specialists. Likewise, production demands during the GLF would have put pressure on party officials to return technical specialists to their posts. Within one year, 662 of the 810 machine industry "rightists" had been returned to their original work units.[12] In the textile industry of Guangzhou, a total of 49 alleged "reactionaries, bad elements, and rightists" were labeled as such by mid-1959, out of 7,243 employees in the city's entire textile industry.[13] The Anti-Rightist Campaign appears to have claimed significantly fewer victims in industry than was the case among employees in educational institutions and government offices. More documents on this period will have to be declassified before we can know precisely why an apparently smaller proportion of rightists

[9] Harper, "Party and the Unions in Communist China," 112–13.
[10] SMA, Series A36-1-304. [11] SMA, Series A36-2-273. [12] SMA, Series A36-2-273.
[13] GMA, Series 227-61.

were found in industry than in other areas such as educational and government institutions.[14]

Decentralization

The sudden decentralization of administrative authority from the center to the provinces in the fall of 1957 meant that factories once subordinate to central government agencies were now turned over to the governments of provinces, autonomous regions, and directly administered cities (e.g., Beijing, Tianjin, and Shanghai).[15] This change in administrative relationships meant that municipal and provincial party committees, which had opposed the concentration of power within central ministries, could exert far more power over industrial policy than had been the case during the FFYP. In late 1957, provincial, municipal, and county governments moved quickly to take administrative control over thousands of factories. Nationwide, the 9,300 enterprises under central administration in 1957 were reduced to 1,200 by the end of 1958.[16] The thousands of enterprises under new administrative supervision still had to remit the bulk of their profits to the central government, but provincial-level governments were permitted to retain a 20 percent share of enterprise profits.[17] Those enterprises that remained with central government departments were generally found in heavy industry, metallurgy, energy, power generation, and other goods deemed critical for national security.

The decentralization directive came following an important policy change at the Eighth Party Congress in August of 1956.[18] At this meeting, the head of the Central Committee's Industrial Work Department, Li Xuefeng, announced that state enterprises would replace the Soviet-inspired "one-man management" system with something known as the

[14] The original leader of the CCP underground at the Shenxin Number Six Mill, Wang Jiasheng, was a victim of the Anti-Rightist Campaign. Despite his credentials as a party member with superior organizational abilities and a strong ideological posture, his having once participated in a Nationalist-sponsored union in 1947 was sufficient to have him sent to the countryside. SMA, Series A36-2-273.

[15] Donnithorne, *China's Economic System*, 151–3; Andors, *China's Industrial Revolution*, 61; Schurmann, *Ideology and Organization*, 202–7.

[16] Sun, *Shanghai shehuizhuyi*, 325.

[17] Donnithorne, *China's Economic System*, 152–3.

[18] The positions of various CCP leaders and the debates over decentralization and industrial policy more generally at the Eighth Party Congress can be found in Bachman, *Bureaucracy, Economy, and Leadership in China*, 160–70.

"factory manager responsibility under the leadership of the party committee."[19] In this case, the latter referred to enterprise party committees, which formally attained a high degree of administrative power within enterprises in addition to the political leadership that they had always exercised.[20] As seen in the previous chapter, the enterprise party committee at the Shenxin Number Six Mill had already captured control of administrative issues at the expense of factory directors and other managers. Despite the Central Committee's announcement, the lines between policy and administration remained blurry. If collective or consultative decision making was now the goal, did factory managers have to turn to the enterprise party committee for approval of every step taken in the day-to-day work of running a factory? As several treatments of this critical juncture in China's industrial management have noted, collective leadership by party committees remained both highly ambiguous and, depending on the enterprise, was limited by the technical knowledge of enterprise party committee members.[21]

The State Council's formal directive on decentralization, "Regulations on the Improvement of the Industrial Management System," was published in the November 18, 1957 edition of *People's Daily*.[22] The announcement noted that the industrial management system in China had two shortcomings. First, "some enterprises suitable for local management" were under the supervision of industrial departments of the central government, while "local administrative organs enjoy too little authority over industrial management." Second, "the person in charge of an enterprise has too little authority over that enterprise while the central industrial administrative department has too much control over the business of that enterprise." While the State Council directive enumerated specific targets and rules for profit retention, it was remarkably ambiguous about who or what constituted "persons in charge of an enterprise." Also notable in its absence was any mention of specific powers designated for party committees, either in local government or within enterprises. The directive did clearly spell out the classification

---

[19] Andors, *China's Industrial Revolution*, 61–2; Donnithorne, *China's Economic System*, 196–7.

[20] You, *China's Enterprise Reform*, 37–9.

[21] Schurmann, *Ideology and Organization*, 290–1; Andors, *China's Industrial Revolution*, 63–4; Donnithorne, *China's Economic System*, 197.

[22] An English translation of the directive can be found in *Survey of China Mainland Press*, no. 1665, Dec. 5, 1957, "State Council's Directive Concerning Improvement of Industrial Management System."

of enterprises that should be decentralized. Only a small number of textile industry enterprises and those under the Light Industry and Food Industry Ministries were to be transferred to local governments. Enterprises in heavy industry and machine manufacturing, as well as large-scale mines, chemical plants, power stations, oil refineries, and military enterprises would remain under the control of central government ministries.

The politics and potential coalitions supporting or opposing the decentralization decree and the GLF that followed have been discussed extensively.[23] How decentralization affected intraenterprise labor management and existing factory institutions has been less directly explored, however. We might begin by repeating the important observation first made by Franz Schurmann: decentralization in 1957 did not give enterprise directors greater autonomy (as had been the case in Yugoslavia), but instead resulted in the transfer of administrative power to local party officials. Schurmann labeled this as "decentralization II."[24] This pattern of decentralization gave party committees at the provincial level (that is, provinces, autonomous regions, and cities with provincial rank) the ability to make and implement investment and production plans for enterprises within their territory. Decentralization II had direct consequences for party committees within enterprises as well. Enjoying as they did ties with local party officials, enterprise party committees gained control over production tasks, in addition to the political work previously assigned to them during the FFYP. If the policy of the late 1950s was to "guarantee the absolute leadership of the party in industrial production," enterprise party committees were the party's key link within factories to do so. This often meant that even if an enterprise had not been formally turned over to local control, enterprise party committees laid claim to administrative issues that rightly belonged to factory management. Subsequent CCP reports would label the seizure of administrative powers by party committees as the problem of "party and administration not divided" (*dang-zheng bu fen*).[25]

Notwithstanding the State Council's decentralization directive to place a limited number of enterprises from light industries under the control of local authorities, provincial and municipal party committees

---

[23] Bachman, *Bureaucracy, Economy, and Leadership*, 191–213; Lee, *Industrial Management and Economic Reform*, 61–2; Schurmann, *Ideology and Organization*, 195–210.
[24] Schurmann, *Ideology and Organization*, 175–8.
[25] GMA, Series 8-244.

exerted substantial direct control over some of the largest enterprises in heavy industry, in addition to those in other sectors. Reports by the Shanghai and Guangzhou MPCs from this time began to refer to certain factories as "party committee factories" (*dangwei chang*) or "factories directly under the municipal party committee" (*shiwei zhishu chang*).[26] These terms imply that local party committees had taken on an explicit administrative function and that some enterprises were classified as "belonging" to party committees, regardless of the government bureau to which the same enterprise might report.

In Shanghai, 480 out of 536 industrial enterprises formerly belonging to central government ministries were transferred to local authorities in 1957. The number of workers in the remaining centrally administered Shanghai enterprises totaled 57,000, whereas employment in the decentralized enterprises amounted to 343,000.[27] The transfer of enterprise administration to local authorities was tantamount to direct control by municipal party committees, not local branches of central ministries. Nationally, 80 to 95 percent of the enterprises formerly under the control of the Ministry of Light Industries, the First Machinery Ministry, and the Ministry of Chemical Industries were now operated by the MPCs and their Industrial Work Departments.[28]

Because Shanghai was one of three cities at this time with the administrative rank of a province, the State Council's decentralization directive gave Shanghai authorities the ability to take control of many of the city's enterprises. The city of Guangzhou, on the other hand, was formally under the administration of the Guangdong Provincial Government. Still, Guangdong provincial authorities transferred administrative control over virtually all of Guangzhou's largest factories to the city government and specifically to the Guangzhou MPC's Industrial Work Department. The Tongyong Machine Tools Factory, the city's largest, came under the control of the Guangzhou Machine and Electric Industries Bureau, which was supervised by the MPC's Industrial Work Department.[29]

Three of the four Shanghai and Guangzhou enterprises discussed in this book underwent some change in administrative relationships

[26] SMA, Series A36-1-320, SMA, Series A36-2-213, GMA, Series 8-244.
[27] Sun, *Shanghai shehuizhuyi*, 325–6.
[28] Shiping Zheng, *Party vs. State in Post-1949 China: The Institutional Dilemma* (New York: Cambridge University Press, 1997), 101.
[29] Tang, *Guangzhou gongye sishinian*, 233.

between 1958 and 1960. The Shenxin Number Six Mill combined with two adjacent plants in 1958 to form the Yangshupu Mill, but the latter remained under the administrative control of the Shanghai Municipal Government's Textile Bureau. Shanghai MPC documents referred to this factory as a "party committee factory," and the city's party committee had especially close ties to the plant (see Chapter 6). The Jiangnan Shipyard in September 1960 was transferred to the administration of the new Third Machinery Ministry's Ninth Bureau. This change in central government agencies supervising the shipyard actually preserved, and possibly strengthened, the Shanghai MPC's control over the Jiangnan Shipyard. Throughout the late 1950s and early 1960s, the MPC Industrial Work Department appointed and set the pay for a series of factory directors and party secretaries as well as workshop and work section directors. In Guangzhou, the Huangpu Shipyard, which had been named "Factory 201" for security purposes, was transferred to the First Machinery Ministry in 1960 and also became a "factory directly under the Municipal Party Committee." The Guangdong Textile Mill remained under the Textile Industry Bureau of Guangzhou but continued to be classified as one of dozens of factories that were "directly under the Municipal Party Committee." The authority of municipal party committees over labor management in these and many other principal production units in Shanghai and Guangzhou had discernible consequences on labor allocation, wage and bonus distribution, and enterprise welfare policy.

Labor Allocation

Decentralization in 1957 was followed quickly by a massive increase in China's industrial labor force. Enterprises, now under less stringent control of local authorities, haphazardly "recruited from society" to fulfill utopian production targets set by local officials who had little knowledge of industry, much less macroeconomic administrative capabilities. Between late 1958 and early 1959, an estimated three million peasants migrated to urban areas, but the increase in the industrial labor force was put at twenty million new workers in 1958 alone. This amounted to more than twice the number of new entrants into the ranks of industrial employment in the previous eight years. In 1960, state plans called for 2 million new workforce entrants, but in just the first eight months of the year, enterprises had added 3.4 million new workers.[30] Efforts to recruit

---

[30] Yuan, *Zhongguo laodong jingjishi*, 211–12.

new labor were facilitated in 1960 by the spreading and deepening famine that drove millions of rural residents to urban areas in search of work.

Employment statistics in Shanghai and in the enterprises under study here reflect the loss of state control over labor allocation during the GLF. The size of the labor force in Shanghai rose from 3.6 million in 1957 to 4.3 million by 1960. Within Shanghai's state sector, the number of employees increased during the same period from 1.74 million to 2.23 million. The population of Shanghai as a whole went from 6.9 million in 1957 to 10.6 million in 1960.[31] Many enterprises also recruited "lane labor" (*lilong gong*), a semiemployed labor force made up primarily of women who were fixtures in the back lanes and alleys of the city and who took work on a temporary basis. At the Yangshupu Mill, employment reached over ten thousand in 1958 (the highest level in any year since in the long history of the mill).[32] At the Jiangnan Shipyard, the number of production workers rose from 6,347 in 1957 to 8,976 the next year, an increase of 41 percent.[33]

In Guangdong province, planning commission figures show that the number employees in state enterprises nearly doubled, increasing from 1.25 million in 1957 to 2.38 million by 1960.[34] Another source estimates that industrial employment (in state and joint enterprises) soared from 381,500 in 1958 to over 1.1 million in 1959, a figure that excludes commune factories and neighborhood workshops.[35] State enterprises in the city of Guangzhou saw an 81 percent increase in employment between 1957 and 1960.[36] The Huangpu Shipyard, with 1,100 employees in 1956, had 1,678 by 1959, representing a 50 percent increase.[37]

This surge in local and enterprise employment was accompanied by an explicit political attack on the technical experts and personnel officials who had sought to impose a bureaucratic order within shop floors and who had constrained growth in the labor supply during the FFYP. Workers in Shanghai and Guangzhou factories submitted literally millions of large character posters in 1958 criticizing the technical emphases of the FFYP and demanding that technicians and engineers join them in

[31] Sun, *Shanghai shehuizhuyi*, 869–70.
[32] Shanghai Number Thirty-One Mill Archives, Labor and Wage Department, Series 59.
[33] Jiangnan Shipyard Factory History Research Office, "Renshi laodong guanli," 175.
[34] Guangdong Economic Planning Commission, ed., *Guangdongsheng jingji jihua*, 1: 702.
[35] GPA, Series 219-1-46.
[36] Tang, *Guangzhou gongye*, 48.
[37] Author's correspondence with Huangpu Shipyard official, May 16, 1995.

production tasks on the shop floor. At the Jiangnan Shipyard, workers penned fifty-three thousand messages that blasted the "waste and conservatism" of the past, such as rules that limited the use of raw materials and detailed accounting procedures that controlled the distribution of parts and labor.[38] With this "sending down" of technical personnel to production teams, party secretaries at the workshop, work section, and production team levels seized control of managerial functions, including even financial tasks in some cases. According to a later report by a central party work team, party secretaries in Shanghai and the Northeast had modified the popular national slogan of the GLF, "politics takes command" (*zhengzhi guashuai*), into "the party secretary takes command" (*shuji guashuai*).[39] Party secretaries at each level dominated day-to-day operations of enterprise unions, Communist Youth League branches, and production and planning. Some factories, not specified in a subsequent Guangzhou MPC Industrial Work Department report, even adopted an anarchical policy of "non-management" (*wuren guanli*). These were enterprises that practiced the "Eight Selfs" (*ba zi*), in which workers arranged their own plans, output quotas, technology, blueprints, operations, inputs of semiprocessed goods, quality inspection, and accounting. What was worse, the authors of the report noted, financial authorities had surrendered to this craze. Local branches of the People's Bank of China distributed cash to any worker who came in with purchase orders. Employees who knew the enterprise's bank account number could withdraw funds to procure whatever items they needed for their factories.[40]

Disdain for technical specialists who supposedly had too little practical knowledge resulted in party committees in factories "sending down" thousands of office staff to the ranks of production workers. At the Jiangnan Shipyard the number of managers and technicians declined from 1,201 in 1957 to 607 in 1959.[41] The number of managers and staff at the Yangshupu Mill fell from 1,924 in 1958 to 579 the next year, as offices were cleared out and white collar staff sent to the production lines.[42] The portion of office staff, (or "employees removed from production") that had increased several-fold during the FFYP, was reduced

---

[38] SMA, Series A36-2-491; SMA, Series A36-1-136.
[39] GPA, Series 219-1-46.   [40] Ibid.
[41] Jiangnan Shipyard Factory History Research Office, "Renshi laodong guanli," 175.
[42] Shanghai Number Thirty-One Mill Factory Director's Office, "Shangmian sanshiyichang zhigong bian" (Shanghai Number Thirty-One Mill, Workers and Staff Section), mimeo, n.d.

dramatically. A retrospective report based on an investigation conducted by central party work teams sent to Shanghai and the industrially developed provinces of Heilongjiang and Liaoning found that staff reductions in the GLF brought the portion of managerial staff in the total workforce down from 20 to 40 percent to only 2 to 4 percent.[43]

The decentralization of administrative relationships outside the enterprise was replicated within the factory. Functional departments and offices turned over planning and production decisions to workshop supervisors and production team leaders.[44] Personnel formerly in finance, accounting, planning, and other offices were sent down to factory floors to participate in labor and exchange technical knowledge with workers. Coupled with the threat of being targeted for rectification in the Anti-Rightist Campaign, the decentralization movement within factories severely weakened the authority that technical specialists had enjoyed during the FFYP.

The restructuring of enterprise administration in effect abolished many of the specialized departments that had been developed during the FFYP. A 1958 report from the Guangdong Textile Mill stated that with the Increase Production and Economize Campaign and the Rectification Campaign (e.g., the Anti-Rightist Campaign) in 1957, the number of departments had been reduced from sixteen to eleven, including the abolition of the workshop level above work sections and production teams.[45] Similar changes are reflected in the shifting fates of the Labor and Wage Section of the Jiangnan Shipyard. In 1958 the shipyard abolished its Labor and Wage Section and merged its functions within the Planning Section. With the restoration of labor quotas, time wages, and more carefully coordinated labor allocation, the Labor and Wage Section was renewed in 1960, only to be once again eliminated and its functions subsumed within another department in 1963.[46] During the GLF, specialized personnel departments in many factories were either abolished or weakened, as local party committees took charge of personnel appointments for positions well down the factory hierarchy. The Shanghai MPC approved numerous workshop party committee secretaries in the

---

[43] GPA, Series 219-1-46.

[44] Andors, *China's Industrial Revolution*, 82–3.

[45] GMA, Series 227-36. Managerial staff as a percentage of production workers had not yet been brought under the municipal textile bureau's desired goal of 10 percent, but was so by late 1959 (GMA, Series 8-245).

[46] Jiangnan Shipyard Factory History Research Office, "Renshi laodong guanli."

Jiangnan Shipyard.[47] The Guangzhou MPC's Industrial Work Department carried out all promotions within enterprise party committees of its factories, and was also responsible for sending down cadres to participate in labor.[48]

As a consequence of having white-collar staff participate in the operations of production teams and having managerial functions vested with teams, conflict ensued between team leaders and erstwhile office administrators.[49] Shop floor supervisors, long the enemies of scientific management under both capitalism and socialism in China, saw their powers enhanced considerably. The significance of the shop floor supervisor as a skilled leader of persons, rather than an administrator of rules and technical procedures, is treated at length in Schurmann's discussion of personnel and organizational ethos in the Maoist era. Schurmann claimed that not since the early stages of China's industrial development had foremen enjoyed the ability to hire and fire workers and to set their wages.[50] Stephen Andors, citing a Nanjing newspaper account, noted that in some cases a foreman of the late 1950s had been a shop floor boss during the 1930s and 1940s.[51] It would be an overstatement, however, to read this period as the simple revival of past practices associated with the "foreman's fiefdom" or, as Schurmann did, to argue that the production team leader of the late 1950s and early 1960s replicated the role of the foremen in labor gangs of the 1920s and 1930s.[52] The workshop director or production team leader after 1957 enjoyed considerably greater autonomy than under the rigors of central planning and administration of the FFYP, but these individuals were also constrained by political doctrine and by those up the factory's party committee hierarchy from freely hiring and firing workers. The historical record lacks sufficient evidence to support the claim that labor supervisors in the late 1950s and early 1960s enjoyed anywhere near the level of authority they once had to recruit, allocate, and dismiss workers. However, because many of these bosses were also representatives of the enterprise party committee at the shop floor level, they did gain by the post-Leap period (further analyzed in the second half of this chapter) important new political resources with which they ruled workers under them.

---

[47] SMA, Series A36-1-75; SMA, Series A36-1-76.   [48] GPA, Series 8-244.
[49] Andors, *China's Industrial Revolution*, 79–83.
[50] Schurmann, *Ideology and Organization*, 260–1.
[51] Andors, *China's Industrial Revolution*, 82.
[52] Schurmann, *Ideology and Organization*, 294.

During the GLF, workshop, work section, and production team leaders used the campaign atmosphere to push workers to their physical limits in order to fulfill production quotas. In Guangzhou, some bosses demanded that the workday be extended by two hours, including adding shifts on Sundays, with no overtime pay. When a union committee on worker safety at a metalworking factory questioned a workshop director about the safety of having his employees engage in sixteen-hour work days, the supervisor rebuffed such caution by noting, "This is the Great Leap Forward. All normal rules are out."[53] Party committee representatives, Communist Youth League members, and older workers led production drives during work shifts, now renamed as "eight-hour combat missions."[54]

Enterprise Welfare

The political discourse of the GLF included frequent demands to curtail the wasteful payments made to the beneficiaries of state socialism under the FFYP. The Guangzhou Municipal Labor Union reported that the "working masses" during a campaign to "oppose bureaucratism and waste" (also called the Double Oppose Campaign) demanded that unreasonable subsidies and wages be abolished and that working hours be lengthened to include voluntary labor. The "working masses" had also proposed the elimination of subsidies paid to managers, staff, and shop floor supervisors, as well as the termination of "retained wages," or the supplemental payments to compensate those whose pay had been lowered by wage reform. It had also been suggested that all bonuses for overtime work be donated to the state. Finally, the "working masses" made demands that wide-ranging subsidies paid to employees for expenses such as rent, school fees, transportation costs, bike purchases, hair cuts, soap, and toilet paper all be eliminated.[55] It is not clear from the reports if the "working masses" who advocated these radical proposals were the temporary and contract laborers excluded from the benefits of their full-time counterparts, yet one can imagine such "have-nots" making demands that would have brought their better off colleagues down to their own level.

In any case, proposals to reduce enterprise welfare measures put union and factory officials in a difficult position. Well aware of the "high-tide of communism" that was sweeping the country, these egalitarian

[53] GMA, Series 92-192.   [54] SMA, Series A36-2-491.   [55] GMA, Series 92-192.

proposals appeared to have political support from the center. On the other hand, enacting them risked a backlash (either overt or covert) by well-established full-time state workers, and at the very least serious productivity declines. Trade union officials in Guangzhou, writing in the summer of 1958, noted that the welfare-reduction proposals would threaten the livelihood of many full-time state workers. A decision by managers at the Fuqiao Dyeing Mill to close the preschool for employees' children angered parents, who said of management, "They want us to throw our children into the sea!" The Guangzhou Municipal Labor Union's party committee, unsurprisingly, took an ambiguous stance on these proposals. Subsidies and the overquota output bonuses were, it argued, "an indispensable part of the national wage system." But welfare measures that had hurt production or caused divisions among workers, they noted, should be abolished. Predictably, these union officials suggested that any enactment of reductions in employee benefits should first receive approval from the relevant district, municipal, or provincial party committees.[56]

With the massive increase in payrolls during the late 1950s, factory managers found themselves with far more employees to provide with basic services. At the Guangdong Textile Mill, the funds originally intended for production bonuses were converted to welfare expenditures to accommodate the rapidly expanding workforce. The mill had over 6,000 employees by the end of 1958 after starting the year with 4,630 on the payroll.[57] Instead of distributing the planned amount of 84,573 yuan on output bonuses, mill managers spent more than double this, with three quarters of it directed not to incentive wages but to health care and other benefits.[58] At the Huangpu Shipyard, which had 1,678 employees by 1959, officials claimed that they now provided their employees with over 21,400 square meters in welfare facilities. Presumably a 2,000-seat arena on the factory grounds and a 300-seat tea house, both built in 1958, accounted for much of the square-meters figure.[59] As had been the case during the FFYP, the Huangpu Shipyard and the Guangdong Textile Mill benefited from their relations with the Guangzhou MPC's Industrial Work Department. They and other enterprises classified as "party committee factories" received generous allocations for welfare measures. A 1959 Guangzhou MPC report noted that out of 4.9 million yuan distributed for enterprise welfare projects to 159 enterprises in the city, nearly

---

[56] Ibid.   [57] GMA, Series 227-47.   [58] GMA, Series 227-36.
[59] Author's correspondence with Huangpu Shipyard official, May 16, 1995.

one-fifth of this sum (923,000 yuan) went to just four "party committee factories."[60] Moreover, any enterprise in the city wishing to make adjustments to welfare expenditures had to first receive approval from the Guangzhou MPC's Industrial Work Department.[61]

In Shanghai, the rapid workforce expansion at the Yangshupu Mill to over 10,000 in 1958 meant that factory managers had to undertake extensive new welfare measures. As a result, mill management built two new dining halls that could feed 500 persons at a time, a day care center that could accommodate over 1,000 children, and nearly 2,900 square meters of new dormitory space for male and female employees. In addition, a new medical clinic measuring 915 square meters was completed at this time.[62] Labor insurance expenditures at the mill amounted to 26 percent of the wage bill in 1958.[63]

The expansion of welfare facilities at well-connected state enterprises during the GLF should not overshadow the problem that government and party officials faced in providing for the much larger labor forces of the time. In Shanghai's textile industry, for example, the all-important labor insurance coverage for workers failed to keep up with the expansion in the number of employees. At year-end 1954, a total of 204,747 workers received labor insurance coverage out of 257,248 employed in the textile sector (nearly 80 percent). By 1959, however, the number of textile workers covered by labor insurance totaled 301,942, but the workforce had risen to 414,290 (73 percent coverage). This gap in the social safety net may not have represented a large change in percentage terms, but it did mean that over 100,000 of Shanghai's textile industry employees were working without labor insurance. In the city's machinery and metalworking sector, employing 312,666 workers in 1959, a total of 230,142 received labor insurance coverage (73.6 percent).[64]

Wages and Bonuses

The previous two chapters demonstrated the practical obstacles and strident opposition to material incentives in the wage and bonus system that central government authorities imposed on enterprises during the FFYP.

---

[60] GPA, Series 227-58.   [61] GPA, Series 92-192.
[62] Shanghai Number Thirty-One Mill Factory Director's Office, "Shangmian sanshiyichang zhigong bian."
[63] Shanghai Number Thirty-One Mill Archives, Labor and Wage Department, Series 59.
[64] SMA, Series C1-2-4414; SMA, Series C1-1-190.

Without adequate technology and accounting personnel, an overquota bonus system became too difficult to administer in the diverse industrial landscape of China. Moreover, workers who did pursue additional income through the bonus system drew resentment from those assigned to more challenging work posts and from older workers who either lacked the skills to operate new machinery or who looked down upon those pursuing material incentives as the spoiled beneficiaries of state socialism.

The sudden expansion in the ranks of the state workforce in 1958 naturally raised the contentious issues of wages and bonuses. At first, the new workforce entrants were placed on the bottom rungs of the wage scale or given the rank of apprentice or part-time laborers. Such distinctions were important because they reduced the eligibility for enterprise welfare provisions accorded existing members of the workforce. Moreover, given the hostility to piece rates voiced by many workers during the FFYP, it was not surprising that calls went up for the abolition of piece rates and overquota bonuses during the GLF. With the political blessings of the Maoist leadership, cries arose from workers in factories throughout China for an end to incentive pay. A prominent editorial in Shanghai's *Jiefang Ribao* (*Liberation Daily*) announced in September 1958 that Jiangnan Shipyard workers had abolished piece-rate payments.[65] Large character posters sprang up throughout factories in Shanghai calling for the termination of incentive pay. Within six months, according to MPC documents, piece rates and incentive bonuses had vanished in Shanghai enterprises.

The piece-rate bonuses that relied solely on quantity were replaced in many factories with a "blended" bonus, a supposedly comprehensive evaluation that took into account a number of other, highly subjective qualities that were to be discussed, out in the open, in a democratic fashion by "the masses." These new criteria included the quality of a worker's output in addition to the quantity, consideration of a worker's safety record, overall "attitude," and the ability to cooperate with others. Staff and production workers together participated in these bonus evaluations, which the Shanghai MPC's Industrial Work Department officials called a "political education as well as a summing up of production."[66] According to recollections by personnel officials from the present-day Shanghai Number Thirty-One Mill, the strictest evaluations in the mass setting were for party members and potential party recruits as well as

[65] SMA, Series A36-1-248.   [66] Ibid.

those in the Communist Youth League. Such politically ambitious individuals received especially close scrutiny in bonus evaluations, and if workers voiced any criticism of the aspiring activist, the candidate would very likely be denied any increase in pay.[67]

In Guangzhou's large-scale state factories that had experimented with material incentives during the FFYP, workers proudly announced the abolition of piece-rate bonuses.[68] The city had 215 factories that used such systems, involving nearly 32,000 workers, over half of whom were in the textile industry. Workers at the Quanxin Knitting Mill submitted posters that criticized piece rates for emphasizing individualism and self-interest. They also noted that piece-rate pay tended to cause workers to refuse orders from their superiors, as workers became absorbed in the pursuit of exceeding the quota. Supporting the "politics takes command" slogan of the time, Guangzhou workers were said to have proclaimed, "We want politics, not cash, to take command."[69]

As a result of having terminated piece-rate wages and overquota bonuses, workers paid through such systems suffered a decline in income of anywhere from 10 to 30 percent.[70] Enterprise managers who had abolished material incentives sought to make up for the decline in workers' incomes. Some enterprises took measures to provide workers with temporary wage subsidies and relief payments.[71] Another makeshift solution permitted family members of workers to join them in the workplace. The wages paid to relatives, though meager in most cases, thus supplemented the income lost as a result of the termination of incentive pay. Much of the expansion in collective welfare measures documented previously in several Shanghai and Guangzhou enterprises might be explained as an effort to substitute income lost from the abolition of piece rates. Guangzhou MPC officials explicitly ordered enterprise managers to put the money they would have spent on piece-rate wages and production bonuses toward the establishment and expansion of collective welfare measures.[72]

The abolition of piece rates and other forms of material incentives, coupled with the dramatic expansion of the workforce, meant a nationwide decline in average wages paid to state enterprise workers. Thus,

---

[67] Author's interview, Factory Director's Office and Personnel Department, Shanghai Number Thirty-One Mill, January 14, 1995.

[68] Guangzhou Labor Bureau, "Guangzhoushi laodong zhi," Wages, 56–8.

[69] GMA, Series 92-216.

[70] Yuan, *Zhongguo laodong jingjishi*, 248; GMA, Series 92-216.

[71] Yuan, *Zhongguo laodong jingjishi*, 248.   [72] GMA, Series 92-216.

while the national wage bill for workers in state industrial enterprises rose from 5.1 billion yuan in 1957 to 10.3 billion yuan in 1959, average yearly earnings per person in state industry fell from 690 yuan to 514 yuan in the same period.[73] For full-time state industrial workers, the national average wage was only slightly higher, at 544 yuan in 1959.

RE-(DE)CENTRALIZATION AFTER
THE GREAT LEAP FORWARD

In response to the industrial recession brought on by the GLF, CCP leaders in the early 1960s imposed comprehensive retrenchment policies and a drastic reduction in budgetary transfers to state enterprises. With national finances in ruin, the State Council gave directives to enterprise managers to scale back welfare measures. Central industrial ministries were also ordered to keep a tight rein on wages in an effort to prevent their rate of growth from outpacing that of productivity increases. Li Fuchun, a vice premier of the State Council in charge of industry, called for strict controls: "As production inches forward, wages and benefits move at a fraction of that" (*shengchan chang yi cun, gongzi fuli chang yi fen*).[74] At a work conference in Lushan in the fall of 1961, party leaders announced the "Articles for State Industrial Enterprises," later shortened to simply the "Seventy Articles."

The Seventy Articles sought to reverse the excesses and imbalances in industry that had resulted from the GLF. If the rank of individual articles is any indication of priority, then halting capital construction projects, the third article, was one of the foremost concerns of the CCP. Other retrenchment measures included having state factories return various commodities and other inputs transferred to them during the GLF to their original units. Separate articles prohibited the unauthorized transfer of labor (including technicians) and the practice of recruiting from the countryside. Over seven articles sought to limit the workday (to eight hours) and to stipulate leave policies for illness, childbirth, and holidays. Another four articles restored piecework and overquota bonus systems.

While the Seventy Articles endorsed many of the labor policies associated with the FFYP, it would be inaccurate, however, to interpret the Seventy Articles as a return to "one-man management." One of the

---

[73] State Statistical Bureau, *Zhongguo laodong gongzi*, 157–8.
[74] GPA, Series 231-1-192.

articles explicitly endorsed the Eighth Party Congress's doctrine of having the "factory director under the leadership of the party committee," a policy that had been a repudiation of one-man management. Another article called on enterprise party committees to mobilize administrative cadres for regular participation in production. The Seventy Articles did attempt to reestablish and redefine certain duties and powers for enterprise workers' congresses and enterprise unions, but enterprise party committees remained firmly in control of both of these institutions.[75]

It is also important to note that the Seventy Articles did not reverse the process of decentralization begun in 1957. In effect, the Seventy Articles and other Central Committee measures taken in the early 1960s recentralized powers within provincial party committees that had been devolved to cities, counties, districts, etc. during the GLF. Provincial party committees remained more powerful than central government ministries.[76] As had been the case since the mid-1950s, party officials at the district and municipal levels continued to be closely involved in the administration of large factories in their cities. The Industrial Work Department of the Shanghai MPC maintained power over personnel appointments for enterprise managers, technicians, and other cadres, including their work post designation and level of pay.[77] In 1964, the Central Committee's Industrial Work Department was renamed the Industrial and Communications Political Department, a move that Barnett attributed to other party departments modeling themselves on the Political Department of the PLA.[78] Post-Leap administrative "recentralization" amounted to the consolidation of power by provincial-level party committees at the expense of county and district committees. For large state enterprises that were already classified as "party factories," such administrative changes had little influence on the ability of municipal party committees to micromanage labor issues within enterprises.

---

[75] For an English translation of the Seventy Articles for Industry, see Union Research Institute, ed., *Documents of the Chinese Communist Party Central Committee, Sept. 1956–Apr. 1969* (Kowloon, Hong Kong: Union Research Institute, 1971), 689–93. See also Rawski, *China's Transition to Industrialism*, 54–6.

[76] Zheng, *Party vs. State*, 103.

[77] SMA, Series A36-2-258.

[78] A. Doak Barnett, with Ezra Vogel, *Cadres, Bureaucracy, and Political Power in Communist China* (New York: Columbia University Press, 1967), 4, fn. 2.

Labor Allocation

While the Seventy Articles imposed an immediate ban on enterprises recruiting surplus labor, within a few years factory managers received official blessing to recruit for certain positions without having to go through the approval process involving Ministry of Labor officials. This generally meant the ability to bring in short-term hires when necessary, without having to provide the pay and perquisites of full-time employees. In contrast to the GLF years, rural migrants and others on the outside of the state employment sector were not accorded full-time positions, and labor mobility across regions was strictly controlled. Liu Shaoqi, whose career was at its height in these years as State Chairman and the apparent successor to Mao, strongly urged factory managers to recruit temporary workers who could be returned to rural areas during the growing season. Workers hired under this policy, known as "working-and-farming" (*yigong yinong*), were not entitled to the wages and benefits of their full-time counterparts.[79] In both Guangzhou and Shanghai, small- and medium-size enterprises widely used temporary and contract labor. The State Council between 1963 and up to the eve of the Cultural Revolution in May 1966 issued strict orders for factory directors to control wage and labor costs by increasing the number of temporaries and worker-peasants in the labor force.[80]

Central state officials also encouraged factories to transfer surplus labor to other enterprises by consulting with local labor bureaus and the supervising industrial ministry.[81] While many factory directors still had an incentive to hoard excess labor as an assurance that they had sufficient personnel to fulfill production quotas, some factory directors also tried to comply with state calls to raise productivity. State officials in Beijing were acutely aware of the highly sensitive nature of this layoff policy, and encouraged party committees and enterprise directors to "strengthen ideological work" and prevent the inevitable "disturbances" by those laid off or sent back to the countryside.[82]

Official statistics on the number of workers dismissed during this period look impressive enough: between 1961 and mid-1963, state officials succeeded in reducing by 19.4 million workers an industrial labor

[79] Yuan, *Zhongguo laodong jingjishi*, 216–17.
[80] SMA, Series B1-1-1642; Yuan, *Zhongguo laodong jingjishi*, 215–19.
[81] SMA, Series B1-1-1642.   [82] Ibid.

force estimated at 50.4 million, largely through sending back to the countryside the twenty million who had flocked to the cities in 1958.[83] The vast majority of these dismissals came from small enterprises that planners in the industrial bureaucracy had been unable to control during the height of the GLF. In larger enterprises, economic retrenchment and job cutbacks led to the politically risky and generally unpleasant task of firing large numbers of older workers. By the early 1960s, many workers who had entered the labor force before 1949 were now too old for employment in the arduous and physically demanding work tasks involved in cotton mills or in other labor-intensive industries. A report by a Shanghai work team from the Textile Ministry and the All-China Textile Union announced plans in May 1962 to dismiss 83,540 mill workers, or about 24 percent of the city's textile industry workforce. It also announced plans to close 251 out of the city's total 693 textile mills.[84] All of these measures had to meet with the approval of the MPC's Industrial Work Department. The cutbacks targeted two groups: one was an estimated 11,300 "lane laborers" and temporaries, most of whom had entered the textile workforce during the GLF, with the vast majority being women. Their enterprises had given many of these workers official or full-time status, making it very difficult for mill managers to fire them.[85] Temporary and newly titled official workers were unwilling to return to the countryside voluntarily.

The other group targeted for dismissals led to a much more politically sensitive problem for enterprise managers and party committees than the sending back of recent hires. This group was the venerable pre-1949 working class, and here too women made up the majority of those to be fired. While the size of this group to be "mobilized" for early retirement was put at about 5,850 or 7 percent of the 83,540, another estimated 25,000 were to be organized for "small commercial sector" work. This meant large-scale layoffs of "pre-liberation" workers at factories that had been visible symbols of the pre-1949 labor movement in Shanghai. One such factory was the Shenxin Number Nine Cotton Mill, where 942 of 6,300 employees were to be dismissed. Among these 942 workers, 86 percent were women, the average age was 38, and the average length of continuous service at the mill was 15 years. Shanghai Textile Union cadres reported that dismissals such as those at Shenxin Number Nine represented an especially sensitive problem. These workers stood to lose not only their jobs but also their urban registration and accompanying

---

[83] Yuan, *Zhongguo laodong jingjishi*, 212–16.   [84] SMA, Series C1-2-3710.   [85] Ibid.

benefits, including labor insurance. "Labor insurance was given to us by the Communist Party and Chairman Mao," argued one mill worker. "It's a better safeguard than sons and daughters, so if we go back [to the countryside] now, everything is finished." Another worker, a 39-year-old woman without children, did not accept the argument that union and CCP cadres made to her about how these retirements were necessary to improve the national economy. "Chairman Mao has problems? I've got problems too," she said. "Others can rely on their children for food. I have to rely on Chairman Mao for food when I'm old." Not surprisingly, many mill hands were said to have expressed their willingness to work without wages for two or three years rather than endure the loss of benefits and the hardship of living in the countryside. Cadres from Shenxin Number Nine, many of whom had been promoted from the ranks of workers, warned that the policy of forcibly retiring "old workers" would result in a "negative political influence" on the overall mill workforce. By late April 1962, only 250 of the 942 designated for forced retirement had "volunteered" to do so, with only 67 of these having left their jobs. Moreover, this refusal to comply with central and local policy took place at a mill that union officials held up as *exemplary* in its handling of dismissals.[86]

Elsewhere in the city's textile sector, the reaction to dismissals turned acrimonious, and at times, violent. The Shanghai Number Eight Cotton Mill, along with three other factories, reported "disturbances" involving the forcible retirement of workers and their return to rural areas. The Shanghai Number Eight Mill "sent down" a group of twenty women, including five party members and a work section head. An uneasy standoff ensued one day in early August 1962 after the entire group returned to Shanghai and went straight to the office of the mill's party secretary to demand reinstatement.[87] (The report on the incident does not make clear whether they succeeded.) Cutbacks of older workers triggered more desperate reactions by older workers who had lost their access to enterprise welfare. At the Shanghai Number Nine Mill, a group of forcibly retired workers returned to the plant and "wailed and fought" (*kukunaonao*) with cadres, surrounded them, tore at their clothes, and went to their homes to "plunder food" (*qiang fanchi*). One male worker at the same mill who was waiting in line with his co-workers to go through the dismissal procedures allegedly incited them to plunder a nearby rice shop. He called out to the cadres at the mill, "You

[86] Ibid.   [87] SMA, Series C1-2-3731.

Communists plunge the knife in and pull it out in one stab. You've taken away all property, and now there's no food to eat . . . we'll just have to plunder for our food, first at the rice shop, then among employees."[88]

In other Shanghai industries, reductions in enterprise workforces were more simply a matter of dismissing those workers who had been brought in as temporaries and apprentices during the GLF. For example, at the Jiangnan Shipyard, the number of full-time workers declined from 12,553 by 1960 to roughly 10,000 in 1965, but over half of these cutbacks came in reducing the number of apprentices, from 1,566 to 151. It is also worth noting that the portion of managers and technicians in the ranks of the workforce expanded gradually during the early 1960s. At the Jiangnan Shipyard, the 21 percent of the workforce who were managers and technicians by 1965 reflected the same level that had existed in 1953, at the start of the FFYP.[89]

Enterprise Welfare

The retrenchment policies of the early 1960s led party and industrial officials to explore ways to cut back on the benefits that factories offered to employees. Yet as the dire consequences of the famine and recession set in and factories had to deal with widespread shortages of raw material, most enterprises now had significantly more workers to feed, clothe, and house than ever before. As the provision of goods and services to employees continued under severe scarcities of the early 1960s, the livelihood of workers declined considerably.

Reports from 1961 and 1962 by the Shanghai MPC Industrial Work Department documented the spread of edema and other illnesses among urban workers. Edema results from malnutrition, and it was common among Chinese peasants in the famine-stricken countryside in 1959–61. Thus, the occurrence of edema among workers at the largest factories in Shanghai may have loomed as a source of grave concern to local party officials who were also being instructed to cut back the labor force through forced early retirements. One investigation of five factories belonging to the Shanghai MPC's Industrial Work Department found that nearly 1 percent of all employees suffered from edema. The incidence of edema among cadres was almost triple that, at 2.7 percent. In addition, high blood pressure, chronic illness (*manxingbing*), and

---

[88] SMA, Series C1-2-3710.
[89] Jiangnan Shipyard Factory History Research Office, "Renshi laodong guanli," 175.

other stress-related maladies were common among the industrial work-force.[90] A total of 858 Jiangnan Shipyard workers, nearly 7 percent of all employees, were diagnosed with tuberculosis. One workshop at the shipyard reported twenty-eight cases of edema, twenty cases of hepatitis, and nineteen workers with high blood pressure. The MPC report concluded the obvious when it stated that workers at the Jiangnan Shipyard and several other factories investigated were not getting sufficient nutrition from the factory mess halls or from home.[91] These and other illnesses were not confined to Shanghai. A survey in Guangzhou during the late 1950s had found over 14 percent of workers with tuberculosis and pulmonary disorders, including over 20 percent at the Xietonghe Machine Factory, one of the city's largest.[92]

Given the signs of severe shortcomings in enterprise welfare provision, many enterprises were permitted to turn to self-sufficient measures to feed and house employees, including raising extrabudgetary funds. A few Shanghai factories got into the business of commercial fishing. Two textile mills and two machine plants pooled their resources to purchase a fishing vessel, then distributed the catch to their respective dining halls (a portion was also sold at markets). Enterprise officials at the Jiangnan Shipyard outfitted two of its own ships for fishing and hauled in over 18,000 *jin* after they hired an experienced captain to guide them to the right fisheries.[93]

Officials from Guangdong Province Planning Commission reported in late 1964 widespread expenditures on new construction for auditoriums, dining halls, and other buildings on factory compounds. Enterprise party committees not only condoned such extrabudgetary expenditures but in many cases it was party leaders within the factories who were encouraging and leading the effort.[94] Management at the Fanyu Nitrogen Fertilizer Plant in Guangzhou built a large apartment complex for company employees, consisting of three three-story buildings that dwarfed the factory. The incongruous sight prompted a member of a visiting delegation of Vietnamese officials to remark, "This enterprise is like a child – its body is small but its eyes are big."[95]

---

[90] SMA, Series A36-2-545.   [91] SMA, Series A36-2-548.   [92] GPA, Series 219-1-21.

[93] SMA, Series A36-2-546. The diversification of revenue-raising ventures by state-owned enterprises in China, a common practice in the 1990s, clearly has precedents from a time when state budget transfers to enterprises were also constrained.

[94] Guangdong Economic Planning Commission, *Guangdongsheng jingji jihua*, 2:110–11.

[95] Ibid., 2:136.

Table 5. *Capital Construction Investment in Shanghai, 1957–1966*

Year	Total CCI	Nonproductive CCI	Nonproductive CCI for Residential Housing	Nonproductive CCI as % of Total CCI	Residential Housing as % of Total CCI
1957	371	116	46	31.3%	12.4%
1958	974	135	45	13.9%	4.6%
1959	1,223	180	52	14.7%	4.3%
1960	1,223	239	48	19.5%	3.9%
1961	491	67	22	13.6%	4.5%
1962	219	32	14	14.6%	6.4%
1963	331	72	24	21.8%	7.3%
1964	502	114	36	22.7%	7.2%
1965	511	121	39	23.7%	7.6%
1966	465	102	27	21.9%	5.8%

Units: million yuan (current yuan).
Source: Sun Huairen, *Shanghai shehuizhuyi*, 881.

Factory directors and enterprise party committees received strict warnings about uncontrolled, unapproved spending on projects classified as nonproductive. The percentage of capital construction investment that went to nonproductive uses declined dramatically from the levels of the FFYP, when Shanghai exceeded the national average in this category. Table 5, which continues the time series on CCI begun in Table 4, shows that in nominal terms, nonproductive CCI soared from 1957 to 1960, when it reached 239 million yuan. It fell to 67 million yuan in 1961 and by more than 50 percent the following year to 32 million yuan. Between 1963 and 1966 the portion of CCI that was nonproductive exceeded 20 percent, but in absolute terms nonproductive CCI remained below the peak years of the FFYP. Relative to the nation as a whole, the portion of Shanghai's CCI that was nonproductive matched the national average of 15.4 percent for the Second Five-Year Plan (1958–62).[96] The share of Shanghai's nonproductive investment in CCI rose to over 20 percent after 1963, also in step with the national average for the years preceding the Cultural Revolution.

Overall national capital construction investment suffered a dramatic decline in 1962 and 1963, but by 1964 it had exceeded the peak year of

[96] State Statistical Bureau, *Zhongguo guding zichan touzi*, 98.

the FFYP (1956), with state investments in capital construction reaching 11.2 billion. For nonproductive projects, however, there was a dramatic decline from the expenditures of the FFYP. Nonproductive investment (including residential housing) declined from a GLF peak of 5.6 billion yuan in 1960 to 2.2 billion yuan the following year. Nonproductive investment throughout the 1960s never exceeded the 3.8 billion average during the FFYP, only doing so in 1971. All of these figures are nominal yuan, but this only reinforces the point that the post-GLF period saw substantial declines in the levels of expenditures on housing, hospitals, and other welfare measures for state workers.[97] In short, state enterprises were expected to provide housing, medical care, insurance, and other welfare amenities for a drastically expanded workforce (relative to FFYP levels) with substantially reduced budgets.

Wages and Bonuses

In many factories, management restored piece rates and other incentive pay systems in the early 1960s. The portion of the state enterprise workforce on such pay schemes expanded from a level of 5 percent in 1960 to 20 percent in 1963.[98] The reintroduction of overquota bonuses and the tightening of wage controls during the first half of the 1960s did not, however, bring enterprise managers into line with state goals of raising productivity and adhering to socialist principles of economic development. Party officials complained at length that wages and bonuses were still largely based on "mass appraisals."[99] Despite the explicit sanctions of the Seventy Articles, bonus criteria remained vague and often included "political attitude" in their assessment.[100] In part this loss of objective criteria may have arisen from the permanent debilitation of enterprise and local union branches in administering wage adjustments. Union rectification and related purges in 1957 had led to "their complete and final exclusion from wage administration."[101]

The first comprehensive adjustment to wages following nationwide wage reform in 1956 came three years later, during the frenzied production of the GLF. In the 1959 wage adjustment, "political thought" (*zhengzhi sixiang*) and material incentives were supposedly integrated in determining who would be eligible for the long-awaited wage increases.[102] Despite the impression of "state control" over the wage

[97] Ibid., 96.   [98] Yuan, *Zhongguo laodong jingjishi*, 256.   [99] Ibid., 260.
[100] Ibid., 257–8.   [101] Howe, *Wage Patterns*, 78.   [102] GMA, Series 227-58.

adjustment, ultimate authority over who received wage increases was passed down to the shop floor and production team levels. In Guangdong province, for example, the Provincial Labor Bureau received from the State Planning Commission and the Ministry of Labor an allotment of funds (45 million yuan in this case) to be used for wage increases. The provincial authorities then parceled out 5.1 million yuan to the Municipal Labor Bureau of Guangzhou. Officials at the city level determined how much of this amount would be spent on giving current workers wage grade promotions and how much would be distributed to new workers and apprentices for their initial grade setting.[103] Specific industrial bureaus at the city level subsequently issued instructions to factories on which kinds of workers should be eligible for wage adjustments. In the Guangzhou textile industry, factory directors were under orders to target two priority areas for wage increases: 1) older workers and 2) "the most unreasonable and obvious" instances of discrepancies between a worker's skill and current wage level. Reflecting the politics of the time, only 10 percent of staff were to be eligible for wage promotions, while 40 percent of production workers could be considered for pay hikes.

As was the case in every wage adjustment in China between the 1950s and 1980s, labor and industry officials gave factory directors a fixed sum to be distributed as wage increases. The factory directors then passed along the decision on which individuals would actually receive wage adjustments to workshop directors, who consulted with production team leaders. The latter gathered their information from "mass meetings" with workers, open sessions in which fellow employees publicly praised or criticized their co-workers. Not surprisingly, highly arbitrary criteria emerged, despite the party's efforts to make skill and production the overriding concern.

However, economic conditions were so strained that the 1959 wage adjustment provided only token increases to a handful of older workers and to the newest entrants to the workforce, many of whom had been transferred from other enterprises or from the countryside. In the Guangzhou textile industry, only some 4,300 employees out of nearly 44,000 workers citywide ultimately received wage increases. A subsequent report issued by the Textile Bureau on the 1959 wage adjustment complained that the procedure that year virtually neglected skill standards and called for a new round of adjustments to remedy this

[103] GMA, Series 92-216.

problem.[104] In future years, tensions would mount as these workers received the low income of a grade 1 or 2 employee, but the state lacked the financial capacity to enact a nationwide wage adjustment that would offer relief to low income workers who had families to support. Party reports on the 1963 national wage adjustment warned against "egalitarian methods" in wage distribution and demanded bluntly that those who produced should get more, and those who did not should get less.

Intensifying Corruption

Loosened administrative controls and an incremental expansion in enterprise welfare funds generated by the modest economic recovery in the post-GLF period led to widespread corruption within Chinese factories by the early 1960s. A report by the Shanghai MPC's Industrial Work Department in early 1963 noted with shock several instances of embezzlement by factory union cadres in charge of collecting and administering enterprise pension and welfare funds, along with several other accounts. The guilty parties in 115 cases of fraudulent withdrawals from such enterprise funds during 1962 were all either party cadres or enterprise union officials. Money from such schemes was being spent on lavish banquets and various forms of "bourgeois" entertainment. Other documents from this period report that cadres were hoarding ration coupons.[105]

Workers were hardly innocent of "capitalist" or "bourgeois" behavior. At the Jing'an Cotton Mill in Shanghai, party investigators discovered that the factory's drama troupe was staging "harmful" plays that involved "obscene movements and behavior." At the Shanghai Machine Tools Factory, the behavior of workers in their dormitories was scandalous. After hours, workers would listen to Nationalist Party radio broadcasts from Taiwan, read "pornographic novels," and engage in gambling, drunken brawls, and illicit sex.[106] The revival of capitalist influence, or entrepreneurship at least, was also apparent. A Jiangnan Shipyard employee who had been sent down to the countryside a few years before had set up a flourishing car repair yard in the Hongkou district of Shanghai, where by 1963 he reportedly earned as much as 10,000 yuan. (This was a huge amount of cash, almost twenty times greater than the annual pay of a typical factory worker earning 30–60 yuan a month.)

---

[104] GMA, Series 227-58.   [105] SMA, Series C1-1-285.   [106] Ibid.

Such "underground enterprises" were reported in both Shanghai and Guangzhou. Party authorities in Shanghai remarked, "Some are workers by day and bosses by night. They establish underground factories. Some make huge profits, some cruelly exploit the labor of the people, some corruptly plunder state finances." The party attributed these activities to a "revival of the power of capitalism." As a report noted, "The obvious enemy in the revival of capitalism is the old pre-Liberation landlords and capitalists, but the not so obvious enemy is the revival of new capitalist elements within the ranks of the working class."[107]

Party work teams sent to basic units from municipal and provincial party committees carried out an escalating sequence of campaigns in the early 1960s. The Shanghai MPC calculated that by late 1961 a total of fifty-two campaigns had taken place at the Jiangnan Shipyard since 1958, an average of thirteen per year. Party officials led a production campaign called the "rectification in the quality of military goods." There were also campaigns directed at production management, skill enhancement, wage adjustments, and bonus assessments. Military advisers sent to the shipyard to oversee top-secret defense-related production were largely resented and reviled by workers and technicians for their arrogance and their bookish dedication to details and procedures.[108] (The record for campaigns in this period appears to have been held by the Shanghai Electric Machinery Factory, which underwent eighty-seven campaigns between 1958–61.) Other campaigns included one to eliminate illiteracy, another to support the peasantry, and one to remove relatives who had occupied work posts during the GLF (a campaign known as the "returning home of family members" [*jiashu huijia*]).[109]

Nationwide, campaigns attacked the malfeasance of factory officials and administrators. In 1962–3, local party committees carried out a Five-Antis Campaign. Unlike its eponymous counterpart in 1952 that investigated private factory owners and managers, this campaign saw work teams investigate the actions of factory cadres in state enterprises. This new class of factory officials was accused of brazenly undermining government policy and abusing power. The investigations took place in the summer of 1963 in Shanghai. The main reason for embezzlement of union finances and other funds in factories, the Shanghai MPC noted in a report, was that many basic-level cadres lacked a sense of responsibility and had been influenced by "bourgeois ideology."[110]

---

[107] SMA, Series A36-2-632. [108] SMA, Series A36-2-512.
[109] SMA, Series A36-2-491. [110] SMA, Series C1-1-285.

During the Socialist Education Movement and the Four Cleans, work team investigations into the behavior of cadres intensified. The Socialist Education Campaign was a broad campaign to instill political loyalty among the ranks of workers. The Four Cleans was aimed at exposing and punishing the abuses of authority and acts of party disloyalty by those in power. Both initiatives bore the stamp of party officials in the center, especially Liu Shaoqi, who favored the top-down investigations and punishment of cadres rather than the mass mobilizational style of Mao Zedong. While scholars have pieced together the dynamics of these campaigns for rural areas of China, we still know little about how these unfolded within factories.[111] If the campaigns were anything like what took place in the countryside, the Four Cleans and the Socialist Education Campaign would have involved work teams investigating and punishing with sometimes extreme forms of violence anyone accused of corruption or other transgressions. Those whose personnel file indicated a "bad class" background by having relatives who had once been capitalists, landlords, or Nationalist officials were especially vulnerable.[112]

Campaigns had become an established pattern of factory life by the early 1960s. Work teams or party committees within the enterprise mobilized propaganda resources and rank-and-file workers to achieve some goal. Party committees engaged in political work and educational indoctrination of the working class. They led frequent socialist labor competitions in which workers who produced the most with the fewest materials won "spiritual" prizes such as being designated a model worker rather than the material reward of bonuses and extra pay. Factory party committees propagated the unselfish acts of model workers, and increasingly in the 1960s, the PLA infused a martial content into production lines. The intensification of this rhetoric, however, correlates almost directly with the spread of corruption and venality pervasive in Chinese factories and society more generally in the early 1960s. Despite hearing all the platitudes about the glories of socialism, technicians at the Jiangnan Shipyard who had witnessed the rapid rise of Japan's economy

---

[111] Richard Baum, *Prelude to Revolution: Mao, the Party, and the Peasant Question, 1962–1966* (New York: Columbia University Press, 1975); Richard Baum and Frederick C. Teiwes, *Ssu-Ch'ing: The Socialist Education Movement of 1962–1966* (Berkeley, CA: Center for Chinese Studies Monographs, 1968); Anita Chan, Richard Madsen, and Jonathan Unger, *Chen Village: The Recent History of a Peasant Community in Mao's China* (Berkeley, CA: University of California Press, 1984), 41–102.

[112] Walder, *Communist Neo-Traditionalism*, 92.

expressed the view that capitalism was no worse if not a better system than socialism:

> The newspapers all talk about America being in some kind of economic crisis, with unemployment, factories closing, students dropping out of school, and writers who can't earn a living. But what about us? Isn't it the same? Factories are closing, workers have to support agriculture, and we technicians work three or four years and our wages are still not enough for a person to live on, much less to support a family. In essence [the two countries] are the same. Slogans are just nice-sounding.[113]

Factory party committees throughout the country responded to the spiritual malaise and material scarcities of the early 1960s by relying on the persons who represented living tributes to the improvements that socialism and the CCP had brought. Party committees turned to the group who had been identified six years earlier as the "backbones" of politics and production – the "old workers" who had toiled in factories during the pre-1949 era. At the Jiangnan Shipyard, the Shanghai Number Thirty-One Mill, and other factories all over Shanghai and Guangzhou, "old workers" engaged in "recollections and contrasts" (*huiyi duibi*) to show how much better the working life was under socialism than under the cruelty of capitalism and imperialism.[114] These veterans dutifully reported and catalogued their hardships before "liberation" in party-sponsored oral histories and in meetings with newer workers. For many of these older workers, changes to their livelihood were dramatic indeed. In the old days, they had labored under the cruelties of the contract system or at best, under the uncertainties of the labor market and the arbitrary punishments of a shop floor boss. Today, they enjoyed the guarantees of a job, labor insurance, medical care, and generous living quarters. Many also noted the pride of seeing one or more of their children working with them in the same enterprise.

As moving as some of these narratives may have been to the younger cohorts of the workforce, they did little to relieve the material scarcities of workers. In one district in Guangzhou, enterprise party committees

[113] SMA, Series A36-2-548. This file contains "Situation Reports" (*qingkuang baodao*) of internal party documents circulated to cadres.
[114] Records of these interviews are the basis for many of the publications on labor history in China. The rationale behind using old workers' recollections to educate the working class can be found in GPA, Series 231-1-192 and the Shanghai Number Thirty-One Mill Archives, Labor and Wage Department, Series 63-16.

used "recollections and contrasts" by older workers to dampen demands among younger workers for higher pay just prior to the nationwide wage adjustment in 1963. The strategy proved ineffective when workers promptly pressed for wage increases at production team meetings.[115] Recollections by their seniors meant little to apprentices and new workers struggling to support their own families on 30 yuan a month. After all, older workers received favored treatment during wage adjustments and in the distribution of housing space, while more recent entrants into the workforce could only gain "spiritual" bonuses for their efforts.

Party committees and the party networks that diffused rapidly throughout the industrial workplace saw their hold strengthened in the early 1960s by gaining control over the distribution of material goods as well as political rewards within the factory. With labor mobility frozen and scarce living needs available almost exclusively from the enterprise, workers had little choice but to participate in these politicized networks. Shop floor bosses could exercise considerable control over how excludable goods such as housing and wage adjustments would be distributed. When large-scale rationing of basic commodities began in the early 1960s, labor supervisors gained additional power by influencing who could receive ration coupons. Party investigations into the sources of tensions among workers found several cases of nepotism and "undemocratic" practices, especially among supervisors. In the Shanghai Number Seventeen Cotton Mill, for example, a workshop director and CCP member who came from the Pudong district promoted only fellow Pudong residents to be deputy directors of production teams. Older workers at the Shanghai Number Five Cotton Mill complained that only youthful party members were being promoted to the position of deputy director of production teams.[116] At the Shanghai Number Two Cotton Mill, the vice-chair of the union had risen to her position despite having been a "Number One" in the days before 1949. By the early 1960s she was acting just as she had in the bad old days, according to workers. A report claimed that "not only is she constantly eating – in the canteen, in the kindergarten, in workers' rooms – but she also has control over the workers' hardship fund. Workers also must give her gifts, 'borrow' money from her, and do housework for her."[117]

Workshop directors and production team leaders enjoyed more power than at any time since the 1940s. It was not always the case that the same

---

[115] GPA, Series 231-1-192.   [116] SMA, Series C16-2-178.   [117] SMA, Series C1-1-285.

individuals who had been labor bosses before 1949 were now back in direct control over the workers under them, although there were a few examples of such continuity. The resources of the socialist shop floor boss differed in several important ways from his or her pre-1949 counterpart. The production team leader or the workshop director no longer had the power to hire and fire, thanks to state labor allocation and formal and informal sanctions against firings. But the worker in socialist China also no longer had the opportunity to change workplaces or jobs. In cities in pre-1949 China, labor mobility within urban labor markets had been curtailed by the power of gangs and guilds. In post-1949 China, interregional, interindustry, and interfirm labor mobility was subject to formal state controls. By the late 1950s, those seeking employment in another city or another factory had to first gain the approval of their work supervisor and factory administrators, who were unlikely to grant the request given the incentives to hoard inputs, including labor.

The Cultural Revolution and Decentralization

Far more documentary evidence will have to be uncovered about the first three years of the Cultural Revolution in factories and the military repression that followed after 1969 to make reasoned assertions about how labor management changed during this period. The initial stage of the Cultural Revolution in factories revisited, albeit with far more violence, the pattern found in the GLF, when party committees flung open the factory doors to outsiders and provided full-time status to scores of new workers. Factory managers and those who eventually replaced them provided "egalitarian" benefits to all employees without regard to their status and rank. Efforts to use more temporary and contract workers during the early 1960s were repudiated and considered ruses to "manage, block, and oppress" workers.[118] Also like the GLF, the Cultural Revolution years were marked by dramatic simplification of enterprise management, with functional departments being replaced by "groups" (*zu*) with broad powers over labor, finance, planning, and other issues. Under a State Council decree of 1970, the number of enterprises under direct control of the center was reduced from roughly 10,500 in 1965 to only 142.[119] Finally, in yet another reprise of the GLF and its aftermath, the excesses of free hiring and granting of full-time status to temporary and contract workers were quickly denounced and curbs placed on such

[118] Yuan, *Zhongguo laodong jingjishi*, 280.   [119] Lu, "Origins and Formation," 69–71.

practices. The Gang of Four and its supporters in Shanghai and elsewhere issued orders in the spring of 1967 for factories to exercise strict controls over new hiring and to suspend immediately the practice of converting apprentices and other part-time workers to official status.[120] The mobilization of workers during the early stages of the Cultural Revolution was shaped to some degree by the *danwei* structure. As Perry and Li note, "the institution of the *danwei* induced not only dependency, but also defiance" toward enterprise party leaders.[121]

The factional battles that raged throughout the country ultimately brought military intervention by 1968. Units of the People's Liberation Army seized control of the revolutionary committees in factories and launched a crackdown which, as Walder remarks, "ushered in a period of repression and terror that was as severe as anything seen since 1949 and that has to this day gone largely unchronicled."[122] A sequence of three campaigns between 1968 and 1971 targeted vaguely defined "enemies" and triggered state violence to a degree that has prompted parallels with the Stalinist purges of the 1930s. Throughout the 1970s, the domination of party committees in enterprises resulted in a near paralysis of managerial functions. Lacking any formal material incentives, disciplinary measures, or the ability to dismiss employees, managerial authority lapsed into political persuasion and mobilization. Workers remained dependent on their enterprises for basic necessities and lacked any formal means of increasing their incomes.

The decentralization movement of 1957–8 and the subsequent recentralization of power to provincial party committees transferred authority once and for all away from functional divisions such as ministries and commissions to territorial units. As noted in the previous chapter, municipal party committees had already begun to intervene in contentious intraenterprise issues such as wage and labor allocation during the FFYP. In some cases, as seen in Guangzhou, the Industrial Work Department of the MPC had attained direct administrative controls over a number of large enterprises in the city as early as 1953.

The rejection of one-man management and its bureaucratic forms of administration represented a significant departure from China's

---

[120] Shanghai Number Thirty-One Cotton Mill Archives, Labor and Wage Section, Series 67-21; Yuan, *Zhongguo laodong jingjishi*, 289.

[121] Elizabeth J. Perry and Li Xun, *Proletarian Power: Shanghai in the Cultural Revolution* (Boulder, CO: Westview Press, 1997), 194.

[122] Andrew G. Walder, "The Chinese Cultural Revolution in the Factories: Party-State Structures and Patterns of Conflict," in *Putting Class In its Place*, Perry, ed., 190.

experiment with Soviet-style command economics in the 1950s and from the limited functions that party committees had exercised within factories during the pre-1957 period. Between the late-1950s and the mid-1980s (with the notable exception of 1966–9), the power of party committees to investigate managers and workers, as well as the controls that such committees had over day-to-day operations, surpassed those of party committees in Soviet factories during any time in the history of the former Soviet Union.[123]

It was this period that also witnessed the creation of networks of politicized rewards that has been described at length by Andrew Walder. As recounted vividly by several Chinese informants in Walder's study, the workplace politics of the Maoist period divided rank-and-file workers into political activists and the less committed followers who competed for limited resources through personalized relations to party authorities on the shop floor.[124] Party networks greatly enhanced state power over what had been in previous decades a contentious and politically influential Chinese labor movement. Patron-client relationships formed the central nexus of exchange that Walder characterized as "communist neo-traditionalism." Inasmuch as the empirical evidence drawn from this and preceding chapters has relied on archives of various organizations in the party, government, and mass organizations of the PRC, it is difficult to add any further understanding of such patron-client ties on the factory floor. In these reports, party cadres and others who offered their first-hand observations of labor problems within factories did not single out personal relations between labor supervisors and workers or the existence of factions as a problem. The authors of such reports may have failed to observe such practices, but it is also possible that overt forms of patron-client relations and divisions between rank-and-file workers and party activists emerged most prominently during or after the Cultural Revolution. It was at this time that revolutionary committees at the municipal and factory levels would have replaced the close ties that had existed between the enterprise party committee and the functional departments of municipal party committees in the pre-1966 period.

The decentralization of power to localities in the late 1950s – what one scholar has said represented "the largest transfer of power from Beijing to the provinces that China had ever seen"[125] – had the unintended effect

---

[123] Walder, *Communist Neo-Traditionalism*, 113–22.   [124] Ibid., 166–86.
[125] Zheng, *Party vs. State*, 101.

of centralizing intraenterprise authority in the hands of enterprise party committees. The latter, backed by MPC Industrial Work Departments, dominated all other intrafirm institutions in subsequent decades. The supremacy of enterprise party committees led to substantial changes in enterprise labor management from what had existed during the FFYP. However, enterprise party committees did not create new labor management institutions as much as they cemented, with some modification, those institutions that were salient *prior to* China's adoption of state socialism: labor supervisors gained substantial personal authority over the workforce (though not to the degree enjoyed in the 1930s); wage determination evolved into a rigid seniority system with narrow wage differentials; initiatives to establish scientific management and material incentives were scrapped as they had been in limited experiments in the 1930s and 1940s; and finally, enterprises throughout China became by the early 1960s – to repeat the phrase an American observer applied to Nationalist government enterprises in Chongqing in the late 1940s – "communities in themselves," sealed off from the outside world and dominated by party activists with links to patrons in party committees at higher levels. After rapid changes in factory-level labor institutions in the 1940s, 1950s, and early 1960s, these institutions remained relatively impervious to external political, social, and economic forces in subsequent years. Some of these institutions would in fact be the most resistant to change as otherwise significant economic reforms in China's industrial sector ensued beginning in the 1980s.

8

Conclusion

IN its effort to gain the support of and ultimately control China's small but critical industrial working class, the CCP drew upon the "debris of the old order," to revisit Tocqueville's metaphor. Just as prerevolutionary institutions whose emergence Tocqueville charted prior to 1789 enhanced the power of the state in postrevolutionary France, so too in China did institutional changes within factories in the 1930s and 1940s culminate in a central organizing vehicle for the Chinese state in the 1950s. While the Chinese state post-1949 significantly expanded its control over the industrial sector and the laborers within it, innovative national policies and top-down mobilization efforts were embedded in and influenced by an existing structure.

The *danwei* as it evolved in Chinese industry can be understood as a matrix of labor management institutions overlaid at different periods between the 1930s and the late 1950s. Economic and political crises of various sorts described in the preceding chapters mandated state intervention in the relationship between employers and workers. During such periods of crisis, state officials devised new institutions of labor management and workers and managers embedded these institutions within existing norms and rules. For example, when central government officials introduced the eight-grade wage scale, managers and workers within factories resisted the skill-based criteria of the national wage regime. For political and technical reasons, managers and workers maintained an informal wage regime that favored older workers at the expense of newer workforce entrants. Chapters 5, 6, and 7 traced this and other processes by which managers and workers both adopted new rules of state socialism and adapted them to existing labor management institutions.

The course of evolutionary change in the Chinese workplace can be traced through each of the following institutions.

Foreman's Fiefdom. Intermediaries who supply laborers to factory owners during the incipient stages of industrialization can be found as a distinct group in nearly all developing economies. This social sector, found organizationally in guilds and labor racketeering gangs in Chinese cities as noted in Chapter 2, was threatened by the global spread of scientific management and modern personnel practices emanating from the industrialized countries in the first decades of the twentieth century. The timing of Taylorism and late industrialization, along with the unfolding of revolutionary politics in the 1920s and 1930s in China, led to an unusual relationship between labor intermediaries and state officials. Managers at many large firms in China established personnel departments and readily adopted the principles of scientific management then popular among Western corporations. The Nationalist regime, which came to power in conjunction with a contentious labor movement, supported opponents of scientific management and personnel administration by its informal alliance with labor intermediaries, who were nowhere stronger and more intermeshed in the Nationalist state than in Shanghai. Factory managers in Shanghai and elsewhere found it impossible to dispense with contractors and the trained labor that they controlled. Economic and political factors that drove the formation of the "foreman's fiefdom" would reemerge in admittedly different contexts in subsequent decades to reproduce a similar pattern of weak managers and dominant factory floor supervisors.

State labor allocation during the command economy took away important powers from pre-1949 shop floor bosses. Production supervisors who had once enjoyed extensive controls over the labor force and the labor process saw their powers considerably weakened by political campaigns and the introduction of central planning during the 1950s. Under the command economy, factory foremen and forewomen could no longer fire and hire workers, nor arbitrarily determine their pay. With the decentralization of administrative power in 1957, however, factory workshop and production team bosses regained important administrative and political controls. The production-territorial hierarchy of workshop, work section, and production team that concentrated authority in one individual at each level also accorded the bosses at the nodes of this structure – workshop supervisors, section leaders, and production team heads – the ability to exercise personal authority as the arbiters of a worker's political "expression" (*biaoxian*) and, as some have argued, the accompanying pay, rewards, and punishments that a worker might receive from the enterprise.[1]

Workplace Welfare. The Japanese invasion of China beginning in 1937, and the security threats that led up to that conflict, placed the Nationalist government firmly in control of China's key industrial sectors. During the war, Nationalist labor policy resulted in laws prohibiting job switching and urging that enterprise managers structure factory communities to isolate and control workers while providing them with wide-ranging basic necessities. After the war, as the Nationalist government controlled an ever-larger number of enterprises and workers, there was no particular reason for enterprise welfare provision to continue. It in fact expanded as Nationalist officials introduced the practice to state-owned enterprises in coastal cities and urged the same on private sector managers. While there was a clear political motive behind Nationalist labor policy, it was also driven by incessant inflation, which reached staggering proportions by the late 1940s. As hyperinflation erased the purchasing power of wages, enterprise managers responded by providing food and other basic commodities to workers.

The collapse of the currency and Communist military victories in 1948–9 led to the precipitous decline in industrial production, and business closures cut off many workers from their only reliable source of food stocks – their places of employment. CCP officials who took over cities in 1949 faced as one of their first challenges the difficult process of removing cash from the economy to fight inflation while distributing sufficient consumer staples. One way out of the problem was to channel food and other basic necessities through consumer co-ops based in enterprises (where speculators could not purchase goods and manipulate their prices). Enterprise welfare provision in the late 1940s, in terms of employee housing and medical care, was rudimentary compared to what it would become in the 1950s, but the importance of this practice is less in quality than in the expectations that it created among workers. To be employed meant to be provided with housing, medical care, meals, cultural resources, etc.

National and local governments, whether the Nationalist regime of the late 1940s or its Communist successor in the early 1950s, directed enterprises to fulfill welfare services that local authorities could not afford

[1] Walder, *Communist Neo-Traditionalism*, 132–43.

without great cost. In the uncertain environment of the late 1940s and early 1950s, it was far easier to continue such enterprise welfare provision than to dismantle existing practices and create a costly welfare program within urban governments. And to the degree that enterprise welfare provision contributed to antiinflationary efforts, it was all the more reasonable to expect this practice to continue at the enterprise level. Later, the low-wage, low-consumption imperatives of the command economy necessitated the expansion of enterprise welfare provision, though this was concentrated in state-owned factories and less so in the recently nationalized collective sector.

Compressed Seniority Wages. Hyperinflation of the late 1940s also had the effect of compressing wage differentials, as noted in Chapter 3. State policy to tie wages to cost-of-living indexes in the late 1940s, in combination with wage ceilings to control wage and price inflation, caused the growth in average wages to outpace the growth in income for the highest wage earners. As a result, by 1949 wage differentials across light and heavy industries, and across occupations within the same industry and even the same enterprise, were highly distorted in favor of less-skilled sectors and workers. The high-employment textile sector saw relative wages rise in the late 1940s, while industries that used more skilled labor, such as machinery, shipbuilding, and steel, suffered relative declines in wages. The same wage structure inversions took place across occupations within the same industry and even enterprise. For example, a technician might have earned little more or even less than an unskilled worker within the same factory. CCP officials in the early 1950s sought to correct such distortions by clamping down on wage increases in light industrial sectors and less skilled occupations and by raising wages in heavy industrial sectors and skilled occupations. Wage reform in the 1950s, in short, was an effort to restore wage differentials to their prehyperinflation ratios of the 1940s.[2]

This process of wage realignment in the 1950s met with measured resistance among workers and managers, as Chapters 5 and 6 showed. While wage reform corrected the most obvious distortions, narrow wage differentials among production workers remained. At the enterprise level, wage personnel classified most workers into a middle range of the eight-grade wage scale. Subsequently, new workers would be classified at the bottom rungs regardless of their skill, and wage adjustments became

---

[2] Howe, *Wage Patterns*, 47.

a matter of job tenure rather than skill. As a result, Chinese factories developed wage differentials that were much narrower than those found in other command economies. Inflation-era wage compression was in effect institutionalized in a de facto seniority system that simply rewarded marginal wage increases based on years of service to the enterprise.

Between the 1950s and the late 1970s, material incentives were ideologically anathema to certain CCP leaders. But within shop floors, the opposition to such production bonuses arose from conflict among older and younger workers and from the complexities involved in administering such an incentive system. Older, pre-1949 workers, some of whom had been promoted to supervisory positions, resented the substantial bonuses that new entrants to the workforce could earn after mastering a new technique or the operation of a machine. Given the aging technology in many older Chinese factories at this time, too much emphasis on production bonuses could also wear out equipment. Overquota production bonuses led to frequent disputes among rate setters, accountants, supervisors, and workers. The resolution of such conflicts ultimately resulted in a victory for older workers when the CCP abolished all such incentive schemes by the late 1950s. Politically and practically discredited, production bonuses never amounted to more than a small fraction of workers' incomes in the ensuing decades.

Party Penetration and Mobilization. The introduction of mass campaigns and the establishment of political networks within factories emerged during the 1950s as a direct result of the CCP's goal to transform the Chinese industrial workplace. The onset of campaigns in the early 1950s and the decentralization of administrative authority to local party committees in the late 1950s altered the existing framework of labor management institutions within Chinese factories. Managers were vulnerable to political charges after the mass campaigns and eventually subordinate in authority to enterprise party committees. The latter gained substantial status and power by their relationships to local party committees, and in certain cases many of the most important factories in Chinese cities became known as "party committee factories." This subordination of management to local political authorities had important consequences for labor management institutions. As Chapter 7 showed, the rise of "party committee factories" significantly altered the stringent wage and labor regimes of the mid-1950s. Enterprise party committees supported the elimination of production bonuses and the enhancement of administrative powers for labor supervisors. Moreover, party committees down to the production team level gained authority at the expense of accountants, quality inspectors, and other functionally specialized departments. Compared to their Soviet counterparts, enterprise party committees in Chinese factories achieved a greater degree of control over administrative issues and pursued in a far broader capacity the political mobilization of the workforce.

Chapter 6 also showed that the role of local party committees and their industrial work departments varied in certain respects across the cities of Shanghai and Guangzhou. While both municipal party committees engaged in close supervision of labor issues such as wage reform, Shanghai's MPC was far more deeply engaged in political supervision of formerly private sector enterprises and of critical sectors such as shipbuilding. In Guangzhou, on the other hand, the MPC's Industrial Work Department pursued the goals of raising production, rationalizing enterprise labor management, and essentially organizing a diffuse and underdeveloped industrial sector. This difference in the roles of local party committees was likely a reflection of the wide variation in the size of the two cities' industrial sectors and the political influence of the working class, with Shanghai measuring higher than Guangzhou on both dimensions.

Noting this variation in how local party committees approached the problem of labor management should not overshadow the fact that in both sectors of both cities, many of the same labor management institutions emerged during the same periods. While one might note certain differences in the quality and quantity of welfare provision across shipyards and textiles, or in the technical details of the wage structure, the overall pattern depicted in the previous chapters is one of convergence in labor management institutions. This would be a predictable outcome when one considers that the period under discussion was one of transition to a centrally planned economy, but as the preceding chapters have shown, it is not possible to explain China's labor management institutions as the simple by-product of a command economy. If this were the case, we should find similar shop floor institutions in other command economies, but those of China varied enough from those of the Soviet Union and other cases to challenge this explanation.

First, authority relationships differed in important ways between Chinese and Soviet factories. Foremen in Soviet factories by the late 1930s had actually gained the authority to hire and fire workers, to assign skill categories to individual workers, and to penalize and punish workers

239

as they saw fit. In a sense this represented a return to past, even prerevolutionary practices: "foremen were as they had once been – masters of the shop floor."[3] The provision of welfare services to industrial workers was also found in different vestiges in Soviet and other command economies. In order to maximize investment capital, the state would minimize consumption by channeling goods and services through enterprises. Yet in China, state enterprises owned 90 percent of urban housing stock; in the Soviet Union municipalities owned and operated urban dwellings.[4] Moreover, in the Soviet Union, where job turnover arising from labor shortages was acute, a worker could switch jobs frequently and still have access to enterprise-based welfare services. In China, job switching was nearly impossible by the late 1950s, and usually the only way in to a work unit was through state allocation to entry-level positions such as apprenticeships. Workplace welfare became highly stratified around a core state sector and a peripheral collective sector in which benefits lagged well behind those granted to state workers. In another departure from the shop floor institutions of command economies, Chinese managers and workers abolished overquota bonus incentives common in state socialist enterprises.

For some, the notable differences between the two largest command economies might reflect not so much the divergent institutional processes that I have traced for the Chinese case but something deeper within the actual cultural milieu of the Chinese factory. Indeed, some have suggested that among the most significant continuities between pre- and post-1949 factories in China could be those that derive from consistent beliefs, values, and preferences associated with employer-employee relations and the Confucian tradition in which many of China's revolutionary leaders were raised.[5] This important point suggests a challenge to, or at least a revision of, the institutionally focused analysis given here.

---

[3] Lewis H. Siegelbaum, "Masters of the Shop Floor: Foremen and Soviet Industrialization," in *Social Dimensions of Soviet Industrialization*, William G. Rosenberg and Lewis H. Siegelbaum, eds. (Bloomington, IN: Indiana University Press, 1993), 186. See also David R. Shearer, *Industry, State, and Society in Stalin's Russia, 1926–1934* (Ithaca, NY: Cornell University Press, 1996), 223–4.

[4] Xiaobo Lü and Elizabeth J. Perry, "The Changing Chinese Workplace in Historical and Comparative Perspective," in *Danwei*, Lü and Perry, eds., 10.

[5] Deborah Davis, "Patrons and Clients in Chinese Industry," *Modern China* vol. 14, no. 4 (1988): 495–6.

Conclusion

CULTURE AND INSTITUTIONAL CHANGE

Workers, managers, and state officials in China during the period covered in this book appeared to manifest certain preferences for the organization of factory labor, and one could fairly interpret such preferences as deriving from commonly held norms, values, and beliefs about the meaning of work and the employment relationship more generally. The most salient examples include the provision of nonwage benefits such as housing to employees, the exercise of personal authority by shop floor supervisors, and relatively narrow distinctions in wages. It is clearly not the case that these tendencies existed as persistent, immutable continuities between the 1930s and the 1960s. They emerged, expanded, and contracted at particular times. Yet if this book has explained the creation of the Chinese industrial workplace from the perspective of institutional emergence and evolution, it would be fair to ask about the conceptual distinctions between culture and institutions. To say that certain labor management institutions accumulated over time to constrain the behavior of workers, managers, and state officials, might be another way of saying that culture shaped action.

The shared understandings among factory managers, state officials, and workers are not difficult to find. As seen from the discussion in Chapters 2 and 3 in particular, some state and private enterprise managers sought not simply to impose a rational bureaucratic administration on factories in the incipient stages of China's industrialization, but also to exert a certain degree of paternalistic authority over the enterprise. Conceived in terms of a family, the enterprise community, whether that of Xue Mingjian's textile mill in Wuxi, the Guangdong Textile Mill in Guangzhou, or Ma Deji's Jiangnan Shipyard in Shanghai, was one in which members worked in harmony together without distinctions of class, gender, ethnicity, or other possible divisions. And it was the role of the proper manager to educate and cultivate the enterprise community, if necessary by isolating it from the malign influences of the outside world. This largely Confucian-informed vision of the industrial workplace of course hardly existed in practice: factory owners and managers turned to labor contractors for staffing their production facilities, and factory welfare programs such as they existed in the 1920s and 1930s did little to erode class or other distinctions within the workforce. Yet in China, factory directors before, during, and after state socialism have styled themselves as leaders of communities as much as administrators of production.[6]

Chinese workers also manifested over time a fairly consistent set of preferences regarding the employment relationship. Unlike their counterparts in other late industrializing countries such as Japan or the Soviet Union, Chinese workers appear to have exhibited very little of the job-switching behavior that characterized the Soviet and Japanese experiences. With the possible exception of the war years in 1937–45, when Nationalist officials imposed laws prohibiting labor mobility, the record shows that Chinese workers more often than not sought to preserve their positions within enterprises, and fought to maintain them when employers wanted to cut the workforce. Moreover, workers in Chinese enterprises demanded and pursued the expansion or restoration of benefits such as housing, food, and other nonwage provisions. The discussion of wage policy and practice in the preceding chapters clearly demonstrated an overriding aversion among many workers to output-based pay that managers attempted to impose at various times between the 1930s and the 1950s. Though workers may not have preferred the personalized authority relationships of the "foreman's fiefdom," its later incarnations in the Maoist period, and the shop-floor cultures that they spawned, Chinese workers consistently resisted efforts to depersonalize the employment relationship with a rule-bound labor regime of personnel administrators. Despite the different working class cultures based on native place, gender, and skill that characterized life within the factory, Chinese workers exhibited certain consistent preferences and pursued interests based on such preferences.

Thus, the workers and managers who created and modified labor management institutions in China over the decades sometimes interpreted these institutions as cultural in nature, and they sometimes used cultural arguments to pursue what were more clearly material interests. Yet the central problem remains that of the relationship between culture and institutions. The question is whether and to what extent the preferences manifested among workers and managers were exogenous to institutions and the process of institutional formation. My account of the emergence of labor management institutions can provide only partial answers to this important question.

---

[6] For reform period perspectives on how factory directors viewed their roles as leaders of communities, see Andrew G. Walder, "Factory and Manager in an Era of Reform," *China Quarterly* 118 (1989): 249–53.

The role of culture in institutional formation and change is evident in North's discussion, noted in Chapter 1, regarding the interaction between informal and formal institutions. To the extent that informal institutions, referring to "conventions and codes of behavior,"[7] can be equated with culture, then we might agree with North that such conventions operate as a kind of constraint on the acceptance of certain formal institutions. Within a given factory, for example, informal institutions can influence how formal institutions operate, and even whether they operate effectively. This focus on the interaction between formal institutions and cultural norms serves as a useful framework for understanding the emergence of factory regimes in China and elsewhere, but it is clearly context specific. The previous chapters have shown that crises and various responses to them by officials, managers, and workers generated what might be fairly characterized as "conventions and codes of behavior." These informal institutions later influenced how formal institutions functioned, as North posits. For example, informal institutions such as enterprise welfare provision, narrow wage differentials, and the broad powers of shop floor bosses emerged as responses to crises during the processes of industrialization and state formation in the twentieth century. Such contingent solutions endured as they continued to resolve basic problems of labor recruitment, compensation, and organization within industrial enterprises. When the CCP imposed institutions of the planned economy in the industrial sector in the 1950s, a labor regime emerged that reflected command economy labor management nested within a preexisting set of older, more durable institutions.

CRISES AND FACTORY INSTITUTIONS

One could argue that the labor institutions sometimes thought of as "national employment systems" particular to a given country developed in close conjunction with episodes of crisis involving state intervention and responses from managers and workers. For example, many accounts of "lifetime employment," seniority wages, and company unions found in Japan view such practices and organizational forms as reflections of hierarchical relationships found in Japanese culture.[8] There is little doubt that the values, norms, and beliefs shared by most Japanese have influenced the development of labor-management institutions in Japan. Yet

---

[7] North, *Institutions, Institutional Change*, 4.
[8] Abegglen, *The Japanese Factory*.

cultural arguments have difficulty in accounting for changes in employment patterns in industrial enterprises over time, especially before and after the Second World War.[9] Some scholars have argued that Japan's experience of "late development" meant that Japanese state officials, factory managers, and workers faced entirely different challenges and constraints and therefore responded with organizational solutions that differed markedly from the labor management patterns found in earlier developers, such as Britain and the United States.[10]

Many features of the Japanese employment system can be traced to the onset of industrial development during the late nineteenth century.[11] External international threats and domestic political challenges forced state officials to quickly create a base of industrial workers. The mobility of skilled labor in heavy industry was an especially serious obstacle to this goal and to sustained industrial production. Thus, the *nenko* system of seniority-based wages, an important institution in Japan, arose as a solution to the extraordinarily high rates of turnover in Japanese factories. Managers and state officials had to offer incentives for workers to remain in place. Subsequent to this resolution of the problem of turnover, however, seniority wages remained as an institution that shaped the conflict among workers, factory owners, and the state during the unionization battles of the 1920s and beyond. The communal and familial unity of employees in large Japanese factories emerged out of the experience of the years immediately after the war, when food shortages and other scarcities created a "community of fate" whose members were tied together by a shared experience of crisis.[12] In Japan, labor management institutions that developed at particular moments persisted beyond the conditions that created them. Both China and Japan underwent transformations of their political systems during the mid-twentieth century, yet workplace institutions proved to be more durable than state officials and others expected. Such institutions also shaped patterns of industrial relations. Unions in Japan sought to preserve seniority wages; by contrast, workers in China sought to preserve a highly intensive yet also exclusive welfare structure of benefits delivered through the enterprise. As in China, labor management institutions in Japan emerged

---

[9] Cole, *Japanese Blue Collar*.

[10] Dore, *British Factory – Japanese Factory*; Taira, *Economic Development and the Labor Market in Japan*.

[11] Gordon, *The Evolution of Labor Relations*.

[12] Gordon, "Conditions for the Disappearance of the Japanese Working-Class Movement."

not simply during state-led industrialization but also in an environment of crisis.

Other cases also suggest that the outcome of conflict between workers and owners to stabilize employment is often decisively influenced by state intervention during periods of war or economic crisis.[13] In the United States, the crises in production during two wars and the Great Depression, as business and labor historians have shown, brought new institutions of labor management that would define employment for much of the post-1945 era, up to the early 1980s.[14] It was during wartime that core industries and firms established collective bargaining, formal job descriptions, and internal promotions, also known as "internal labor markets." Some have asserted that the establishment of the National War Labor Board during the Second World War was the critical force in "nationalizing a conception of routine and bureaucratic industrial relations" and "fixing a system of industrial relations on the shop floor."[15] Post-1945 labor relations brought sustained prosperity to both labor and management, but at the cost of foregoing alternative possibilities of workplace organization in which workers may have gained greater participation in managerial decisions.[16]

Well before this twentieth-century intervention of the federal government in the workplace, however, certain institutions in the American factory were already in place. Drawing upon the findings of Charles Sabel and others who have illustrated the importance of ideas in the development of employment systems, labor historian David Brody notes that postwar "workplace contractualism" was strongly shaped by workers' conceptions of justice and legal norms that existed before the 1940s.[17] As Brody explains it, workers conducting specific tasks on general purpose machines and assembly lines defined their grievances in terms of management's failure to "play by the rules," or to offer standard wage rates for the same task. Following court decisions between the 1930s and the 1950s, the federal government only affirmed and

---

[13] James N. Baron, Frank R. Dobbin, and P. Devereaux Jennings, "War and Peace: The Evolution of Modern Personnel Administration in U.S. Industry," *American Journal of Sociology* vol. 92, no. 2 (September 1986): 350–83.

[14] Jacoby, *Employing Bureaucracy*.

[15] Nelson Lichtenstein, "Industrial Democracy, Contract Unionism, and the National War Labor Board," *Labor Law Journal* 33 (August 1982): 524.

[16] Ibid.

[17] David Brody, "Workplace Contractualism in Comparative Perspective," in *Industrial Democracy in America: The Ambiguous Promise*, Nelson Lichtenstein and Howell John Harris, eds. (New York: Cambridge University Press, 1993), 176–205.

standardized agreements that emerged during labor-management battles in the 1930s, according to Brody. Workplace values or "conceptions of industrial justice" caused labor laws and policy, not the other way around.[18]

Using the terms proposed here to explain the origins and development of labor management institutions in China, it is not difficult to synthesize these two arguments for the U.S. case. The crises of the 1930s and 1940s brought federal government intervention and new formal institutions of labor management, yet the new policies were mediated by the preexisting institution of standardized wage contracts. It is worth noting that, in contrast to China at roughly the same time, industrial welfare declined sharply as the U.S. federal government established a national (as opposed to enterprise-based) pension administration and other social welfare programs. In the United States as elsewhere, employment patterns arose from the long-term accumulation of institutions.

There would have been no "work unit" as we know it without the CCP's effort to impose revolutionary changes on the Chinese workplace in the 1950s, but it is not difficult to conceive that certain elements of the industrial work unit, most notably welfare provision, enterprise party committees, and seniority wages, would have become institutional elements of life in Chinese factories absent a CCP victory in 1949. Indeed, some evidence to assess this counterfactual claim exists in Taiwan in the 1950s – where the condition of "Communist rule" was obviously not present as a causal factor but a factory regime with strikingly similar traits to that found in the PRC existed in the 1950s.

BUILDING WORKPLACE INSTITUTIONS: TAIWAN IN THE 1950S

Nationalist Party officials, faced in 1949 with the task of administering a much smaller yet significant number of industrial enterprises on Taiwan, "transported" labor management institutions from the mainland. The National Resources Commission, as noted in Chapter 3, had established and operated enterprises in critical sectors since the 1930s – largely in response to security concerns and eventually the onset of war. By the late 1940s, NRC enterprises employed over 260,000 workers and staff.[19] After the Nationalist retreat to the island, the Ministry of Economic Affairs and the NRC maintained control of the "commanding heights"

---

[18] Brody, "Workplace Contractualism," 199.   [19] Kirby, "Continuity and Change," 132.

of Taiwan's economy. It may not come as a surprise therefore that the labor institutions created during the years of foreign invasion and civil war on the mainland continued in the early 1950s on Taiwan, especially in enterprises belonging to the NRC and state corporations. While Employee Welfare Committees had been established in almost all state enterprises during the 1940s, NRC-managed enterprises had developed a variant of the EWCs, known as "Employee Improvement Associations" (*yuangong lijin hui*). An NRC report (in English, possibly for official U.S. consumption) on Employee Improvement Associations some time in the early 1950s proudly noted that the main purpose of such groups was "to direct members in their out-of-duty activities, such as recreation, education and training, aid and benefit[,] and cooperative shopping." Enterprises provided subsidies for the education of their employees' children, for employee medical expenses and insurance, and other living costs. The report said that in the more than one hundred factories and mines employing over 50,000 personnel, "experience has told us that these associations have helped to cultivate [a] cooperative spirit, improve production, eliminate personal difference and institutional friction."[20]

Outside this core of advanced industry and labor harmony transported from the mainland, NRC officials observed, local workers in the nonstate sector were poorly organized and needed educating. "Since this island has been for 50 years under Japanese rule, and [is] used to the colonial way of living, most of the workers do not quite understand the value of labor organization. They still cling to the old Japanese convention of having no group activities." Regardless of the source of Taiwanese workers' apparent unwillingness to cooperate, the report's authors urged the relevant labor departments in the government to organize nonstate workers for the same purposes as their state sector counterparts.[21] (The attribution of "no group activities" to "Japanese convention" stands in obvious contrast to many other characterizations of factory culture in Japan.)

In 1950, the Executive Yuan established a "Labor Welfare Study Group" consisting of representatives from the Interior Ministry, the NRC, and the "national" and Taiwan labor federations. The conclusions of this high-level Nationalist study group, compiled in a secret report in June 1951, bears a striking resemblance to the reports on factory labor management authored in the early 1950s by the GMD's Communist

[20] MEA, Series 24-03-49.   [21] Ibid.

Party rivals on the mainland.[22] Officials from both parties, after all, were grappling with labor welfare and organization issues in what for most were strange and unfamiliar locales. Moreover, in many cases management and labor could literally not understand one another, the latter having little if any knowledge of the language (Mandarin) or the ideology (Leninism and/or Sun Yat-sen thought) in which their supervisors communicated.

Premier Chen Cheng noted in his introduction to the Study Group's report that workers on the mainland currently toiled thirteen hours a day and only received the equivalent of under 50 Taiwan dollars per month, not enough to maintain one person's livelihood, much less a family's. "On the other hand," Chen observed, "our labor treatment is far better than that of the Communist bandits in several respects. This difference between our labor treatment measures and those of the enemy should be demonstrated to workers in various locales." The Study Group report, despite its references to Communist "bandits," was written in a tone and substance that could have been found in many CCP reports at that time. Some of the problems identified in the Study Group report are the same as those that the CCP found in mainland factories. There were wide disparities in the distribution of benefits and "inversions" of wages in factories of the same industry, as well as a proliferation of "hidden" wages, side payments to workers that amounted to wage subsidies. The GMD Study Group proposed measures that would have been familiar to its rivals on the mainland: the establishment of enterprise union-managed welfare funds in state, provincial, and private sector enterprises; the expansion of employee housing and medical facilities; the provision of daily goods to employees; and the construction of collective welfare facilities such as child care centers, dining halls, showers, and hair salons. The Study Group also reported on the successes and popularity of the government's labor insurance program, which had over 140,600 workers in 639 units registered by May 1951.

The Study Group noted that state-owned factories and mines all had party branches (*dangbu*) ranging in size from 6 to 226 members, made up almost exclusively of mainland rather than Taiwan-born workers. These factory party branches were linked to the territorial party branch for the area in which the enterprise was located. While workers expressed little interest in party affairs, or even knowledge of party

---

[22] Ministry of the Interior, "Laogong fuli kaocha baogao" (Report on Investigation of Labor Welfare), in MEA, Series 24-03-48.

activities, factory unions had managed to stoke much interest by organizing May 1 Labor Day festivities and selecting "model workers" for accolades. The positive atmosphere, according to the report, was attributable to the absence of labor-management disputes in state factories. However, the report asserted, the "leadership powers" (*lingdaoquan*) of the factory union should belong to the factory party branch. This meant that all important union measures must be first presented to that factory party branch and its local territorial organization for consideration. The "supervisory powers" over unions should be carried out by the local government's social and administrative departments. In another observation that resonates with the experience of mainland state factories in the 1950s, the Study Group criticized the overstaffing of state enterprises with too many managers and administrative workers, saying that too few managerial personnel were willing to "set a good example and become one with the workers and their lives" (*yu gongren shenghuo dacheng yipian*). This was in stark contrast to private industry, the report noted, where managers were few and the ones who were in charge were indeed willing to "become one with the workers."[23]

The extent to which the recommendations of this elite Study Group on labor welfare in Taiwan were carried out over the next years is less important than the similarities in conceptions of the ideal factory labor management environment as envisioned by Nationalist and Communist Party officials. The Nationalist Party at this time had a very strong "planning" orientation, including officials who were openly enamoured of Soviet-style command economics.[24] This might explain some of the labor measures being discussed by Nationalist leaders in the 1950s, but more significant was the obvious fact that the provision of enterprise-level welfare measures and efforts to establish party networks within factories were both initiatives that the Nationalists had attempted on the mainland during and after the War of Resistance Against Japan. In a still-tenuous security outlook in the early 1950s, state intervention in the core of industrial enterprises under the NRC and other agencies was a necessity. In a more stable economic environment, enterprise welfare provision, including pensions, insurance, and other measures, was more attainable than in the highly disruptive hyperinflationary environment

---

[23] Ibid.

[24] Chen-kuo Hsu, "Ideological Reflections and the Inception of Economic Development in Taiwan," in *The Role of the State in Taiwan's Development*, Joel D. Aberbach, David Dollar, and Kenneth L. Sokoloff, eds. (Armonk, NY: M.E. Sharpe, 1994), 313.

of the late 1940s. Having a shared history of institutional development before 1949, factories in mainland China and in Taiwan reflected similar patterns of state-labor relations.

EPILOGUE: OLD FACTORIES, NEW INSTITUTIONS

The institutional transformation of the 1940s and 1950s in Chinese factories chronicled in this book has been followed by a subsequent and equally transformative period of institution building in the 1980s and 1990s. It is not necessary here to retell the story of reforms in industrial labor management over the past two decades. It is instructive, however, to recount observations and discussions with officials from the Shanghai and Guangzhou enterprises whose socialist and presocialist pasts have made up the bulk of the preceding chapters, and how some of the oldest enterprises in China are experiencing reforms of their labor management institutions.[25] These observations were gleaned from interviews and factory visits in 1994–5 over the course of my conducting research for this book.

One of the first questions that arises to a visitor to state-owned textile mills in Shanghai and Guangzhou today is an obvious, if rather delicate one: "Where are the workers?" Both of the textile sector enterprises surveyed in the preceding chapters had by the mid-1990s established production "off-site" in less expensive suburban areas or even in neighboring provinces in the case of the Shanghai Number Thirty-One Mill. The buildings where production once took place were left empty and silent. These and other buildings within the factory compound were literally being auctioned off, as rental properties to outside investors. The enterprises had also put factory property to more lucrative commercial or residential real estate ventures. (As I was leaving the Shanghai Number Thirty-One Mill one day in early 1995, officials were eagerly awaiting a meeting with investors from a Taiwan manufacturer looking to lease or purchase a building on the factory compound.) Inside the various workshops where limited production did take place, much of the spinning machinery sat silent. Some of it, a Shanghai Number Thirty-One

---

[25] Several earlier studies have shown that the reforms of state industry resulted in an expansion of enterprise provision of social welfare services. See for example, Lowell Dittmer and Xiaobo Lü, "Personal Politics in the Chinese *Danwei* Under Reform," *Asian Survey* vol. 36, no. 3 (March 1996): 246–67; Naughton, "Economic Foundations," 182–3; Walder, "Factory and Manager," 243–4.

Mill official remarked, might be highly valued by collectors in England, who were said to be scouring Shanghai's mills to purchase these "industrial antiques" and ship them back to the country from which they had come during the first decades of the twentieth century. Elsewhere at the mill, piecemeal production continued, but the walls that might have once been festooned with large character posters and pictures of model workers were now bare and dust covered, adding to the drab environs that bespoke an enterprise whose productive years, in Shanghai at least, had long since passed. The visit to the Guangdong Textile Mill, where a Chinese colleague and I showed up unannounced after many weeks of having failed to gain official permission, was expectedly attenuated. But here too it was readily apparent that the enterprise was engaged in very little on-site production. Its managers were seeking foreign investors and anyone interested in leasing property within the factory compound, which was located in a high-rent district of Guangzhou not far south of the Pearl River.

Far more activity was apparent at the two shipyards, with their expansive work sites and massive docks for assembling and repairing ocean vessels. While visits to these enterprises resulted in fruitful conversations and a number of useful documents being shared with me, officials at both shipyards informed me that foreigners were not permitted to tour the production facilities. (An understandable explanation coming from the Huangpu Shipyard, which in 1995 was engaged in repair work on naval vessels for the PLA Navy's South China Sea Fleet. A questionable excuse coming from the Jiangnan Shipyard, which enlisted a dozen or so foreign technicians as consultants in its construction and repair facilities.)

The substantive interviews that took place at three of the four enterprises revealed a number of interesting observations on how managers and party functionaries understood labor management institutions of the present and past.[26] After the exchange of pleasantries and introductions, I inquired if there were any older workers whom I might interview about their recollections of factory work in the 1950s and possibly earlier. The universal response at all four enterprises was one form or another of "no, they retired long ago." Besides, several officials told me, most retired workers who had been employed during the decades I was researching

---

[26] At the Huangpu Shipyard, the Shanghai Number Thirty-One Mill, and (briefly) the Guangdong Textile Mill, I interviewed officials from the Factory Director's Office or the Labor and Personnel section. At the Jiangnan Shipyard I interviewed officials from the Factory History Office.

were so advanced in years that "their thinking isn't clear anymore" (*naozi bu qingchu*). Not that there was any shortage of retirees – officials noted with an odd mixture of pride and disdain the heavy burden that their enterprises were compelled to shoulder in the form of medical expenses, pensions, subsidies, housing, and other welfare measures for retirees. A 1992 document from the Jiangnan Shipyard estimated that the number of retirees, then at 5,304 or 36 percent of the existing workforce, would rise to 60 percent of the workforce by 2002.[27] At the Shanghai Number Thirty-One Mill, according to a 1992 factory document, there were a total of 5,905 retirees in an enterprise with 6,725 active employees (retirees there made up 88 percent of the current workforce).[28] Both Shanghai enterprises had set up Retiree Management Committees (*tuiguanhui*) to manage the work of delivering services and looking after the livelihoods of the thousands of retirees across the city and even other provinces. They did this by establishing "liaison stations" (*lianluozhan*) or "group leaders" (*zuzhang*) to which retirees in a particular district of the city could report problems, and whose job it was to visit retirees in their homes from time to time to check on their living conditions.

The interviews with factory officials also provided insights into how current staff members viewed labor management institutions under the command economy, though most had only experienced its later phases of the late 1960s and 1970s. Virtually everyone began by recalling with incredulity the monthly salary they had earned when they entered the workforce during or just prior to the Cultural Revolution: 30 to 36 yuan. Nor were there any bonuses or much in the way of subsidies then, several officials noted. "After 1958 the whole wage system was under great pressure," a Jiangnan Shipyard official explained. "No one dared pursue incentive bonuses or to work beyond production quotas."[29] One personnel staff member at the Huangpu Shipyard repeated the official line on the old days when she said, "In the past you always got your pay regardless of your work. In those days everyone was 'eating out of the big pot' (*chi da guofan*), and there was no way to actively bring into play the power of labor."[30] A Shanghai Number Thirty-One Mill official explained

[27] Jiangnan Shipyard Factory History Research Office, "Renshi laodong guanli," 184.
[28] Shanghai Number Thirty-One Mill Factory Director's Office, "Shangmian sanshiyichang zhigong bian."
[29] Author's interview, Jiangnan Shipyard Factory History Research Office, December 26, 1994.
[30] Author's interview, Huangpu Shipyard officials, May 3, 1995.

how workers during the 1950s and 1960s had in some ways greater status than managers: "In the past, enterprise officials had no power to manage workers. Workers were treated as state property (*guojia caichan*) and they couldn't be casually dismissed or pushed around."[31] In addition, another official at the same mill noted, because older workers had made a contribution to the nation for their service before "liberation," it was only natural that they should receive generous compensation thereafter.[32]

If retirees and "old workers" had contributed their share to the nation and were now being duly, if expensively, compensated by their enterprises, what of the reforms? What had the sweeping changes in the economy brought to the workplace? The first issue officials raised in response to this question was the institution of labor contracting. In 1986, the State Council issued regulations that allowed enterprise managers to recruit new labor through short-term, usually three year, contracts that were in theory renewable at the end of the term.[33] The policy of labor contracts applied to new hires, meaning that existing workers were "grandfathered" and remained "permanent labor" (*guding gong*), though some interviewees referred to this part of the workforce as "official labor" (*zhengshi gong*). An enterprise with a declining workforce would therefore have a smaller proportion of employees on contracts. The Shanghai Number Thirty-One Mill, for example, which initiated labor contracts in 1986, by 1995 had only 20 percent of its workers on contracts, with the remainder classified as official labor.[34] The Jiangnan Shipyard had 1,471 of its 12,855 employees in 1992 on labor contracts, though officials in 1995 informed me that the shipyard would soon implement an "all-employee contract system" (*quanyuan hetong zhi*).[35] Officials at the Huangpu Shipyard in Guangzhou reported that almost

---

[31] Author's interview, Shanghai Number Thirty-One Mill Factory Director's Office and Personnel Department, January 14, 1995.

[32] While officials in Shanghai used the construction "before/after liberation" (*jiefang yiqian, jiefang yihou*) when referencing events before and after 1949, it was far more frequent in Guangzhou to hear the term "before/after nation-building" (*jianguo yiqian, jianguo yihou*).

[33] Doug Guthrie, *Dragon in A Three-Piece Suit: The Emergence of Capitalism in China* (Princeton, NJ: Princeton University Press, 1999), 86–91; John Child, *Management in China*, 162–4; William A. Byrd, *Chinese Industrial Firms under Reform* (New York: Oxford University Press, 1992), 8–9; Yuan, *Zhongguo laodong jingjishi*, 300–7.

[34] Author's interview, Shanghai Number Thirty-One Mill Factory Director's Office and Personnel Department, January 14, 1995.

[35] Author's interview, Jiangnan Shipyard Factory History Research Office, December 26, 1994.

all of its 3,500 production workers were on labor contracts of generally three years, though some workers had labor contracts of between five and fifteen years. Huangpu Shipyard officials commented that the enterprise's generally uncompetitive pay rates had led to over 1,000 workers leaving the shipyard during the preceding ten years. Having longer term contracts might help mitigate the turnover problem, but officials said they were also trying to lessen turnover by expanding and improving employee benefits.

An important part of the labor contract system as it evolved in the 1990s was the development of Labor Dispute Resolution Committees within state enterprises. As stipulated in the 1995 Labor Law, these committees have nine members represented by employees, management, and the enterprise union. In 1995 interviews, most enterprise officials dodged direct answers to the question of how many contract disputes had been heard by their dispute resolution committees. Officials at the Shanghai Number Thirty-One Mill said that its workforce had averaged fewer than ten dispute cases per year since 1986. Disputes had arisen over "misunderstandings" and "violations" of labor contracts. The implementation of the then-new 1995 Labor Law was expected to clarify ambiguities in the labor contracts and their dispute resolution.

On the enterprise visits I also asked about employee welfare measures. All the enterprises offered housing or rent subsidies to their employees. Generally it was the case that unmarried workers lived in factory dormitories within the compound, while workers with families were provided with free apartments or with very low nominal rents in neighboring "new villages" (*xincun*). The Shanghai Number Thirty-One Mill, for example, had expanded the number of its factory dormitories for women from two to four, which now housed nearly 900 workers. Between 1978 and 1990 the same mill had built in the surrounding neighborhood 25,810 square meters of family apartments for employees, and added another 18,000 square meters of apartments between 1990 and 1992.[36]

Wage determination, like recruitment and welfare provision, had also undergone substantial change. At the Shanghai Number Thirty-One Mill, there had been no piece-rate wages between 1958 and 1983. During nationally coordinated wage adjustments, a handful of workers would have their pay grade adjusted upward. It was not necessarily the case that party members were the ones who received such promotions,

---

[36] Shanghai Number Thirty-One Mill Factory Director's Office, "Shangmian sanshiyichang zhigong bian."

officials explained. If anything, party members had to demonstrate their asceticism and not ask for wage promotions.[37] All this changed in the mid-1980s, when State Council directives gave enterprise directors substantial authority to determine the enterprise wage bill. Managers were able to experiment with production-based bonuses and other incentive systems. The size of the wage bill, once a simple function of total employees, was now linked directly to the amount of profits and taxes generated by the enterprise. As these rose, so could the wage bill. Because factory directors could control the growth of new hires, the average pay per employee rose significantly (less so when inflation is taken into account).[38] With the emergence of labor contracts, wages and incentive bonuses could be clearly spelled out.

Yet this transition to new institutions of wage determination has been far from seamless. Setting wage levels and distributing subsequent wage adjustments, now the purview of factory directors rather than central officials in Beijing, continued to cause problems among managers and workers. A Huangpu Shipyard personnel official noted that the process of wage determination still led to "egalitarian" results with differences in base pay being papered over through subsidies and other nonwage income. This official commented, "It's a face-losing situation to give one person less money and someone else more money."[39] Enterprise personnel departments now calculated an employee's pay by adding up several income categories for which an employee was eligible. First, a basic wage was calculated through a matrix of pay grades (while enterprises could draw up these pay grades, many, including the Huangpu Shipyard, used the pay grades of the Guangdong Provincial Labor Bureau). Following this basic wage, a worker was eligible for living subsidies (*shenghuo jintie*); a "workpost wage" (*gangwei gongzi*) determined by any number of criteria including undesirable conditions such as heat and noise; a seniority bonus based on years at the enterprise; and a production bonus for surpassing a given quota. Because enterprises had the autonomy to experiment with and add any number of other items to wage determination, this pattern varied widely. An official with the Guangzhou Municipal Labor Bureau with whom I discussed wage policy in 1995 criticized state enterprise managers for their frequent practice of

---

[37] Author's interview, Shanghai Number Thirty-One Mill Factory Director's Office and Personnel Department, January 14, 1995.

[38] Yuan, *Zhongguo laodong jingjishi*, 364–9.

[39] Author's interview, Huangpu Shipyard officials, May 3, 1995.

attaching item after item, especially subsidies, to the base pay of workers. This was, he said, an example of "reforming chaotically" (*gailuan*). Because of the opaque accounting methods in most state factories, it was impossible to know how much revenue and profits were being channeled to employees in the form of welfare measures, subsidies, and other "hidden wages."[40]

The all-important connections between enterprise party committees and their patrons in the Industrial Work Department of the Municipal Party Committee were severed during the early 1980s. Political Departments (*zhengzhi bu*) had been formed within enterprises and MPCs in 1964, replacing Industrial Work Departments. Political Departments carried out an escalating series of campaigns starting that year. In 1982, the Political Departments at the Huangpu Shipyard and many state enterprises were dissolved.[41] As a result, enterprise party committees no longer hold the authority over day-to-day decisions that they once enjoyed.[42] In post-Mao China, one could argue, it has been the very receding of party committee dominance at the local level and the emergence of alternative nonparty networks that have brought far-reaching change to China and could continue to do so over the long run. Party committees continue to have some say in personnel decisions, subject to approval by party committees further up the hierarchy. In fact, the authority of the party committee is often trumped by the factory director, who is likely to sit on the enterprise party committee, if not chair it by jointly holding the position of enterprise party secretary.[43] Officials at the Jiangnan Shipyard explained that today, the enterprise party committee acts as a "board of directors" (*dongshihui*) that offers general guidance on issues and to which factory directors must report.[44] The

---

[40] On the problems associated with "irregular wage income," see You, *China's Enterprise Reform*, 128–33.

[41] Huangpu Shipyard Party Committee Organization Department, "Huangpu zaochuanchang zuzhishi ziliao" (Materials on the Organizational History of the Huangpu Shipyard), mimeo, 1989.

[42] For an account of how the powers of factory party committees have been superseded by those of factory directors, see An Chen, "Democratic Reform of Management Structures in China's Industrial Enterprises," *Politics & Society* vol. 23, no. 3 (September 1995): 390–1.

[43] The Chinese government announced in March 1997 its plans to bolster the power of party committees in state-owned enterprises to monitor and investigate managerial activities. Pamela Yatsko, "Party's Over," *Far Eastern Economic Review*, June 5, 1997:59.

[44] Author's interview, Jiangnan Shipyard Factory History Research Office, December 26, 1994.

selection of an analogy to the Western corporation is revealing in an environment in which Chinese leaders are attempting to introduce modern capitalist management structures to hold factory managers responsible for profits and losses. Within the enterprise workforce, party membership had declined substantially by the mid-1990s. Party membership has declined to 7 or 8 percent of the workforce at the Shanghai Number Thirty-One Mill, down from an estimated 15 to 20 percent during the 1970s.[45]

The erosion of party networks during the economic reforms also undermined the personalized political authority that supervisors enjoyed in the Maoist era. It is now factory directors and personnel and wage departments that exercise authority over hiring and pay decisions. It is no longer the case that a shop floor boss can influence, through wage reform or job placement, a worker's chances for promotion or job transfer. One official at the Shanghai Number Thirty-One Mill disputed the idea that factory supervisors had ever enjoyed substantial personal authority, arguing that workshop directors and production team leaders in the command economy simply followed state plans. "Labor policy was very strict then. The state set everything. A workshop director would get in trouble if he altered labor policy." If anything, according to this official, workshop directors and team leaders today have more power than in the past, because they can report violations of contracts and are designated to enforce the enterprise's own rules and policies.[46]

With the receding of planned labor allocation and the adoption of contract labor as an enterprise institution has come the ability of enterprises to "recruit from society." Given the fact that the enterprises I visited in 1994–5 were in the process of cutting back on the size of their workforces, recruitment was not an especially difficult problem except for highly skilled labor. Both the Jiangnan Shipyard and the Huangpu Shipyard relied on technical schools managed by their enterprise for a steady supply of technicians. Nonetheless, a Jiangnan Shipyard official remarked that "young, skilled workers want to leave the factory to go work for foreign enterprises, and this is a big problem."[47] The textile mills, with most of their production now based outside of their respective cities, recruited local labor. Officials at the Shanghai Number Thirty-One Mill

---

[45] Author's interview, Shanghai Number Thirty-One Mill Factory Director's Office and Personnel Department, January 14, 1995.

[46] Ibid.

[47] Author's interview, Jiangnan Shipyard Factory History Research Office, March 6, 1995.

and other specialists I spoke with noted that local labor bureaus still exercised approval power over the labor recruitment plans submitted by enterprises, and that this veto power was significant. State enterprises in particular had to justify their use of labor from outside the city and other efforts to "recruit from society." Many enterprises still turned to local labor officials for assistance in obtaining new workers.

China's state-owned enterprises are in many respects living relics of the past. This is true in a literal sense, given the aging equipment and technology in state factories, as well as in a deeper political sense. State enterprises represent a past that even the current leadership of the CCP has rejected as a costly undertaking to deliver guaranteed employment and social services to workers and to mobilize millions for political and production purposes. As SOEs are dismantled, downsized, corporatized, and otherwise sold off to nonstate investors, new firm-level institutions have emerged from a similar process of negotiation and conflict among state officials, employers, and workers that characterized China's transition to socialism. To date, this process takes place in the absence of autonomous associations of workers and employers. Yet with the conversion of state enterprises to nonstate forms of ownership, there is a strong demand for new firm-level labor institutions to cope with the uncertainties of the market economy.

Archives Consulted

SHANGHAI

Shanghai Municipal Archives (SMA)
Jiangnan Shipyard, Factory History Archives
Shanghai Number Thirty-One Cotton Mill Factory Archives
Chinese Business History Research Center (CBHRC), Institute of
  Economics, Shanghai Academy of Social Sciences

GUANGZHOU

Guangdong Provincial Archives (GPA)
Guangzhou Municipal Archives (GMA)

TAIPEI

Ministry of Economics Archives (MEA), Institute of Modern History,
  Academia Sinica

Bibliography

Abegglen, James. *The Japanese Factory: Aspects of its Social Organization.* Glencoe, IL: The Free Press, 1958.

Andors, Stephen. *China's Industrial Revolution: Politics, Planning, and Management, 1949 to the Present.* New York: Pantheon Books, 1977.

Andrle, Vladimir. *Workers in Stalin's Russia: Industrialization and Social Change in a Planned Economy.* New York: St. Martin's Press, 1988.

Bachman, David. *Bureaucracy, Economy, and Leadership in China: The Institutional Origins of the Great Leap Forward.* New York: Cambridge University Press, 1991.

Barnett, A. Doak. *China on the Eve of Communist Takeover.* New York: Frederick A. Praeger, 1963.

Barnett, A. Doak, with Ezra Vogel. *Cadres, Bureaucracy, and Political Power in Communist China.* New York: Columbia University Press, 1967.

Baron, James N., Frank R. Dobbin, and P. Devereaux Jennings. "War and Peace: The Evolution of Modern Personnel Administration in U.S. Industry." *American Journal of Sociology* vol. 92, no. 2 (1986): 350–83.

Baum, Richard. *Prelude to Revolution: Mao, the Party, and the Peasant Question, 1962–1966.* New York: Columbia University Press, 1975.

Baum, Richard, and Frederick C. Teiwes. *Ssu-Ch'ing: The Socialist Education Movement of 1962–1966.* Berkeley, CA: Center for Chinese Studies Monographs, 1968.

Bendix, Reinhard. *Work and Authority in Industry: Ideologies of Management in the Course of Industrialization.* New York: Wiley Press, 1956.

Berger, Suzanne, and Michael J. Piore. *Dualism and Discontinuity in Industrial Societies.* New York: Cambridge University Press, 1980.

Berliner, Joseph S. *Factory and Manager in the USSR.* Cambridge, MA: Harvard University Press, 1957.

Bian, Morris Linan. "Development of Institutions of Social Service and Industrial Welfare in State Enterprises in China, 1937–1945." Paper presented at the annual meeting of the Association for Asian Studies, 1998.

Bian, Yianjie. "*Guanxi* and the Allocation of Urban Jobs in China." *China Quarterly* 140 (1994): 971–99.

——— *Work and Inequality in Urban China.* Albany, NY: State University of New York Press, 1994.

Blecher, Marc. "Communist Neo-traditionalism: Work and Authority in Chinese Industry." *Pacific Affairs* vol. 60, no. 4 (1987–8): 657–9.

Boisot, Max, and John Child. "The Iron Law of Fiefs: Bureaucratic Failure and the Problem of Governance in the Chinese Economic Reforms." *Administrative Science Quarterly* 33 (1988): 507–27.

Brandes, Stuart D. *American Welfare Capitalism, 1880–1940*. Chicago: University of Chicago Press, 1976.

Brody, David. "Workplace Contractualism in Comparative Perspective." In *Industrial Democracy in America: The Ambiguous Promise*, edited by Nelson Lichtenstein and Howell John Harris, 176–205. New York: Cambridge University Press, 1993.

Brugger, William. *Democracy and Organisation in the Chinese Industrial Enterprise, 1948–1953*. New York: Cambridge University Press, 1976.

Burawoy, Michael. *The Politics of Production: Factory Regimes Under Capitalism and Socialism*. London: Verso Press, 1985.

——— *Manufacturing Consent: Changes in the Labor Process under Monopoly Capitalism*. Chicago: University of Chicago Press, 1979.

Burawoy, Michael, and Janos Lukacs. "Mythologies of Work: A Comparison of Firms in State Socialism and Advanced Capitalism." *American Sociological Review* vol. 50, no. 6 (1985): 723–37.

Bush, Richard C. *The Politics of Cotton Textiles in Guomindang China, 1927–1937*. New York: Garland Publishing, 1982.

Butterfield, Fox. *China, Alive in the Bitter Sea*. New York: Times Books, 1982.

Byrd, William A. *Chinese Industrial Firms Under Reform*. New York: Oxford University Press, 1992.

Chan, Anita, Richard Madsen, and Jonathan Unger. *Chen Village: The Recent History of a Peasant Community in Mao's China*. Berkeley, CA: University of California Press, 1984.

Chan, Ming K. *Historiography of the Chinese Labor Movement, 1895–1949*. Stanford, CA: Hoover Institution Press, 1981.

——— "Labor and Empire: The Chinese Labor Movement in the Canton Delta, 1895–1927." Ph.D. diss., Stanford University, 1975.

Chen, An. "Democratic Reform of Management Structures in China's Industrial Enterprises." *Politics & Society* vol. 23, no. 3 (1995): 369–410.

Chen, Feng. "Subsistence Crises, Managerial Corruption, and Labour Protests in China." *The China Journal* 44 (July 2000): 41–63.

Chesneaux, Jean. *The Chinese Labor Movement, 1919–1927*. Translated and edited by H.M. Wright. Stanford, CA: Stanford University Press, 1968.

Child, John. *Management in China During the Age of Reform*. New York: Cambridge University Press, 1994.

Chinese Academy of Social Sciences, Institute of Economics. *Shanghai minzu jiqi gongye* (Shanghai's Domestic Machine Industry). 2 vols. Beijing: Zhongguo shehui kexue yuan, 1966.

Chinese Communist Party, Shanghai Municipal Committee, Party History Research Office and Shanghai Municipal Labor Union. *Shanghai dishier mianfangzhi chang gongren yundongshi* (The History of the Labor

Movement at the Shanghai Number 12 Cotton Spinning and Weaving Mill). Beijing: Zhonggong dangshi chubanshe, 1994.

———*Shanghai disanshiyi mianfangzhi chang gongren yundongshi* (The History of the Labor Movement at the Shanghai Number Thirty-One Cotton Spinning and Weaving Mill). Beijing: Zhonggong dangshi chubanshe, 1991.

———*Shanghai jiqiye gongren yundongshi* (The History of the Labor Movement of Shanghai Machinists). Beijing: Zhongguo gongchandang dangshi chubanshe, 1991.

Chung, Chongwook. "Ideology and the Politics of Industrial Management in the People's Republic of China, 1949–1965." Ph.D. diss., Yale University, 1975.

Coble, Parks, Jr. *The Shanghai Capitalists and the Nationalist Government, 1927–1937*. Cambridge, MA: Harvard University Press, 1986.

Cochran, Sherman. *Big Business in China: Sino-Foreign Rivalry in the Cigarette Industry, 1890–1930*. Cambridge, MA: Harvard University Press, 1980.

Cole, Robert E. *Japanese Blue Collar: The Changing Tradition*. Berkeley, CA: University of California Press, 1971.

David, Paul. "Clio and the Economics of QWERTY." *American Economic Review* vol. 75, no. 2 (1985): 332–7.

Davis, Deborah. "Patrons and Clients in Chinese Industry." *Modern China* vol. 14, no. 4 (1988): 487–97.

Diamant, Neil J. *Revolutionizing the Family: Politics, Love, and Divorce in Urban and Rural China, 1949–1968*. Berkeley, CA: University of California Press, 2000.

DiMaggio, Paul J., and Walter W. Powell, eds. *The New Institutionalism in Organizational Analysis*. Chicago: University of Chicago Press, 1991.

Ding Yisheng. "Ming bu xuchuan zhi Shenxin laogong zizhiqu" (The Well-deserved Reputation of the Shenxin Labor Self-rule District). *Wuxi zazhi* 22 (February 1937): 15–24.

Dittmer, Lowell, and Xiaobo Lü. "Personal Politics in the Chinese *Danwei* Under Reform." *Asian Survey* vol. 36, no. 3 (1996): 246–67.

Donnithorne, Audrey. *China's Economic System*. New York: Frederick A. Praeger, 1967.

Dore, Ronald. *British Factory – Japanese Factory*. Berkeley, CA: University of California Press, 1973.

Duara, Prasenjit. *Culture, Power, and the State: Rural North China, 1900–1942*. Stanford, CA: Stanford University Press, 1988.

Eastman, Lloyd E. "Nationalist China During the Sino-Japanese War, 1937–1945." In *Republican China 1912–1949, Part 2*. Vol. 13 of *The Cambridge History of China*, edited by John K. Fairbank and Albert Feuerwerker, 547–608. New York: Cambridge University Press, 1990.

———*The Abortive Revolution: China Under Nationalist Rule, 1927–1937*. Cambridge, MA: Harvard University Press, 1974.

Eckstein, Alexander. *China's Economic Revolution*. New York: Cambridge University Press, 1977.

———*China's Economic Development: The Interplay of Scarcity and Ideology*. Ann Arbor, MI: University of Michigan Press, 1975.

Bibliography

Editorial Committee for "Archival Materials on the Defense Industry of Modern China." *Zhongguo jindai bingqi gongye dang'an shiliao* (Archival Materials on the Defense Industry of Modern China). 4 vols. Beijing: Bingqi gongye chubanshe, 1993.

Editorial Group for Historical Materials on the Chinese Warship Industry Series. *Zhongguo jindai jianting gongye shiliaoji* (The Collection of Historical Materials on the Modern Chinese Warship Industry). Shanghai: Renmin chubanshe, 1994.

Edwards, Richard. *Contested Terrain: The Transformation of the Workplace in America*. New York: Basic Books, 1979.

Fang, Xianting (H.D. Fong). *Industrial Organization in China*. Tianjin: Nankai Institute of Economics, Nankai University, 1937.

Feuerwerker, Albert. *Economic Trends in the Republic of China, 1912–1949*. Ann Arbor, MI: Center for Chinese Studies, 1977.

Fewsmith, Joseph. *Party, State, and Local Elites in Republican China: Merchant Organizations and Politics in Shanghai, 1890–1930*. Honolulu: University of Hawaii Press, 1985.

Filtzer, Donald. *Soviet Workers and Stalinist Industrialization: The Formation of Modern Soviet Production Relations, 1928–1941*. Armonk, NY: M.E. Sharpe, 1986.

Fligstein, Neil. *The Transformation of Corporate Control*. Cambridge, MA: Harvard University Press, 1990.

Frazier, Martin W. "Mobilizing a Movement: Cotton Mill Foremen in the Shanghai Strikes of 1925." *Republican China* vol. 20, no. 1 (1994): 1–45.

Friedman, Edward, Paul G. Pickowicz, and Mark Selden, with Kay Ann Johnson. *Chinese Village, Socialist State*. New Haven, CT: Yale University Press, 1991.

Fu Zechu. *Zhanqian Guangdong zhi gongye* (Industry in Prewar Guangdong). Nanjing: Zhongyang rixingshe, 1947.

Garon, Sheldon. *The State and Labor in Modern Japan*. Berkeley, CA: University of California Press, 1987.

Gordon, Andrew. "Conditions for the Disappearance of the Japanese Working-Class Movement." In *Putting Class in its Place: Worker Identities in East Asia*, edited by Elizabeth J. Perry, 11–52. Berkeley: Institute of East Asian Studies, 1996.

——— *The Evolution of Labor Relations in Japan: Heavy Industry, 1853–1955*. Cambridge, MA: Harvard University Press, 1985.

Gordon, David M., Richard Edwards, and Michael Reich. *Segmented Work, Divided Workers: The Historical Transformation of Labor in the United States*. New York: Cambridge University Press, 1982.

Granick, David. *Chinese State Enterprises: A Regional Property Rights Analysis*. Chicago: University of Chicago Press, 1990.

"Guangdong fangzhichang zhi yuanqi ji qi jianglai" (The Origins of the Guangdong Textile Mill and its Future). *Xiandai shengchan zazhi*, 1934.

Guangdong Province Economic Planning Commission's Editorial Office for the "Economic Planning Gazetteer." *Guangdongsheng jingji jihua wenjian xuanbian* (Selected Documents on Economic Planning in Guangdong

Province). 3 vols. Guangzhou: Guangdongsheng jingji jihua weiyuanhui, 1990.

Guangzhou Municipal Labor Bureau. "Guangzhoushi laodong zhi" (The Guangzhou Labor Gazetteer). Mimeo, n.d.

Guangzhou Municipal Labor Union, Wage Department. *Gongzi gaige xuanchuan cankao ziliao* (Wage Reform Propaganda Materials). Guangzhou: Guangzhoushi gonghui lianhehui gongzibu, 1956.

Guangzhou Municipal People's Government Labor Bureau, Investigation and Research Office. *Laodong zhengyi huibian* (Reports on Labor Disputes). Guangzhou: Guangzhoushi laodong ju diaocha yanjiu ban, 1951.

Guangzhou Municipal Trade Union Preparatory Committee. *Guangzhou gongyun* (Guangzhou Labor Movement). Guangzhou: Guangzhoushi gonghui lianhehui, 1950.

Guthrie, Doug. *Dragon in a Three-Piece Suit: The Emergence of Capitalism in China.* Princeton, NJ: Princeton University Press, 1999.

Hamilton, Gary G., and Nicole Woolsey Biggart. "Market, Culture, and Authority: A Comparative Analysis of Management and Organization in the Far East." *American Journal of Sociology* 94 (1988): S52–S94.

Hammond, Edward. "Organized Labor in Shanghai, 1927–1937." Ph.D. diss., University of California, Berkeley, 1978.

Haraszti, Miklos. *A Worker in a Workers' State.* Translated by Michael Wright. New York: Pelican Books, 1977.

Harper, Paul. "The Party and the Unions in Communist China." *China Quarterly* 37 (1969): 84–119.

Henderson, Gail E., and Myron S. Cohen. *The Chinese Hospital: A Socialist Work Unit.* New Haven, CT: Yale University Press, 1984.

Hershatter, Gail. *The Workers of Tianjin, 1900–1949.* Stanford, CA: Stanford University Press, 1986.

Hoffman, Charles. *The Chinese Worker.* Albany, NY: State University of New York Press, 1974.

Honig, Emily. *Sisters and Strangers: Women in the Shanghai Cotton Mills, 1919–1949.* Stanford, CA: Stanford University Press, 1986.

Howe, Christopher. *Wage Patterns and Wage Policy in Modern China, 1919–1972.* New York: Cambridge University Press, 1973.

Hsu, Chen-kuo. "Ideological Reflections and the Inception of Economic Development in Taiwan." In *The Role of the State in Taiwan's Development,* edited by Joel D. Aberbach, David Dollar, and Kenneth L. Sokoloff, 307–20. Armonk, NY: M.E. Sharpe, 1994.

Huangpu Shipyard Party Committee Organization Department. "Huangpu zaochuanchang zuzhishi ziliao" (Materials on the Organizational History of the Huangpu Shipyard). Mimeo, 1989.

Huang Xihui. "Guangzhou jindai siying chuanbo xiuzaoye" (The Modern History of Guangzhou's Private Sector Ship Repair and Construction Industry). *Guangdong wenshi ziliao* 61 (1990): 225–62.

Huang Zengzhang. "Minguo shiqi Guangdong shengying gongye gaikuang" (Overview of Guangdong's Provincial-Owned Industry in the Republican Period). *Guangdong shizhi* no. 2 (1989).

Jacoby, Sanford M. *Employing Bureaucracy: Managers, Unions, and the Transformation of Work in American Industry, 1900–1945*. New York: Columbia University Press, 1985.

Jacoby, Sanford M., ed. *Masters to Managers: Historical and Comparative Perspectives on American Employers*. New York: Columbia University Press, 1991.

Jiangnan Shipyard Factory History Research Office. "Jiangnanchang de renshi laodong guanli" (Jiangnan Shipyard Personnel and Labor Management). Mimeo, n.d.

—— "Factory Chronology." Mimeo, n.d.

—— "Tongji ziliao" (Statistical Materials). Mimeo, n.d.

"Jiefang qian Guangzhoushi siying jiqi gongye gaikuang" (Background on Pre-Liberation Guangzhou's Private Sector Machine Industry). *Guangzhou wenshi ziliao* 23 (1981): 73–106.

Kallgren, Joyce K. "Social Welfare and China's Industrial Workers." In *Chinese Communist Politics in Action*, edited by A. Doak Barnett. Seattle, WA: University of Washington Press, 1969.

Kaple, Deborah A. *Dream of a Red Factory: The Legacy of High Stalinism in China*. New York: Oxford University Press, 1994.

Katznelson, Ira, and Aristide R. Zolberg, eds. *Working-Class Formation: Nineteenth-Century Patterns in Western Europe and the United States*. Princeton, NJ: Princeton University Press, 1986.

Kirby, William. "Continuity and Change in Modern China: Economic Planning on the Mainland and on Taiwan, 1943–1958." *The Australian Journal of Chinese Affairs* 24 (1990): 121–41.

Kornai, János. *The Socialist System: The Political Economy of Communism*. Princeton, NJ: Princeton University Press, 1992.

Korzec, Michael. *Labour and the Failure of Reform in China*. New York: St. Martin's Press, 1992.

Kuromiya, Hiroaki. *Stalin's Industrial Revolution: Politics and Workers, 1928–1932*. New York: Cambridge University Press, 1988.

Lardy, Nicholas R. *China's Unfinished Economic Revolution*. Washington, DC: Brookings Institution, 1998.

Lee, Ching Kwan. "Engendering the Worlds of Labor: Women Workers, Labor Markets, and Production Politics in the South China Economic Miracle." *American Sociological Review* 60 (1995): 378–97.

Lee, Hong Yung. *The Politics of the Chinese Cultural Revolution*. Berkeley, CA: University of California Press, 1978.

Lee, Peter N.S. *Industrial Management and Economic Reform in China, 1949–1984*. New York: Oxford University Press, 1987.

Lichtenstein, Nelson. "The Man in the Middle: A Social History of Automobile Industry Foremen." In *On the Line: Essays in the History of Auto Work*, edited by Nelson Lichtenstein and Stephen Meyer, 153–89. Urbana, IL: University of Illinois Press, 1989.

—— "Industrial Democracy, Contract Unionism, and the National War Labor Board." *Labor Law Journal* 33 (August 1982): 524–31.

Li Cishan. "Shanghai laodong zhuangkuang" (Shanghai Labor Conditions). *Xin qingnian* vol. 7, no. 6 (1920): 1–45.

Lieberthal, Kenneth. *Revolution and Tradition in Tientsin, 1949–1952*. Stanford, CA: Stanford University Press, 1980.

Lin, Justin Yifu, Fang Cai, and Zhou Li. *The China Miracle: Development Strategy and Economic Reform*. Hong Kong: Chinese University Press, 1996.

Li Qing, Chen Wenwu, and Lin Shecheng, eds. *Zhongguo zibenzhuyi gongshangye de shehuizhuyi gaizao* (The Socialist Transformation of Capitalist Industry and Commerce in China). *Guangdong, Guangzhou*, edited by Editorial Leading Group on Guangdong and Guangzhou. Beijing: Zhonggong dangshi chubanshe, 1993.

——— *Zhongguo zibenzhuyi gongshangye de shehuizhuyi gaizao* (The Socialist Transformation of Capitalist Industry and Commerce in China). *Shanghai*, edited by Editorial Committee on Shanghai. 2 vols. Beijing: Zhonggong dangshi chubanshe, 1993.

Liu Dajun, ed. *Zhongguo gongye diaocha baogao* (Report on Industrial Survey of China). 3 vols. Nanjing: Jingji shuxue suo, 1937.

Li Weiyi. *Zhongguo gongzi zhidu* (China's Wage System). Beijing: Zhongguo laodong chubanshe, 1991.

Lu Feng. "The Origins and Formation of the Unit (*Danwei*) System." *Chinese Sociology and Anthropology* vol. 25, no. 3 (1993): 7–92.

Lü, Xiaobo. "Minor Public Economy: The Revolutionary Origins of the *Danwei*." In *Danwei: The Changing Chinese Workplace in Historical and Comparative Perspective*, edited by Xiaobo Lü and Elizabeth Perry, 21–41. Armonk, NY: M.E. Sharpe, 1997.

Lü, Xiaobo, and Elizabeth J. Perry. "The Changing Chinese Workplace in Historical and Comparative Perspective." In *Danwei: The Changing Chinese Workplace in Historical and Comparative Perspective*, edited by Xiaobo Lü and Elizabeth Perry, 3–17. Armonk, NY: M.E. Sharpe, 1997.

MacFarquhar, Roderick. *The Origins of the Cultural Revolution, Vol. 2. The Great Leap Forward, 1958–1960*. New York: Columbia University Press, 1983.

Mann, Susan. *Local Merchants and the Chinese Bureaucracy, 1750–1950*. Stanford, CA: Stanford University Press, 1987.

Mao Zedong. "On the People's Democratic Dictatorship." In *Selected Works of Mao Tse-tung, Vol. IV*. Beijing: Foreign Languages Press, 1969.

March, James G., and Johan P. Olson. "The New Institutionalism: Organizational Factors in Political Life." *American Political Science Review* 78 (1984): 734–49.

Martin, Brian G. *The Shanghai Green Gang: Politics and Organized Crime, 1919–1937*. Berkeley, CA: University of California Press, 1996.

Migdal, Joel S. "The State in Society: An Approach to Struggles for Domination." In *State Power and Social Forces: Domination and Transformation in the Third World*, edited by Joel S. Migdal, Atul Kohli, and Vivienne Shue, 7–34. New York: Cambridge University Press, 1994.

Naughton, Barry. "*Danwei*: The Economic Foundations of a Unique Institution." In *Danwei: The Changing Chinese Workplace in Historical and Comparative Perspective*, edited by Xiaobo Lü and Elizabeth J. Perry, 169–94. Armonk, NY: M.E. Sharpe, 1997.

———*Growing Out of the Plan: Chinese Economic Reform, 1978–1993*. New York: Cambridge University Press, 1995.

Nelson, Daniel. *Managers and Workers: Origins of the Twentieth-Century Factory System in the United States, 1880–1920*. 2nd ed. Madison, WI: University of Wisconsin Press, 1995.

North, Douglass C. *Institutions, Institutional Change and Economic Performance*. New York: Cambridge University Press, 1990.

Peng, Yusheng. "Wage Determination in Rural and Urban China: A Comparison of Public and Private Industrial Sectors." *American Sociological Review* 57 (1992): 198–213.

Pepper, Suzanne. *Civil War in China: The Political Struggle, 1945–1949*. Berkeley, CA: University of California Press, 1978.

Perry, Elizabeth J. "From Native Place to Workplace: Labor Origins and Outcomes of China's *Danwei* System." In *Danwei: The Changing Chinese Workplace in Historical and Comparative Perspective*, edited by Xiaobo Lü and Elizabeth J. Perry, 42–59. Armonk, NY: M.E. Sharpe, 1997.

———"Labor's Battle for Political Space: The Role of Worker Associations in Contemporary China." In *Urban Spaces in Contemporary China: The Potential for Autonomy and Community in Post-Mao China*, edited by Deborah S. Davis, et al., 302–25. New York: Cambridge University Press, 1995.

———"Shanghai's Strike Wave of 1957." *China Quarterly* 137 (1994): 1–27.

———*Shanghai on Strike: The Politics of Shanghai Labor*. Stanford: Stanford University Press, 1993.

———"State and Society in Contemporary China." *World Politics* vol. 41, no. 4 (1989): 579–91.

Perry, Elizabeth J., and Li Xun. *Proletarian Power: Shanghai in the Cultural Revolution*. Boulder, CO: Westview Press, 1997.

Pierson, Paul. "Increasing Returns, Path Dependence, and the Study of Politics." *American Political Science Review* vol. 94, no. 2 (June 2000): 251–67.

Pomfret, John. "Miners' Riot A Symbol of China's New Discontent." *Washington Post*, April 5, 2000.

Porter, Robin. *Industrial Reform in Modern China*. Armonk, NY: M.E. Sharpe, 1994.

Rawski, Thomas G. *Economic Growth in Prewar China*. Berkeley, CA: University of California Press, 1989.

———*China's Transition to Industrialism: Producer Goods and Economic Development in the Twentieth Century*. Ann Arbor, MI: University of Michigan Press, 1980.

———*Economic Growth and Employment in China*. New York: Oxford University Press, 1979.

Redding, S. Gordon. *The Spirit of Chinese Capitalism*. New York: Walter de Gruyter, 1990.

Research Office on China Labor Policy, ed. *Zhongguo laodong lifa* (China's Labor Legislation). Beijing: Renmin chubanshe, 1980.

Richman, Barry M. *Industrial Society in Communist China*. New York: Random House, 1969.

Sabel, Charles F. *Work and Politics: The Division of Labor in Industry*. New York: Cambridge University Press, 1982.

Sabel, Charles, and Jonathan Zeitlin. "Historical Alternatives to Mass Production: Politics, Markets and Technology in Nineteenth Century Industrialization." *Past and Present* 108 (August 1985): 133–76.

Schurmann, Franz. *Ideology and Organization in Communist China*. 2nd ed. Berkeley, CA: University of California Press, 1968.

Shanghai Academy of Social Sciences, Institute of Economics. *Jiangnan zaochuanchang changshi* (Factory History of the Jiangnan Shipyard). Shanghai: Shanghai shehui kexue yuan, 1983.

———— *Rongjia qiye shiliao* (Historical Materials on the Rong Family Enterprises). 2 vols. Shanghai: Renmin chubanshe, 1980.

———— *Hengfeng shachangde fasheng fazhan yu gaizao* (The Birth, Development, and Transformation of the Hengfeng Cotton Mill). Shanghai: Shanghai shehui kexue yuan, 1959.

Shanghai Jiangnan Shipyard Labor Movement History Group. *Shanghai Jiangnan zaochuanchang gongren yundongshi* (The History of the Labor Movement at the Shanghai Jiangnan Shipyard). Beijing: Zhonggong dangshi chubanshe, 1995.

Shanghai Municipal Labor Union, ed. *Jiefang zhanzheng shiqi Shanghai gongren yundongshi* (History of the Shanghai Labor Movement during the War for Liberation). Shanghai: Shanghai yuandong chubanshe, 1992.

Shanghai Number Thirty-One Mill Factory Director's Office. "Shangmian sanshiyichang zhigong bian" (Shanghai Number Thirty-One Mill, Workers and Staff Section). Mimeo, n.d.

———— "Number Thirty-One Mill History." Mimeo, n.d.

Shearer, David R. *Industry, State, and Society in Stalin's Russia, 1926–1934*. Ithaca, NY: Cornell University Press, 1996.

Shi, Tianjin. *Political Participation in Beijing*. Cambridge, MA: Harvard University Press, 1997.

Siegelbaum, Lewis H. "Masters of the Shop Floor: Foremen and Soviet Industrialization." In *Social Dimensions of Soviet Industrialization*, edited by William G. Rosenberg and Lewis H. Siegelbaum, 166–92. Bloomington, IN: Indiana University Press, 1993.

Sil, Rudra. "The Russian 'Village in the City' and the Stalinist System of Enterprise Management: The Origins of Worker Alienation in Soviet State Socialism." In *Danwei: The Changing Chinese Workplace in Historical and Comparative Perspective*, edited by Xiaobo Lü and Elizabeth J. Perry, 114–41. Armonk, NY: M.E. Sharpe, 1997.

Skocpol, Theda. *States and Social Revolutions: A Comparative Analysis of France, Russia, and China*. New York: Cambridge University Press, 1979.

Smith, S. A. "Workers and Supervisors: St. Petersburg 1905–1917 and Shanghai 1895–1927." *Past and Present* 139 (1993): 131–77.

State Statistical Bureau, ed. *Zhongguo tongji nianjian, 1998* (China Statistical Yearbook, 1998). Beijing: Zhongguo tongji chubanshe, 1998.

———— *Zhongguo guding zichan touzi tongji nianjian, 1950–1995* (China Statistical Yearbook on Investment in Fixed Assets, 1950–1995). Beijing: Zhongguo tongji chubanshe, 1997.

———*Zhongguo laodong gongzi tongji ziliao, 1949–1985* (China Labor and Wage Statistical Materials, 1949–1985). Beijing: Zhongguo tongji chubanshe, 1987.

Steinfeld, Edward S. *Forging Reform in China: The Fate of State-Owned Industry.* New York: Cambridge University Press, 1998.

Strauss, Julia. *Strong Institutions in Weak Polities: State Building in Republican China 1927–1940.* New York: Oxford University Press, 1998.

Sun Huairen. *Shanghai shehuizhuyi jingji jianshe fazhan jianshi, 1949–1985* (A Concise History of the Establishment and Development of the Socialist Economy in Shanghai, 1949–1985). Shanghai: Shanghai renmin chubanshe, 1990.

Survey of China Mainland Press, no. 1665, December 5, 1957. "State Council's Directive Concerning Improvement of Industrial Management System."

Taira, Koji. *Economic Development and the Labor Market in Japan.* New York: Columbia University Press, 1970.

Tang Guoliang, ed. *Guangzhou gongye sishinian, 1949–1989* (Forty Years of Industry in Guangzhou). Guangzhou: Guangdong renmin chubanshe, 1989.

Tien, Hung-mao. *Government and Politics in Kuomintang China, 1927–1937.* Stanford, CA: Stanford University Press, 1972.

Thelen, Kathleen. "Historical Institutionalism and Comparative Politics." *Annual Review of Political Science* 2 (1999): 369–404.

Thelen, Kathleen, and Sven Steinmo. "Historical Institutionalism in Comparative Politics." In *Structuring Politics: Historical Institutionalism in Comparative Analysis*, edited by Sven Steinmo, Kathleen Thelen, and Frank Longstreth, 1–32. New York: Cambridge University Press, 1992.

Tocqueville, Alexis de. *The Old Regime and the French Revolution.* Translated by Stuart Gilbert. Garden City, NY: Doubleday Anchor Books, 1955.

Tongji yuebao (Statistical Monthly), nos. 117/118, 123/124 (1947).

Union Research Institute, ed. *Documents of the Chinese Communist Party Central Committee, Sept. 1956–Apr. 1969.* Kowloon, Hong Kong: Union Research Institute, 1971.

United States Department of State. *Internal Affairs of China, 1945–1949.*

———*Internal Affairs of China, 1930–1939.*

Vogel, Ezra F. *Canton Under Communism: Programs and Politics in a Provincial Capital, 1949–1968.* Cambridge, MA: Harvard University Press, 1969.

Walder, Andrew G. "The Chinese Cultural Revolution in the Factories: Party-State Structures and Patterns of Conflict." In *Putting Class In Its Place: Worker Identities in East Asia*, edited by Elizabeth J. Perry, 167–98. Berkeley, CA: Institute of East Asian Studies, 1996.

———"Factory and Manager in an Era of Reform." *China Quarterly* 118 (1989): 242–64.

———"Wage Reform and the Web of Factory Interests." *China Quarterly* 109 (1987): 22–41.

———*Communist Neo-Traditionalism: Work and Authority in Chinese Industry.* Berkeley, CA: University of California Press, 1986.

Ward, Chris. *Russia's Cotton Workers and the New Economic Policy: Shop Floor Culture and State Policy, 1921–1929.* New York: Cambridge University Press, 1990.

Weiss, Linda. "War, the State, and the Origins of the Japanese Employment System." *Politics & Society* vol. 21, no. 3 (September 1993): 325–54.

White, Lynn T. III. *Policies of Chaos: The Organizational Causes of Violence in China's Cultural Revolution.* Princeton, NJ: Princeton University Press, 1988.

Whitley, Richard. *Business Systems in East Asia: Firms, Markets and Societies.* London: Sage Publications, 1992.

Whyte, Martin King, and William L. Parish. *Urban Life in Contemporary China.* Chicago: University of Chicago Press, 1974.

Womack, Brantly. "Transfigured Community: Neo-Traditionalism and Work Unit Socialism in China." *China Quarterly* 126 (1991): 313–32.

Wong, Siu-Lun. *Emigrant Entrepreneurs: Shanghai Industrialists in Hong Kong.* New York: Oxford University Press, 1988.

Wright, Tim. " 'The Spiritual Heritage of Chinese Capitalism': Recent Trends in the Historiography of Chinese Enterprise Management." *The Australian Journal of Chinese Affairs* 19/20 (1988): 185–214.

Wu Weipu. "Guangdong bingqi zhizaochang gailue" (Outline of the Guangdong Arsenal). *Guangdong wenshi ziliao* 9 (1963): 18–28.

Wu Zhixin. "Zhongguo baogongzhi zhi xianyou xingtai" (Present Patterns of the Chinese Contract Labor System). *Laogong yuekan* vol. 5, no. 8 (1936): 1–6.

Xin haijun yuekan (New Navy Monthly), no. 3 (September 1946).

Xue Mingjian. "Gongchang zhuzhong laogong shiye yu benshen zhi guanxi" (Factory Emphasizes the Connection Between Labor Institutions and Self-Interest). *Wuxi zazhi* 22 (1937).

Xu Kan, ed. *Zhonghua minguo tongji nianjian* (Republic of China Statistical Yearbook). Nanjing: Zhonghua minguo tongjiju, 1948.

Xu Weiyong, and Huang Hanmin. *Rongjia qiye fazhanshi* (History of the Development of Rong Family Enterprises). Beijing: Renmin chubanshe, 1985.

Yang, Mayfair Mei-hui. "Between State and Society: The Construction of Corporateness in a Chinese Socialist Factory." *The Australian Journal of Chinese Affairs* 22 (1989): 31–60.

Yatsko, Pamela. "Party's Over." *Far Eastern Economic Review* (June 5, 1997): 59.

Yeh, Wen-hsin. "The Republican Origins of the *Danwei*: The Case of Shanghai's Bank of China." In *Danwei: The Changing Chinese Workplace in Historical and Comparative Perspective*, edited by Xiaobo Lü and Elizabeth Perry, 60–88. Armonk, NY: M.E. Sharpe, 1997.

——— "Corporate Space, Communal Time: Everyday Life in Shanghai's Bank of China." *American Historical Review* 99 (1995): 97–122.

You, Ji. *China's Enterprise Reform: Changing State/Society Relations after Mao.* New York: Routledge, 1998.

Yuan Lunqu. *Zhongguo laodong jingjishi* (History of Chinese Labor Economics). Beijing: Beijing jingji xueyuan chubanshe, 1990.

Zeitlin, Jonathan. "From Labour History to the History of Industrial Relations." *Economic History Review* vol. 40, no. 2 (1987): 159–84.

Zhang Qi, and Chen Guokang. "Guangzhou zhenzhiye" (Guangzhou's Knitting Industry). *Guangzhou wenshi ziliao* 36 (1986): 64–82.

Zheng, Shiping. *Party vs. State in Post-1949 China: The Institutional Dilemma.* New York: Cambridge University Press, 1997.

Zhu Bangxing, Hu Linge, and Xu Sheng. *Shanghai chanye yu Shanghai zhigong* (Industries and Employees in Shanghai). Shanghai: Renmin chubanshe, 1984.

Index